T0325285

PRAISE FOR THE BOOK

Asia's Stock Markets: From the Ground Up provides an approachable and entertaining, yet highly informative, overview of Asia's bourses. The book chronicles the fits and starts of Asia's capital markets development and gives investors frameworks with which to assess opportunities in these markets today".

—**Carson Block**
Founder
Muddy Waters Research

"What a fascinating – and truly one of a kind – business book. van der Linde takes us on a unique journey around Asia's financial markets – from their sometimes unlikely origins to what makes them tick, and work for companies and investors today. Always interesting, he writes with authority on an increasingly relevant subject. *Asia's Stock Markets* is a must-read for both novice and seasoned stock pickers alike. Highly recommended!"

—**Philippe Espinasse**
Capital Markets Expert and
Author of *IPO: A Global Guide*

Van der Linde is one of the most experienced equity analysts and macro strategists in Asia. But, more importantly, he knows how to explain Asia's markets in an entertaining way (including personal anecdotes). He is also a master at making complicated financial concepts simple. (The discount rate on stocks? It works just like a supermarket's early-evening markdowns on the price of fresh sushi). Neophytes to Asia's stock markets will learn much from this book, while being amused along the way. And even experts will find fresh insights and previously unknown nuggets.

—**Garry Evans**
Chief Global Asset Allocation Strategist
BCA Research, Inc.

"Asia stock markets are extremely diverse and can be a bit of a mystery to outsiders. Van der Linde's investment stories and adventures get straight to the essence of these markets and provide an invaluable guide to spotting opportunities in the region."

—**Ronald W. Chan**
Founder and CIO of Chartwell Capital, Hong Kong,
and Author of *The Value Investors:
Lessons from the World's Top Fund Managers.*

"An absolutely superb introduction to the complexity of Asia's equity markets. Packed full of historical information, personal anecdotes and relevant insights from somebody who has lived the region's stock markets for the last 25 years. Highly recommended to anybody with an interest in Asian finance and equity investing".

—**William Bratton**
Former Head of Asian Equity Research at HSBC
and Author of *China's Rise, Asia's Decline*

"*Asia's Stock Market: From the Ground Up* is not just a compelling page turner but is also an authoritative compendium of markets in the world's fastest growing region. The engaging narrative covers topics ranging from Asia's oldest stock market, to Japan's spectacular boom and bust cycle, and China's meteoric rise. Written in a simple yet absorbing style, the book will appeal to both investors and to those simply interested in a good read. This well-researched book is an absolute treat."

—**Umesh Desai**
Author of *The Singapore Blue Chips*

"For years, Herald van der Linde has been a source of sage advice on Asian stock markets for the world's top financial professionals. Now, he distils those years of insight and experience into a work equally accessible – and equally fascinating – for layman, individual investor, and full-time portfolio manager alike."

—**Michael Kurtz**
Hedge Fund Strategist, Hong Kong

ASIA'S STOCK MARKETS
FROM THE GROUND UP

ASIA'S STOCK MARKETS

FROM THE GROUND UP

Herald van der Linde

Text © 2022 Herald van der Linde

Published by Marshall Cavendish Business
An imprint of Marshall Cavendish International

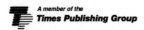

Other Marshall Cavendish Offices
Marshall Cavendish Corporation, 800 Westchester Ave, Suite N-641, Rye Brook,
NY 10573, USA • Marshall Cavendish International (Thailand) Co Ltd, 253 Asoke,
16th Floor, Sukhumvit 21 Road, Klongtoey Nua, Wattana, Bangkok 10110, Thailand
• Marshall Cavendish (Malaysia) Sdn Bhd, Times Subang, Lot 46, Subang Hi-Tech
Industrial Park, Batu Tiga, 40000 Shah Alam, Selangor Darul Ehsan, Malaysia

Marshall Cavendish is a registered trademark of Times Publishing Limited

ISBN 978 981 4974 62 2

Printed in Singapore

Voor mij ouders, Hans en Fenna

'T weark is doan en wie könt 't der wa met doon. Kieken wat 't wordt.

Contents

Ups and Downs in Asia's Stock Markets: a Timeline – MSCI Asia All Country Asia Pacific Index 1995–2020

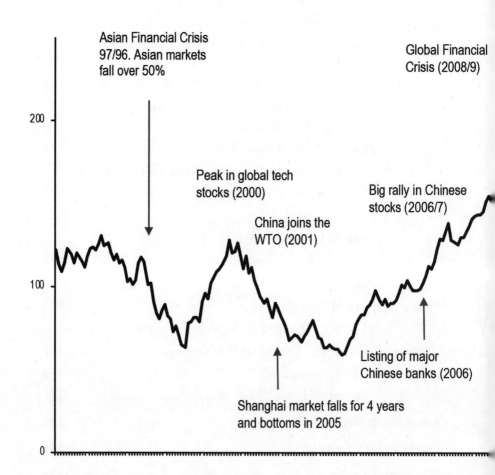

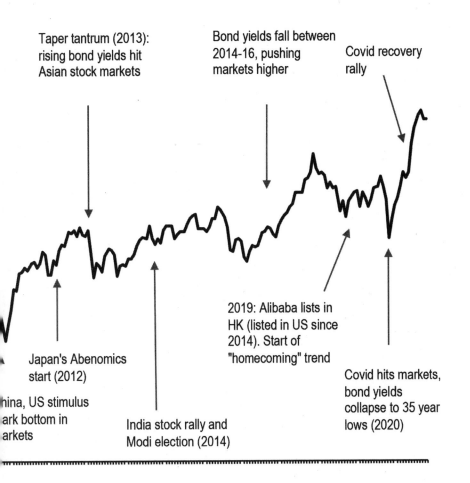

Taper tantrum (2013): rising bond yields hit Asian stock markets

Bond yields fall between 2014-16, pushing markets higher

Covid recovery rally

Japan's Abenomics start (2012)

hina, US stimulus ark bottom in arkets

India stock rally and Modi election (2014)

2019: Alibaba lists in HK (listed in US since 2014). Start of "homecoming" trend

Covid hits markets, bond yields collapse to 35 year lows (2020)

Introduction

This book is a gentle introduction to Asia's stock markets for a general audience. It is for people who do not know much about the markets but, for whatever reason, would like to learn more. They could be seasoned expatriate pilots, academics and other professionals, newcomers to the region, as well as students or young men and women about to start in the finance industry.

The idea is to cut through the alphabet soup of industry jargon to provide a clear understanding of the history of these markets, what makes them tick, how they differ from each other and the forces that will drive them over the next decade. But this is not a dry, technical "how to" textbook. Quite the opposite. There are inspirational success stories, utter calamities and juicy market scandals. This book is spiced with lessons learned and personal anecdotes, all of which the author hopes have contributed towards making him a wiser man after nearly 30 years in the world of Asian investment.

***

The idea behind this book started to ferment over a dinner of Indonesian food and a splendid view of Hong Kong harbour. Andrew, an Airbus captain and close friend of many years, turned to me a little sheepishly, gin and tonic in hand. The conversation went something like this:

What's the stock market doing?
I was surprised. Sports was his thing. And movies. He had never mentioned finance before.

What do you mean? I replied, feigning ignorance. He knew very well that I looked at markets pretty much every day.

We've just sold the flat and I'm not sure what to do with the money. I know very little about this stuff.

Look, I'm not a financial advisor. I deal with big institutional investors. But as a rule of thumb, putting a chunk of your savings that you won't need in the next 10 or 15 years into the stock market is generally a good idea.

But what if the market goes down? I'll lose money.

You're a long-term investor, not a day trader. Think in terms of 15 years, not a week or two. Markets generally go up over time.

Do you think now is a good time to buy? I saw an economist on TV saying that things were going to seriously slow down.

That's possible. But economies and stock markets are very different. Many people think markets move in line with economies. That's often not the case, especially in Asia.

But I have no idea about what stocks to buy. I haven't got a clue about these things. It all seems very complicated.

Andrew, it's not. Honestly. You don't have to buy individual stocks. That's too risky for an investor like you. There are much safer, easier and cheaper ways to invest. There are things called ETFs, exchange traded funds. Don't be put off by the name. They allow you to invest in a whole range of different stocks, which reduces the level of risk. Mutual funds do pretty much the same thing.

My phone rang the next morning. It was Andrew. *Morning, Herald. About that ETF ...*

***

My conversation with Andrew got me thinking. There are many different types of investors. Hawk-eyed hedge fund analysts looking to swoop on mis-priced stocks, cautious pension funds which safeguard retirement pots, a host of professional asset managers and desk-bound day traders, and the new army of individuals who discovered stocks while they were stuck at home during the pandemic … the list is long.

But there also many people like Andrew, who need to know more about what is, after all, a fairly important subject: the future of their savings. This book is for them. Stock prices rise and fall for many reasons – company results, a change in market share or profit margins, the success or failure of a freshly-launched product, the latest release of economic data or the introduction of a new government policy. Most novice investors get that. It's intuitive. But this book also offers a simple guide to some of the other prevailing forces that are not so obvious to the untrained eye, such as the tug of war between stock dividends and bond yields.

When I first started out in the finance industry in Asia, the world was a very different place. Almost everything revolved around the US and Europe, and the Asian markets were mere sideshows. Yes, they were growing fast but were still largely afterthoughts for many overseas investors. Fast forward 30 years and, my goodness, how this has changed, led of course by the emergence of China as an economic superpower.

The changes are, however, much deeper and broader than that. For example, the recent global shortage of semiconductors, the computer chips that make the digital world go round, underlined the importance of the giant technology companies that dominate the market in Korea and Taiwan. Pension pots are also growing rapidly in the region, and much of the money is being invested in Asia's stock markets.

This makes it even more important for people to understand how these markets work. They are all quite different, with their own quirks and idiosyncrasies. They are also, to varying degrees, exposed to global forces such as geo-political tensions between China and the US, and longer-term demographic trends like ageing.

However, the truth remains that, for many, investing in stock markets can be a daunting prospect. Some turn to financial advisors with mixed results. Investors are often bombarded with too much jargon and not a little bullshit that can make their heads spin. This book is for the Andrews of this world, people who want to keep their relationship with investing on a need to know basis and have no desire to become entangled in the opaque language of finance and markets.

This book features a rich cast of characters and tales of triumph and disaster, dismal market crashes and ludicrous peaks. We meet Dirck van Os, who became the world's first stock investor in Amsterdam in 1602. This little slice of history is helpful because both the plumbing and psychology of stock markets have not really changed over the centuries despite innumerable crises.

In India, Rakesh Jhunjhunwala fell in love with the stock market listening to his father argue with friends about share prices, before going on to become one of the richest men in the country. Then there's Samsung chairman, Lee Kun-hee, who in 1993 famously called on employees to "change everything but your wife and children" in the pursuit of leading the company into a new era, one in which quality trumped quantity. Two years later, he ordered the mass burning of Samsung products which he considered to be defective. Only the best was good enough for him. Samsung is now one of the most-recognisable names in global technology.

There are also scandals aplenty. An investment bank in Hong Kong, Peregrine, reached for the sky but instead came crashing down to earth in the mid-1990s by loaning money to the unfortunately named Steady Safe, an Indonesian taxi company. More recently, a Chinese coffee chain called Luckin soon ran out of luck after it was discovered that it was better at faking its accounts than selling coffee. And let's not forget Sino-Forest, the Canadian-listed lumber company – the investors couldn't see the wood for the trees because the trees it said it owned in China simply didn't exist.

Before we start this journey across Asia, let's make one thing absolutely clear: this book does not try to tell you which stocks to buy and it contains no specific investment recommendations. There are entire library shelves devoted to that subject. The companies mentioned are simply part of the narrative that unfolds in the following pages.

Chapter 1 The story begins in 1602, the year when the first prototype stock market began operations in a house in Amsterdam. More than two and a half centuries later, in 1875, Asia's first stock market opened in Mumbai. A little bit of history helps to show that the basic mechanics of stock markets have not changed that much over the years.

Chapter 2 My career in the world of Asian finance began as the most junior of junior stock analysts in Jakarta. Over time, I realised that people have very different ideas about what a stock market is or should be. Many see it as a barometer of the economy, while politicians assume the market is a benchmark for their approval ratings. Both views are wrong, and it is explained why the supermarket shelf-life of sushi can help explain the tug of war between dividend payments and bond yields.

Chapter 3 Human psychology has a lot to answer for and greed, fear and misplaced confidence are three recurring emotions in any stock market. A sharp fall in share prices can lead to panic, while a surge can bring on a severe case of FOMO – fear of missing out. Investors who are in for the long haul should shut out the noise, take it easy, and order another gin and tonic.

Chapter 4 My first day in China back in 1991 was a complete disaster. I was robbed, smacked in the nose and the first plane I flew on landed in a paddy field after skidding off the runway. Like the country itself, China's stock markets have been transformed from financial backwaters to global juggernauts running at breakneck speed. Although the two main markets in Shanghai and Shenzhen are quite different, they are both opening their doors wider to the world at a rapid pace.

Chapter 5 Hong Kong and Singapore remain close financial friends, yet fierce rivals. Stanley Kwan introduced the Hang Seng Index with the help of pen, paper and typewriter, and the Hong Kong market hasn't looked back ever since. It never stands still and is now a magnet for China's tech leaders, while Singapore's market remains heavily dependent on traditional banks and property companies. We also take a brief look at Macau, home to the world's busiest casinos, gangsters and meat cleavers.

Chapter 6 Welcome to India, home to Asia's oldest stock market, which is as diverse as the country itself. Giant pharma and IT firms with international footprints jostle alongside local retailers which have mastered the art of reaching millions of rural consumers in countless villages and small towns scattered across India's vast hinterland. Given the range of languages, tastes and cultures, local knowledge is the key to success.

Chapter 7 Taiwan and Korea have a lot in common. Both economies are dominated by large tech companies which export products all over the world; they also face the challenge of coping with ageing populations. But Korea is a land of global brands, volatile profits and cultural exports. With a few notable exceptions, Taiwan companies tend to make stuff on contract for other people.

Chapter 8 In Southeast Asia, sensual Javanese *dangdut* dancers and a famous Bangkok multimillionaire turned sandwich seller both carry important lessons for investors. These smaller and highly idiosyncratic markets move to their own rhythms as they are less influenced by economic data coming out of China, offering investors the opportunity to diversify their stock portfolios.

Chapter 9 Our journey around the region ends in Japan, the only place in Asia where if you had invested in the stock market in the late 1980s and kept it there, you would have lost money. We look at the extraordinary boom and bust which reshaped the country's stock market and how a number of companies which lead the world in precision engineering, both large and small, offer hope for the future.

Chapter 10 Different styles of investment go in and out of fashion, and they can help us gain a better understanding of how Asian stock markets work. For example, as the pandemic eased, there was an almighty tussle between the growth stocks that benefitted from COVID-19 lockdowns (think internet) and the value companies which stand to prosper once life has returned to normal (think traditional consumer operators, travel and tourism).

Chapter 11 Responsible investing is a red hot topic in investment circles these days. Many want to make a positive contribution to the world we live in and the concept of environmental, social and governance (ESG) investing has evolved from fuzzy green do-goodery to a hard-nosed set of investment rules and principles at a rapid clip. There's much more to come, led by the younger generation, and this will move markets.

Chapter 12 We finish off by taking a peek at what Asia's stock markets might look like in ten years' time. First, we look back to see what we can learn – those who cannot remember the past are condemned to repeat it. And while predicting the future is fraught with hazards, changes in demographics and advances in technology help provide some measure of certainty. By 2030, the silver dollar – money spent by the elderly – and automation will both be powerful forces across Asia.

Now, it's time to hit the road. Imagine that you have just arrived at the main railway station in the centre of bustling Amsterdam …

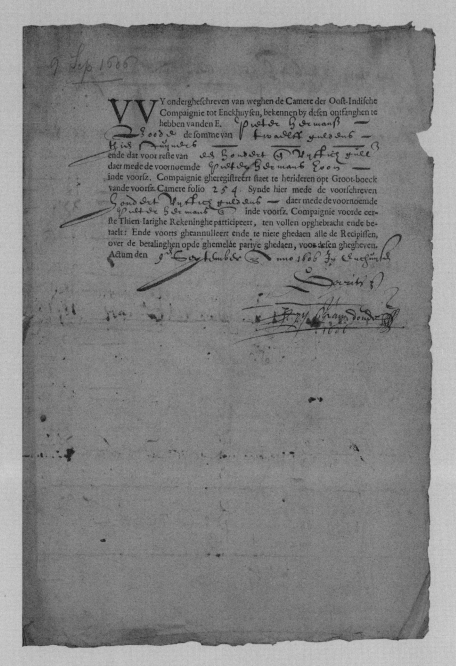

Investors in Dutch East India Company (VOC) shares received a receipt which effectively became tradeable share certificates. The oldest share certificate in the world is dated 9 September 1606 and was in the ownership of Pieter Harmensz, who invested 150 guilders in the VOC in 1602. This was not a small capital investment, about equal to his annual salary. His name is mentioned on the front of the certificate. The inside of the certificate recorded dividend payments and their payment dates. He received his first payment in 1612 and the last recorded payment in 1650. It also shows that, in 1635, the VOC paid out its dividends in bags of cloves. Source: Hoorn, Westfries Archief, Stadsarchief Enkhuizen, toegangsnummer 0120, bergnummer 1587a.

Anno 1612 ade 6 November betaelt voor uetdelinge a 5 7½ p c
onde 150 g Cap: — f 96 . 5 . 0
Anno 1615 ade 2 december betaelt voor uetdes a 42 ½ p c — 63 . 15 . 0
Anno 1618 aert 21 aprill betaelt voor uetdelung
a 62 p c resoluti — 93 . 15 —
Anno 1620 20 mayb uth voor uetdelinge a 37 ½ p c — 56 . 5 —

Anno 1625 . 6 . october voor uetdelinge an 20 p c — 30
1627 . 12 aprill voor uetdelingen 12 ½ p c — 18 . 15 —
1629 . 28 february voor uetdelingen an 25 p c — 37 . 10 —
1631 . 13 feb: voor uetdes an 17 ½ p c — 26 . 5 —
1633 . february voor uetdes w 12 ½ p c — 18 . 15 —
1634 . 13 febr: voor 20 p c to — 30
1635 . 15 aprill voor uetdes no p c — 30
11 july voor uetdelings was 12 ½ p c in raet — 18 . 15 —
24 voor uetdel voor uetdes 12 ½ p c . raet — 18 . 15 —
— 41 . 5 —
1637 21 mart 27 ½ p c in maglie — 37 . 10 —
1638 . 4 january voor uetdes an 25 p c in meel —
1639 . my 13 dordres voor uetd des 10 p c cap delling — 15
1640 in 29 marty voor des 15 p c resoluti may — 22 . 10
voor uetdel an 25 p c in meel — 37 . 10 —
1642 2 6 augusti voor uetde des 25 p c in meel — 37 . 10 —
de voor uetdes an 15 p c in meel des — 22 . 10
1642 . 26 d voor uetdes 25 p c in dichena — 37 . 10
1643 . 20 january voor contant — 25
a 29 september voor 15 p c nagels in voort — 22 . 10
1645 f aprill 20 p c des 15 f raes voort — 63 . 10 —
1646 . 8 october 22 ½ p c p c out — 33 . 15 —
1647 . 15 aprill 25 f to Cont . — 30 — 37 . 10 —
1649 . 18 january 30 f to 25 p c
Cont . 25 f p c voorder
p january 1648 G to 30 p dato — 02 . 10 .
1649
1650 . 1 marty 20 p c Cont — 30 —

Chapter 1

A Bit of History

Nes, 1602

Travellers arriving in Amsterdam make their way through a bustling, high-roofed, 19th century railway station before they find themselves in a large square at the front of the building. Here, swarms of waiting relatives, lovers, business associates and other assorted meeters and greeters swirl back and forth between trams, taxis and a thousand bicycles.

The square opens on to a broad street with a wide canal on the left, both called The Damrak. It's often packed with wandering tourists, rowdy British bachelor parties, overseas students in search of weed, or busy locals pedalling their way disdainfully through the crowd on bicycles, bells jingling. The wide sidewalks are lined with kebab vendors, pizza restaurants and souvenirs shops that draw new arrivals into the city centre a five-minute walk away.

The Damrak opens up to the large and imposing Dam Square, the heart of Amsterdam, with the former City Hall at the centre, a large church on the right and Madam Tussauds, a tourist hot spot, on the left. This is also where the Dutch gather, at the National Monument – to celebrate the end of World War II, protest about whatever is on their minds or simply soak up the atmosphere and people-watch. In a small side street there is a shop I like to visit, home to an elegant, old distiller of gin – *jenever* in Dutch – named Wynand Fockink. Aged *jenever* is a wonderful, long-forgotten spirit with a taste that has much more in common with malt Scotch whisky than Gordon's London dry gin. The shop has been there since 1679.[1]

On the left of Dam Square is The Rokin, a road which opens into a wide boulevard, with a large metro station of the same name. After a few hundred metres, a left turn takes you on to a narrow street, more of an alley really, next to the NRC newspaper building, which provides access to an even narrower alleyway that runs parallel to The Rokin. Enclosed by the tall buildings, it's a very quiet area. Few tourists venture here, unless they have booked a seat at the small Frascati theatre or a table at one of the unpretentious restaurants.

We have arrived at where it all started – Nes. In this nondescript lane, global capitalism was born on the evening of 1 April 1602. It was here that the world's first shares were traded in a house in the centre of Amsterdam belonging to a tall, handsome man with a twisty little moustache. His name was Dirck van Os.[2]

The world's first IPO

The story began a few years earlier on 2 April 1595, when four ships – the Mauritius, Hollandia and Amsterdam, together with the smaller Duyfken, all equipped with the latest gunnery – set sail for Banten, the most important of the trading centres on the island of Java.[3] They arrived more than a year later, on 6 June 1596. The fleet was under the command of Cornelis de Houtman, who had instructions from the expedition's financial backers to explore the viability of sailing all the way to Asia and to identify opportunities to buy pepper, nutmeg and other spices from those faraway lands.

Welcome to the world of 16th century European geo-politics. At the time, the Portuguese were the nemesis of the Dutch in Asia. These formidable mariners had arrived in the region about a century earlier than the Dutch and taken control of the strategically important city of Malacca on the Malay Peninsula. To avoid a possible clash with the Portuguese, the Dutch steered clear of the peninsula by sailing to the southern tip of Sumatra, and then on to the neighbouring island of Java. It was here, in Bantam and various other small towns dotted along the northern coast, that they planned to ply their trade.

Where it all started: a painting of Nes, by Herman P Schouten, 1774. The house of Dirck van Os, now long gone, would have been on the right, at the end of the street, just after the bend. Source: Amsterdam City Archives.

Portrait of Dirck van Os by Cornelis de Visscher. Source: Stedelijk Museum Alkmaar (on loan from Hoogheemraadschap Hollands Noorderkwartier, Heerhugowaard, The Netherlands).

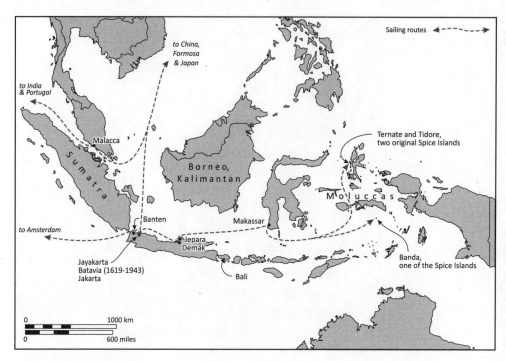

Map of Indonesia with sailing routes. Source: adapted from "Map of the region", *Jakarta – History of a Misunderstood City* (Marshall Cavendish Editions, 2020) pp viii–ix. Map by Brendan Whyte.

This first expedition came at a high price in terms of human lives: of the 240 crew who left Amsterdam, only 87 would make it back alive. Things began to go wrong even before they reached Java. The small fleet had temporarily anchored at Nosy Manitsa, a small island on the southwest coast of Madagascar, when scurvy struck. Reports vary, but between 20 and 30 sailors succumbed to the disease, the blight of the maritime world caused by a lack of vitamin C. Even today, this place is known as The Dutch Graveyard.

Despite the heavy loss of life, the expedition went down in history as a big success. On 14 August 1597, well over two years after setting sail, three of the four ships made it back home – the Mauritius, Hollandia and Duyfken. The Amsterdam had started to leak and had to be torched. This type of bulk carrier – the East Indiaman – was valuable and could not be allowed to fall into the wrong hands.[4] The expedition might have been a commercial failure as few goods were carried back home, but it was now clear that sailing to Asia was possible. It initiated an era of Dutch maritime exploration in the late 16th century, which led to the foundation of the Dutch East India Company in 1602 and the beginning of the Dutch Golden Age.

These dangerous but highly profitable voyages to Asia were often financed by rich individual investors who put cash into a single expedition. The spoils were divided amongst these investors in the form of dividends that were often paid in bags of pepper, nutmeg or other spices that the ships had carried back home. As the profits mounted, the frequency of the expeditions increased.

These voyages were backed by *voorcompagnieën* or pre-companies, the predecessors to the Vereenigde Oost-Indische Compagnie (VOC) or in English, the Dutch East India Company. These trading companies, backed by different Dutch provinces, sent a total of 65 ships to Asia between 1595 and 1602, and the spices the expeditions brought home were sold across Europe at a handsome profit. Some of the money was spent in Amsterdam, spawning all sorts of enterprises, including Wynand Fockink's flourishing gin business near Nes. The small side street was probably considerably busier back in those days. But instead of cooperating, the expeditions of the Dutch provinces competed amongst themselves, much to the benefit of the Portuguese. Then, on 29 March 1602, the government of the new Dutch Republic, under the leadership of Johan van Oldenbarnevelt and Prins Maurits,[5] called a halt to this infighting – and they had a good plan.

Their idea was to amalgamate the *voorcompagnieën* into one large company, the VOC or Dutch East India Company. The company would be run from six different cities, Amsterdam being one, and managed by their representatives, the "board" of the VOC, the Heeren XII. Over time, the VOC would become one of the first truly multinational companies, with its own armed forces and diplomats. It competed with another immensely powerful multinational, Britain's East India Company, which was formed in 1600 to participate in the spice trade.

And so, just before 10pm on Saturday, 1 April 1602, a crowd gathered at the house of Dirck van Os in Nes to establish the Amsterdam chapter of the VOC. One of those present was its bookkeeper, Barent Lampers, who sat behind an imposing, vellum covered volume that became the official register of the first shareholders.

It must have been an extraordinary evening, buzzing with excitement and expectation as the first shares were issued to a total of 1,143 people. And what a motley crew they were: lawyers, carpenters, bakers, shopkeepers, weavers and even seven housemaids lined up to put money into this new venture. The total capital raised in this first "initial public offering" (IPO) – the process by which a private company goes public by the sale of its stocks to the general public – was more than 3.6 million guilders, a fortune at the time. To put this into perspective, in those days, a few hundred guilders would buy a small house in the centre of Amsterdam.

The VOC was a completely different animal from the earlier *voorcompagnieën*. To start with, the company was not liquidated every time the ships returned to Amsterdam and the spoils had been divided.[6] Like many listed companies operating today, this venture was all about thinking about long-term growth. The investors had the right to receive a stream of dividend payments generated by all the VOC's future expeditions.

Aside from putting an end to the infighting between the various Dutch expeditions, this new business model offered another big benefit. Investing in single expeditions was extremely risky. If a ship sank in a storm or was captured by pirates, investors lost all their money. This new model afforded the prospect of the next expedition returning laden with valuable cargo. This meant that risks were much lower. Although this all sounds rather obvious now, the concept of managing risk marked the start of a financial revolution at that time, and this basic principle still drives stock markets today. In the following chapters, we will revisit the idea of multiple expeditions and streams of cash flow quite a few times.

The VOC flourished. By 1611, the Dutch had set up warehouses in a small town on Java's northern coast called Jayakarta. Eventually, they decided to make this their headquarters on the sprawling archipelago that is now Indonesia. To ensure they had full control, they kicked out the British and their East India Company, sidelined the local power brokers and, just for good measure, burned the whole town down. A new city emerged, Batavia, which over the centuries morphed into the metropolis that is now called Jakarta.[7]

The first purpose-built stock exchange

Back in Amsterdam, shareholders were starting to do what shareholders have been doing ever since – buying and selling. The first page of the VOC's share ledger detailed how this was to be done. The buyer and the seller both had to go to East India House,[8] a few minutes' walk from Dirck van Os' house in Nes, and after receiving approval from two directors, the bookkeeper transferred the shares and updated the ledger.[9]

To begin with, trading was far from brisk and it took a year before the first stock trade took place. On 3 March 1603, Jan Allertsz tot London sold his VOC shares for 2,400 guilders to Maria van Egmont. He must have been short of cash because later that day, he sold another 600 guilders worth to a Mrs van Barssum in The Hague.[10] These were the first ever stocks to be traded for the second time – that is, after the IPO – marking the start of secondary stock market transactions, which is a multi-billion-dollar business around the world today.

Profile of Amsterdam, seen from the IJ, by Pieter van der Keere, around 1614 to 1618. The "New Bridge", where stock traders met, is seen prominently in the middle of the picture. These days, the train station blocks this view of the city. Source: Amsterdam City Archives <https://archief. amsterdam/beeldbank/detail/22fb88bf-909b-6f81-999b-396d629b97ad>.

Opposite the Amsterdam railway station is a small bridge, where trams squeal as they turn right from The Damrak to loop towards the central station. Just beyond the "Nieuwe Brug" (New Bridge) is an alley that leads to the Warmoesstraat, one of the oldest streets in Amsterdam. Beyond that lies what was then, and is still today, the city's famed red-light district. In the early 1600s, people who wanted to buy or sell VOC shares met on this unassuming bridge.[11] On rainy days, the traders sought shelter under the porches of the shops on the Warmoesstraat.[12] Once they agreed on a price, it was only a short walk to East India House to finalise the share transfer and update the ledger.

The VOC was starting to prosper and in April 1610, the patient shareholders were summoned to collect their very first dividend after an eight-year wait. But they had already made money. Information is sketchy – neither the exchange clerk nor the VOC itself recorded the prices – but it appears that at the time, shares were trading at double the initial price set in 1602.[13] As for the dividend, they were given 75% of the nominal value of each share – the initial price they paid to buy it on that April day in 1602, not the market value on the day – in mace,[14] the spice made from the reddish covering of the nutmeg seed. Later that year, another 50% was distributed in pepper. This turned out to be a mistake and gave the shareholders an unwanted lesson about the laws of supply and demand. The unintended consequence was that the sudden abundance of pepper saw prices tumble across Amsterdam[15] as everybody turned their dividends into hard currency. Later, it was decided to pay dividends in cash.[16]

Shareholder activism attracts a lot of headlines in the financial media these days. The truth is that it is nothing new. In 1613, a group of shareholders grew frustrated with the directors of the Amsterdam chapter of the VOC. They claimed that the company was far too preoccupied with empire building and military engagements to focus on what it was meant to be doing – making large profits from the spice trade.[17] They were probably right but somehow the issue was resolved and nothing much changed. This was the first attempt to stage a shareholder revolt. By 1622, another debate about the management of the company was in full swing but that, too, proved to be little more than a hiccup. In a

Detailed profile of Amsterdam, seen from the IJ, by Pieter van der Keere, around 1614 to 1618. The "New Bridge" (De Nieuwe Brugh), where stock traders met, is seen prominently in the front of the picture, further back the tower on top of the stock exchange, called "De Beurs", is visible. The letter "s" is somehow hidden in a fold in the drawing. Source: Amsterdam City Archives <https://archief.amsterdam/beeldbank/detail/22fb88bf-909b-6f81-999b-396d629b97ad>.

The Amsterdam Stock Exchange built by Hendrik de Keyser. Different commodities were traded at different corners of the exchange. Stocks were traded in the back, which is visible on this drawing. Source: Wikimedia Commons <https://commons.wikimedia.org/wiki/File:Engraving_depicting_the_Amsterdam_Stock_Exchange,_built_by_Hendrik_de_Keyser_c._1612.jpg>.

later chapter, we will discuss how corporate governance and responsible investing have made quite a splash in Asian stock markets in recent years, but it is perhaps a comfort to know that it was also an issue in the very first days of stock trading.

By that time, it had become clear that trading in the rain on a windy bridge was a rather inconvenient way to buy and sell shares. Initially, traders moved their business to coffee shops, posting the shares they had for sale on the shops' doors. But as trading in VOC shares and a range of other commodities gained in popularity, it was decided that a permanent trading venue was required. The city council appointed architect Hendrik de Keyser to design and construct a building on what is now The Rokin, close to the residence of Dirck van Os in Nes. It was to become the world's first purpose-built stock exchange.[18] The impressive building opened on 1 August 1611 and consisted of a covered stone passage around a large rectangular courtyard where commodities were traded, each in their own designated location. Trading in stocks took place by one of the pillars at the back of the exchange.[19]

Fittingly, the exchange was built on top of a canal and returning ships could pass directly underneath the building on their way to delivering spices to warehouses that lined the city's network of waterways. Despite concerns about cracks in the foundations, the building survived until 1836, when the market was moved to the Beurs van Berlage, near The Damrak, which still serves as the Amsterdam Stock Exchange[20] today.

The flame of capitalism had been lit and soon spread like wildfire across the whole city. Everybody wanted a piece of the action – bakers, housemaids, lawyers, bankers and gin distillers. In 1688, the first bestseller about stock markets was written by an Amsterdam-born Portuguese Jew named Joseph de la Vega. He described how trading in VOC shares held Amsterdam in its grip:[21]

> If one were to lead a stranger through the streets of Amsterdam and ask him where he was, he would answer "among speculators" for there is not corner where one does not talk shares.

The book was written in flowery 17th-century language, with the narrative structured around a philosopher, a merchant and a shareholder in discussion about the stock market. But he also writes about "confusion" about the mechanics of the exchange and warns about dodgy practices and shenanigans by rogue traders of the day. Again, little seems to have changed.

One of these practices, perfectly acceptable these days, was to "go short" – borrow stocks on the assumption that prices will fall and make a profit by buying them back at a lower price. It's the opposite of being "long", buying in the hope that share prices will trade higher. The first investor to go short was Isaac le Maire, a sizeable shareholder of the VOC. He is said to have shorted the company's shares by speculating on its ships being lost at sea, causing such a stink that the practice was eventually banned.[22]

In those early days, purchasing stocks was like buying apples in a market: two parties negotiated a price and made a deal. This is what is now called an "over the counter" (OTC) market. But buyer beware – fake share certificates could be the ruin of investors. It was eventually decided that it would be best to buy and sell through an agent who could check if the counterparty was the real owner of the shares, if the share certificates were legitimate, and had been properly registered in the appropriate ledger. These people were called "stock jobbers" or "stockbrokers".

Molten cheese

The idea of stock exchanges spread like molten cheese, slowly and irreversibly. About 50 years later, in 1657, the management of the British East India Company[23] in London went from funding individual expeditions to backing a continuous stream of voyages, just like the VOC.[24] They also needed a stock exchange.

Trading in gold and silver in London was already taking place in Jonathan's Coffee House, but a proper stock exchange, "New Jonathan's", was opened in 1773 in Sweeting's Alley, now Threadneedle Street and the home of the Bank of England.[25] The London securities market quickly overtook its Amsterdam counterpart and became the more powerful financial centre. And as more shares were traded, the British government began using the market to raise loans (a bond market). By the end of the 17th century, all manner of shares were being traded in London; by 1695, there were 140 listed companies in the market.[26]

In London, however, just like in Amsterdam, rogue traders were the order of the day. Eventually, in 1697, the British government decided that something needed to be done. It introduced legislation to "restrain the number of ill-practice of brokers and stock jobbers"[27] which meant that all trade went through stockbrokers. These brokers were not allowed to deal on their own behalf, only their clients; they had to be registered, wear a special silver medal embossed with the Royal Arms, and could charge a maximum 5% commission fee. Those that didn't comply ended up, if caught, in the pillory for three days.[28]

The Americans were the next to catch the stock market fever. On 17 May 1792, a group of 24 stockbrokers met under the boughs of a buttonwood tree on the corner of Wall Street and Broadway in New York to sign the appropriately named Buttonwood Agreement. They decided to make the nearby Tontine Coffee House their headquarters. Trading initially focused on government bonds but 25 years later, on 8 March 1817, the New York Stock Exchange (NYSE) was opened.

A picture of pillory. Source: Wikipedia <https://en.wikipedia.org/wiki/Pillory#/media/File:John_Waller_in_pillory.JPG>.

Stock exchanges then started to pop up across Asia. The first was set up in Mumbai in 1875. Before that, somewhere around 1850, Indian stockbrokers traditionally met under shady banyan trees in front of the town hall[29] and later at the junction of Meadows Street.[30] But as the number of stockbrokers rose and the streets became congested with agitated traders, they moved to Dalal Street, or Broker Street,[31] a name that became synonymous with India's finance industry (like Wall Street in the US).

At about the same time, Japanese stockbrokers, easily identified on the streets by their distinctive kimonos, gathered to establish the Tokyo Stock Exchange. It opened on 15 May 1878 and two weeks later, on 1 June, the first Japanese shares exchanged hands. Other exchanges were set up in different cities – the Osaka stock exchange, for example – and in 1943, in the middle of World War II, they amalgamated into one large stock market named the Japanese Stock Exchange. This market was shut down at the end of World War II and reopened a few years later, in 1949, as the Tokyo Stock Exchange.

In Southeast Asia, the first city off the mark was Jakarta, called Batavia at the time, and part of the Dutch colonies. It opened in 1912. The Philippines followed a few decades later with two stock exchanges: one in Manila in 1927 and another much later in nearby Makati in 1963. They traded exactly the same stocks in two different locations and the markets eventually merged in 1992 to form the Philippine Stock Exchange.

The first Thai exchange was established in July 1962 in Bangkok. At first, it did not attract a lot of attention and died a slow death. But the Thais gave it another shot and in 1975, the Securities Exchange of Thailand (SET) started trading.[32] Singapore had joined the club two years earlier. After the Korean War ended in 1953, South Korea established the Korean Stock Exchange (KSE). In 1997, a second exchange, the KOSDAQ, was launched to attract new tech companies and other young businesses.[33] It proved to be a huge success.[34]

Most of these new Asian stock exchanges were raucous, bustling "open outcry" markets, with brokers receiving orders from clients on pieces of paper and shouting them to so-called market makers, the holders of an inventory of stock. When it got too noisy, they used hand signals, and to identify brokers in the crowd they would wear special coloured jackets. Traders for the Hong Kong and Shanghai Banking Corporation (HSBC), for example, wore striped red and white jackets. Market makers would identify the trades, use hand signals to communicate with the brokers and then record the share prices and trading volumes on a wall or large blackboard. In the 1990s, these traders became obsolete as computer trading systems did the same job much faster.

China enters the game

The history of China's stock markets deserves a little more attention and is a little more complex. The Opium Wars and the Treaty of Nanking in 1842 allowed the British and other nations to establish footholds in China and obtain access to the country's markets. In Shanghai, in an area called the International Settlement, and Guangzhou (Canton), foreigners traded rubber, coal and other goods under their own laws. Stocks were popular too, and in June 1866, the first list of shares to be traded was nailed to a wall near the Shanghai Customs House.

CUSTOM HOUSE, SHANGHAI.

Shanghai Custom House, from "The world: historical and actual" by Frank Gilbert, 1886. Source: Wikimedia Commons <https://commons.wikimedia.org/wiki/File:The_world-_historical_and_actual_(1886)_(14596896879).jpg>.

Eventually, the sale of shares had to be conducted through appointed stockbrokers to ensure nobody sold pieces of worthless paper and in 1891, the Shanghai Sharebrokers' Association met for the first time. Initially, a few banks, shipping, canal and dock companies were listed on the Shanghai Stock Exchange. It was modest in size, with a total market value of US$23 million in 1871, because large companies that needed capital, such as railroads, preferred to issue shares in London.[35] The Shanghai market was dominated by rubber plantations and by autumn 1910, there were as many as 47 rubber companies listed. Rubber remained the biggest sector until the 1940s.

In 1937, Japan occupied Shanghai and put a halt to share trading on 8 December 1941. It resumed after the war but when the communists seized power in 1949, this beacon of capitalism was closed down again. Meanwhile, the stock market in Hong Kong, set up at the same time as its Shanghai counterpart in 1891, continued to trade.

Deng Xiaoping, China's great reformer, reopened the country's economy to foreigners in 1978. Chinese firms that wanted to list their shares usually went to Hong Kong, but in December 1990, the Shanghai stock market opened again after nearly half a century.[36] China also opened a secondary exchange in the bustling southern city of Shenzhen in 1990 in order to raise funds for technology companies. It proved to be popular and everybody wanted in on new share issues; in 1992, protests broke out when there were not enough forms printed for subscribing to a new share offering.

I remember this very clearly because I was there. But that's something we will pick up later in Chapter 4 on China's stock markets.

Endnotes

1　Wynand Fockink acquired the distillery in 1724. See the Wynand Fockink website: <https://wynand-fockink.nl/history>. Aside from old *jenever*, it sells Dutch liqueurs aptly named "Volmaakt Geluk" (Perfect Bliss), "Bruidstranen" (Bride's Tears) and "Hansje in de Kelder" (Jack in the Cellar).

2　Dirck van Os was one of the initial shareholders of the VOC. But his signature is also found on a document dated 8 January 1609 with the English adventurer, Henry Hudson. Hudson was employed by the VOC to look for a shorter, western-sailing route to India. This he did not find but in the process "discovered" Manhattan in 1609 and sailed up the river, now called the Hudson River.

3   Before this trip, two other attempts to find a passage to Asia by a northern route, through the Arctic, had failed. In 1596, the city of Amsterdam offered 25,000 guilders to fund a third venture through the Arctic. Two ships sailed, one under Jan Cornelisz Rijp, the other under Jacob van Heemskerck, with navigator and cartographer Willem Barendsz as expedition leader. Their aim was to sail to the kingdom of Cathay (China). Instead, they discovered Bear Island and Spitsbergen in the Arctic (now part of Norway). Van Heemskerck's ship became trapped in the ice off the island of Nova Zembla and the crew of 17 were forced to stay there through the long Arctic winter. The Barents Sea was named after the cartographer Barentsz. See de Veer 2010.

4   It was not that the ship was destroyed because the Dutch ships were better or had some new technology that they did not want to fall into the hands of others. Indeed, on the contrary, it appears that Dutch ships were slower than others travelling from Europe to Asia. See Bruijn 1984. Still, ships were considered valuable property not to be fallen into the hands of an opponent.

5   Prins Maurits would lend his name to an island in the Indian Ocean, Mauritius.

6   Initially, the idea was to continue the VOC's business for 21 years, but this was later scrapped.

7   van der Linde 2020.

8   This was the Oost-Indisch Huis on Kloveniersburgwal 48 in Amsterdam.

9   Petram 2011, p 2. An official transfer in the capital books involved transaction costs that were high, amounting to $f2.80$: the bookkeeper charged $f0.60$ per transaction and the stamp tax on the deed of transfer was $f2.20$. Remember, a small house in the centre of the city cost about 200 guilders in those days. Petram 2011, p 18.

10 Petram 2014, p 16.

11 A little further, in the Warmoesstraat, is where commodity traders gathered every day and they were the same merchants that dominated the trade in VOC shares.

12 Petram 2011, p 19.

13 For VOC share prices, see Petram 2011, p 243.

14 Mace, which the VOC distributed to shareholders in the first dividend of 1610, is the covering of the nutmeg seeds. It's called *foelie* in Dutch.

15 Petram 2011, pp 28–29.

16 Starting in 1623, the VOC paid out a dividend every two years, and from 1635 until the company's bankruptcy in the late 18th century, it paid out every year or every six months, with only a few interruptions. But this was not always the case and in the 1630s and 1640s, dividends were still often paid in kind, now primarily in the form of cloves. See Petram's website: <https://www.worldsfirststockexchange.com/2020/10/01/what-was-the-return-on-voc-shares/>.

17 Petram 2011, p 32.

18 The Amsterdam Stock Exchange is considered to be the first stock exchange although trading on exchanges started much earlier, and this was mostly debt paper. People were, however, trading assets thousands of years ago during the Roman Empire. A better way to categorise the Amsterdam Stock Exchange would be as the oldest of the stock exchanges in the world which are still operating. It was, however, the first to construct a special, purpose-built stock exchange.

19 Petram 2011, p 31. Trading only took place at particular hours, every day of the week except Sundays, from 11am to noon and, during summer months (May–August), from 6.30 to 7.30pm.

20 Trading at the Amsterdam Stock Exchange is now done in a new building adjacent to it.

21 de la Vega 1939, paragraph 249, translation used by Petram 2011, p 1.

22 Petram 2011, p 60 and onwards. Technically, he went into a "naked short" as he sold shares that he did not own in speculation that he would buy them at a lower price.

23 The British East India Company (EIC) was founded 1600.

24 Before that time, the EIC repeatedly issued new stocks to fund its fleets and was thus basically a series of separate companies with the same name.

25 The Bank of England is located on Threadneedle Street, which has been its home for the past 250 years and this is why it is sometimes it is called "The Old Lady of Threadneedle Street". Less widely known is that for the first 40 years after its foundation in 1694, the Bank did not have its own building. The Bank first operated from the Mercers' Hall in Cheapside, after which it moved to the Grocers' Hall. See Bank of England's website: <https://www.bankofengland.co.uk/about/history>.

26 By 1824, this had grown to 156. See Chapman 1994, p 12–14. The market capitalisation was GBP4.5m in 1695 and GBP47.9m in 1824.

27 William III 1697.

28 William III 1697 and Chapman 1994, p 10. The bill reads "offending shall forfeit the sum of five hundred pounds and likewise being legally convicted thereof shall for such Offence stand in the Pillory in some public place within the City of London, three days for the space of one hour in the morning of each of the said three days".

29 In Mumbai, where Horniman Circle is currently situated.

30 Now known as Mahatma Gandhi Road.

31 That was in 1842. Dalal is Marathi for "broker". Dalal Street in Mumbai is the address of the Bombay Stock Exchange. When the Bombay Stock Exchange was moved to its current location at the intersection of Bombay Samachar Marg and Hammam Street, the street next to the building was renamed as Dalal Street. It is often used as a metonym for the entire Indian financial establishment.

32 This name was changed to Stock Exchange of Thailand (SET) on 1 January 1991.

33 Before that, smaller and new tech companies had gone to what is called an "over-the-counter" markets, a place to trade stocks without brokers, not unlike buying apples or oranges in a fruit market.

34 Shin 2002.

35 Another factor at play was that the Europeans were interested in railroads to exploit Chinese resources, something opposed by the Chinese mandarins at the time. Thus, it was not something the Chinese wanted to invest in. Between 1881 and 1895, only 18 miles of railways were built per year in China, but when the Chinese government realised how railroads could help the government put down the Boxer Rebellion between 1899 and 1901, a railway boom ensued, though one managed by the government for military purposes. By 1911, 6,000 miles of railway had been laid. See Taylor 2019.

36 On 26 November 1990, the Shanghai Stock Exchange was established, and on 19 December of the same year, it started formal operations. Source: Shanghai stock exchange website.

Chapter 2

Myths and Misconceptions

Morning meetings and investment myths

On a sweltering hot day in late August 1990, after descending from a KLM flight from Amsterdam to Bali, I stood on the tarmac and inhaled an incredible concoction of aromas – a mixture of ripe fruit, fried meat, wet grass and burnt rubber. This was my first trip to Asia and the idea was to go backpacking across Indonesia for a few months.

I hopped around Bali and in the weeks that followed, I made my way east, across a string of islands in eastern Indonesia. On one island, I met a family who lived in Jakarta, Indonesia's capital, there to visit family. I got to know them over the next few days and by the time I headed further east with my student backpack, I had promised to look them up when I was back in Jakarta. A few months later, I arrived in the sprawling metropolis by train at Gambir, the railway station located in the city centre. My first views of Jakarta were shacks along the railway, clothes drying in the sun by the tracks and children playing nearby, waving to train passengers.

I phoned the family and found myself, a few hours later, at their house in Pasar Minggu, a district in south Jakarta. The whole family, their friends and a few neighbours wanted to say hello to this somewhat dishevelled Dutch fellow. In the months and years that followed, I stayed at their home on a regular basis, becoming close friends and, in the process, significantly improving my Bahasa Indonesia skills.

That was my first experience of Asia and I was hooked. I returned the following year, this time to China, a trip that got off to a disastrous start.

More on that later. In the following years, I financed my university studies by moonlighting as a tour guide in China and Indonesia, shepherding groups of 20 to 30 adventurous Europeans around two equally exotic but quite different countries. Remember, this was in the early 1990s and tourism in China was still barely a trickle after the fallout from the Tiananmen Square crackdown in 1989.

I graduated in 1994 and, after navigating one last tour group around China, decided to stay in Asia and look for a job. Eventually, an opportunity as a junior stock analyst with a bank presented itself in Jakarta. There was one minor problem. I had studied economics but had not the faintest idea about finance and accounting, aside from an introduction to finance course I had taken at university. At the advice of my first boss, Rick, I signed up for the three-year chartered financial analyst (CFA) programme, which meant that for a few hours every Saturday, I dived into the theory of finance.

I loved my new job and new home. I shared a house in central Jakarta with two other expats and was soon in tune with the rhythm of city life. Early each morning, I walked out of our garden and grabbed breakfast. This came in the form of *nasi uduk* – a wrapped packet of rice, vegetables and spicy *tempeh* made from fermented soybeans. As the friendly lady who ran the makeshift stall opposite our house prepared my order, our neighbour would come out to spray the street with water to prevent dust, another part of Jakarta life, from blowing into our homes. The heat of the day had not yet arrived and, *nasi uduk* in hand, I would walk a hundred metres to the main road to wave down a taxi for the short journey to work.

By 6.30am, I was at my desk on the 17th floor of a large office block in central Jakarta. It was still quiet on the roads but within half an hour, the traffic would start to snarl into the jams the city was, and still is, famous for. The office buzzed with activity. Clocks displaying the time in Jakarta, Hong Kong, Tokyo, Zurich, London and New York gave the whole enterprise an international feel, the sense that you were part of something much larger and awfully grand. By 7.30am, the morning newspapers had already been devoured and discarded, and we gathered in a room with wide, sweeping views of the city.

The morning meeting, an age-old industry ritual, was about to begin.

This is how equity analysts, sales staff and traders start their day the world over. At its best, the morning meeting is full of insight, razor-sharp analyses and lively exchanges between very clever people who really know their stuff. At its worst, it is full of overblown waffle and limp, tedious presentations with few clear conclusions or investment ideas. One way or another, these precious 30 minutes will set the tone for the working day.

On the conference room table would be a set of printouts prepared by our research associate, Sandra, who came in at an ungodly hour every morning to ensure we had yesterday's closing prices and latest valuations for all the major stocks listed on the Jakarta exchange. The head of equity sales, James, would call the room to order and ask the traders to comment on what had happened in the US markets overnight and Tokyo earlier in the day. Then our economists would dial in from Hong Kong to comment on the latest data releases or statements by Indonesia's central bank. James then handed over to Rick, the head of research, who would introduce the reports the analysts had published overnight.

While traders make split-second decisions about the direction of the market, analysts have a very different job. Trained in accountancy or financial analysis, they play a longer game, steeped (hopefully) in knowledge about the companies they cover. They have the time to read through financial statements, work on spreadsheets, build valuation models, visit factories, meet company executives, check on supply chains, read up on industry trends and visit retail stores. Once they have presented a (in theory) brief assessment of their stock views, the equity sales staff and traders would bombard them with questions to test their convictions and investment theses about individual stocks and broader equity sectors. We had analysts who specialised in areas like Indonesian banks, industrial companies or large retailers. Rick, the head of the team, covered paper producers, which were a really big deal in those days. My first job as a junior analyst was to look at anything that fell outside these categories.

By 8am, the morning meeting was over. The traders were handed order pads and their job was to gauge what might happen to the stocks that they needed to buy or sell that day. If they had to buy shares for a client and they felt the price would move higher, it was best to be aggressive in the morning. But if they thought prices would come down, it was better to wait until later in the day. They looked for anything that might give them a better idea of what would happen – they monitored markets across the region, assessed the pearls of wisdom dropped by the economists and analysts at the morning meeting and, of course, rang their contacts for the latest market gossip. Meanwhile, the sales team started phoning clients to dangle the latest research ideas in front of them.

As the day progressed, buy and sell orders were logged manually in the trading system. In those days, this was quite a process. The bank employed three men who were permanently stationed at the stock exchange, a few kilometres from the office, to shout the orders across the trading floor. This "open outcry" style of trading was noisy, boisterous and often dramatic, making it great fun to watch.[1] E-mail was in its infancy in the mid-1990s, so a young man was employed to feed a sputtering fax machine and send the research reports to clients all over Asia and later to Europe and the US. It took him all day. The hope was that clients would appreciate the service and direct orders to our trading desks. We now live in a completely different world: stock prices are available on screen at the click of a mouse and buyers and sellers are matched electronically. But the essence of the morning meeting – the buzz, the energy and let's not forget the bullshit – have never gone away.

The truth is that stock markets grip the collective imagination. Over the years, I have heard all sorts of different people spout all sorts of ideas about what stock markets are, are not or should be. Politicians see them in terms of approval ratings, mom and pop investors regard them as a proxy for the economy, some think they are exclusive playgrounds for the rich, while others condemn them as casinos or symbols of heartless capitalism.[2] Markets are often described – usually completely out of context – as being "crazy", "irrational", "about to fall off a cliff" or "runaway trains that nothing can stop". If they behave differently from what some people expect, they are described in the media as "complacent" or "disconnected from the real world". This is not to say that stock markets are perfect, far from it. But, more often than not, these criticisms and headlines reveal a misunderstanding of what markets really are.

Before we go any further, these myths and misconceptions need to be addressed. It turns out that history can offer a helping hand as the plumbing of stock markets has not changed that much since that April evening in 1602 when the Dutch East India Company was founded in a house in a backstreet of Amsterdam.

1 The stock market is not the economy

"Why is the Stock Market Rallying When the Economy is so Bad?" blared a headline in *The Wall Street Journal* on 8 May 2020. The coronavirus had hit economies around the world hard, with businesses closing their doors and millions of people losing their jobs. Airlines went bankrupt, banks were struggling and restaurants had to move into food delivery service or face sudden death.

Stock markets, however, went up and up. Many journalists and TV commentators threw their arms into the air and asked how this could be. They assumed that the stock market was some sort of barometer for the health of the economy. That's plain wrong. Studies have shown that there is no relationship between economic growth and the performance of stock markets. Quite the reverse – a stronger economy is often bad news for markets.[3]

In essence, a stock market is nothing more than a bunch of companies that allow their shares to be freely traded on a stock exchange. The total value of all the shares of a company is what is called the market capitalisation of a company or "market cap". It's a simple concept. If a company has 1,000 shares priced at $10 each, the market cap is $10,000. It's true that business is impacted by the state of the economy, that is, how many people have a job, how many products are being bought and sold, the level of investment made in a particular year and how many goods are traded with other countries. But that does not mean that the stock market reflects the strength of the economy.

For example, the US stock market, the largest on the planet with thousands of listed companies, is less of a reflection of the US economy now than it was in the 1970s. The reason is simple. The vast majority of companies in the US – from online retail websites and restaurant chains, to healthcare clinics and shopping malls – are not listed.[4] In Asia, the most extreme example of a stock market that has little to do with its economy is Taiwan. This exchange is dominated by tech companies that make all sorts of gadgets – the stuff that allows 5G telecom networks to run, make your mobile phone buzz or connect it to the Wi-Fi system at home. The products are sold all over the world, but few end up in Taiwan. The strength of Taiwan's economy has little influence on their business. It is demand for these products in the US, China and Europe that really matters. Korea is another example. The big, listed companies, such as Samsung Electronics and Hyundai, operate in global markets. Korea represents only a small portion of their sales.

At the other end of the spectrum, there are stock markets in Asia that do, at least to some extent, reflect the domestic economy. The best examples are China, India, Indonesia and other parts of Southeast Asia. They have a wider range of local businesses listed on their stock exchanges – think banks, retailers, convenience stores operators, domestic car producers and, especially in Southeast Asia, all manner of companies that sell quirky local products not seen elsewhere on the planet. But even here, large parts of the economy do not have a strong presence on the stock market. For example, agriculture represents a big chunk of the economy, but only a few small agricultural companies are listed.

In short, what happens in an economy can have a bearing on listed companies, but it is wrong to say that whatever happens in the economy is reflected in the price of stocks. This has implications for how to get to grips with Asian stock markets. Often, there is no need for a mountain of technical economic analyses.[5] To understand them, we need to look at them from the ground up, identify the biggest players and see what makes these companies tick.

Before we move on, a quick word on the stock market indices that investment companies and the financial media refer to on a daily basis. First, what is an index? It's a benchmark, a way of measuring how a given market, or particular part of that market, is performing. It reflects the value of a small but representative selection of companies. Think the

Hang Seng Index in Hong Kong, the JCI in Jakarta or the Sensex in India. These indices measure the pulse of their respective markets.

For example, the Hang Seng Index covers 50 companies – about 65% of the market cap of the Hong Kong stock exchange – and is often used as a market benchmark by Hong Kong investors. There are many different types of indices – they can track specific markets, individual industry sectors, regions, small companies, or special classes of companies such as the Jakarta Islamic Index. Morgan Stanley Capital International, or MSCI as this global index provider is universally known, now has indices that follow mega-trends in China, such as robotics and renewable energy. From a global perspective, major indices include the MSCI, the Financial Times Stock Exchange (FTSE) and the Standard & Poor's 500 (S&P500).

These indices are important for another reason. Billions and billions of dollars are invested globally in "passive" funds through portfolios that match the components of a particular index. For example, the S&P500 tracks the performance of the largest 500 stocks in the US market. They are called passive funds because they simply follow their benchmark index regardless of the state of the market. No active investment strategy is required. They also offer broad market exposure, low operating expenses and limited portfolio turnover.

2 A stock is not a company

I always enjoy staying at Mandarin hotels and feasting on spicy hotpot, a Sichuan specialty. The Mandarin hotel group and Haidilao, a hotpot chain in China, are both listed, but the fact that I like what they sell tells me absolutely nothing about the attractiveness of their stocks. This is because a stock is not a company. It is, just like in the days of the Dutch East India Company (VOC), a right to a fair, equitable portion of the spoils of that company, the profits or "dividends" as they were known back then. That is why shares are also called "equity", meaning equal rights to the profits. The words stocks, shares and equity all mean the same thing.[6]

The genius of the VOC was that investors were no longer betting all their cash on a single expedition, which meant they had a much better chance of getting dividend payments. The VOC took eight years to pay its first dividend, but these days investors expect annual payments. To make matters easier, companies announce whether they will pay a percentage of all profits or a fixed payment every year. Shareholders get an invitation, often to a large ballroom in a swanky five-star hotel, to vote on how much of last year's profits will be paid in dividends.[7]

Of course, not all companies are alike. In Asia, especially in China, the major shareholder can be the government. For example, China Mobile, a massive state-owned enterprise, sits on a massive pile of cash, as much as RMB451 billion (US$69 billion) at the end of 2020, but the company has not paid it out in dividends for years. This is also the case with other state-owned companies, something that investors should keep in mind. To make a return on their investment, they simply have to hope that the share price goes up.

The VOC was ahead of its time because investors had a stake in all the company's expeditions, voyages being made in a particular year as well as those that would sail in the years ahead. This meant that all of the investors' eggs were not in one basket. This was a very big deal, as it introduced the revolutionary concept of managing risk and having a stake in future expeditions (and cash flows).

As mentioned in the previous chapter, this principle still drives stock markets today. It is important because it helps us to evaluate a stock, or the whole stock market for that matter, in terms of a continuous stream of dividend payments paid out every year until the company ceases to exist. For context, the VOC was around for 200 years, not bad considering that its British and Portuguese rivals were keen practitioners of what can be loosely termed as the "hostile takeover" school of corporate governance.

This introduces a tricky issue. Most people prefer to get paid dividends now rather than in the future.[8] This makes perfect sense as you can put the dividend to work to earn interest. As the saying goes, a bird in the hand is worth two in the bush. So a dividend paid in the future is worth less than a dividend paid now,[9] but how do you measure this? In a word, discounts. This is the process of determining the present value of a future payment or stream of payments.

To avoid getting too deeply into finance jargon, consider the fresh sushi counter in a supermarket. In the morning, the sushi is listed at full price; by the time the supermarket closes, the unsold product will have no value as sushi does not keep. The manager wants, of course, to sell as much sushi as possible. He offers a discount in the early afternoon and increases the discount later in the day and again in the evening. At 10pm when the store closes, whatever is left unsold has to be thrown away. The point to note is that the discount increases as the price of sushi falls throughout the day.

And so it is with discounts to dividend payments. As we peer further into the future, the discount grows and the value of the dividends falls, just like the price of sushi. With stocks, however, we are not talking about hours in a day but payments that stretch out over years. Next year's dividend payments get, for example, a 2% discount, while one paid in 10 years' time might be discounted by 25%. The further into the future the dividend is to be paid, the larger the discount and the lower the value of the dividend.

So far, we have established that stock markets are an agglomeration of listed companies and therefore, by extension, the sum of all dividends paid. And because dividends are based on profits, investors look at the profits generated by the companies listed on the stock exchange (there are exceptions, like China Mobile). Politicians might see stock markets as barometers of their popularity and others might consider it a temperature check on the economy but in the end, it's simply all about dividend payments and the discount rates attached to future payments.[10]

And that brings us to the third misconception about stock markets – the importance of bond markets, and investors who ignore this do so at their own peril.

3 Bond markets matter much more than you think
The first thing you need to know about bond markets is that they don't get nearly as much attention as stock markets. For example, the closing prices of the major stock markets are regularly reported on general news bulletins in many different languages around the world. The second thing you need to know is that the bond market is much larger than the

stock market. The value of the global bond market now exceeds US$105 trillion, while the combined market cap of all the world's stock markets is about US$95 trillion. In the US, trading volumes are also much higher – US$894 billion for bonds compared to US$322 billion for equities.[11]

Unlike Wall Street, Main Street is far more familiar with the stock market than the bond market, which can lead to its financial muscle being underestimated. There is a great quote from Bill Clinton's political adviser James Carville who put it this way:[12]

> I used to think that if there was reincarnation, I wanted to come back as the president or the pope or as a .400 baseball hitter. But now I would like to come back as the bond market. You can intimidate everybody.

On Main Street, the first thing that most people who are new to investing look at is the share price of a company. It goes up, it comes down. Simple. Monday through Friday, you can see if you are making or losing money. Many new investors find the concept of discount rates attached to dividend payments a bit abstract and hard to get their heads around. Actually, the concept is very real, concrete and everywhere around us. These discount rates are shown in newspapers, on websites, financial TV programmes and displayed on small screens in the elevators of fancy office buildings. They are called interest rates or bond yields.

Companies and governments all over the world borrow money by issuing bonds. Just about anyone can buy them – from individuals to giant pension funds – and the concept is simple. The bondholder gets paid a set interest rate every year until the end of the loan period, when the amount of money invested at the start is returned in full. The loan period can vary, but most are somewhere between six months and ten years. As with dividend payments, the longer it takes for the money to be returned, the higher the interest rate. This is called the bond yield, which varies depending on the level of risk.

For example, lending the US government money is a lot safer than investing in a bond issued by a small company. That is why the yield on bonds issued by the US government, regarded as the safest investment in the world, is very low and the yield on Sure Win Absolutely No Risk Enterprises is much higher.[13] There are specialised companies that help here. These ratings agencies assess the financial strength of companies in terms of their ability to meet payments on their bonds, based on a ratings system.

These bond yields influence the interest paid on everything from our bank accounts and mortgage rates to credit cards and bank loans. In short, they affect us one way or another almost every day of our lives. There are all sorts of different bond yields but to keep matters simple, we will focus on one – the discount rate used for ten-year loans to the US government, the so-called ten-year US bond yield. It is the most widely used discount rate for dividends paid by companies listed on stock markets. This is because it is an indicator of broader investor confidence as these bonds are a very safe investment as they have the full backing of the US government.

4 A tug of war

Before we move on, it might be useful to see how the influence of bond yields works in practice. In 2020, the coronavirus hit businesses everywhere. Stock markets initially crashed because profits in 2020 were expected to be much lower than anticipated. As the pandemic spread around the world, it became clear that some of the future profits would also have to be written off. This was in March 2020 and stock markets fell by as much as 30%. But then governments and central banks stepped in and took a number of measures to support their economies. For example, the US central bank, the Federal Reserve, made explicit statements about "keeping interest rates low". Bond yields or discount rates (for our purpose here, they are the same) immediately started to fall.

The stock markets roared back to life as future dividends were not being discounted as much as before. It was as if, suddenly, the sushi did not have to be binned at the end of the day and could be stored in the fridge for another day. There was no need for supermarket managers to aggressively discount the sushi and the price would now be higher. Many commentators threw their arms in the air and claimed markets were disconnected from reality. Hence the headline, "Why is the Stock

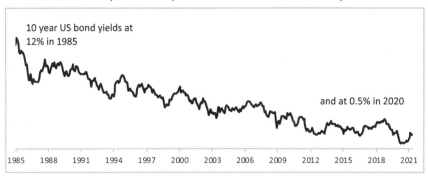

US 10-year bond yields have fallen dramatically

10 year US bond yields at 12% in 1985

and at 0.5% in 2020

1985 1988 1991 1994 1997 2000 2003 2006 2009 2012 2015 2018 2021

Source: Yahoo Finance.

The relentless decline in bond yields

In the early 1980s, buying a house was an expensive business because the interest rate for a 30-year mortgage was as high as 18%. These days, it is about 4%, a massive decline. This has everything to do with lower bond yields – the interest rates charged when firms or governments want to borrow money. And, as the chart shows, they have generally been on the decline since 1981.

Bond yields are set by the laws of supply and demand for loans; the more people or firms want to borrow money, the higher these bond yields go, and vice versa* – when demand falls, so do yields. Look what happened when the COVID-19 outbreak started to sweep across the world – nobody is in the market to borrow money when a pandemic is ravaging the planet.**

Although the downward trend is clear, there have been periods when these yields have risen sharply, which was the case in 1994, 1998 and 2013. These periods are generally associated with lacklustre performance in Asian stocks. Generally speaking, it is true to say that over the years, lower bond yields have provided a considerable boost to Asian stock markets.***

---

* See Fisher 2016. Bond yields have been on the decline since 1985 and whole armies of economists have scratched their head over why this is the case. It turns out that demographics played a role. More older people means more savers putting their money in the market, making it easier and cheaper to borrow money. This means lower bond yields. It's all much more complex and all sorts of other issues, such as a slow pace of innovation, are important, too.

** See Jordan 2020. Basically, the last thing firms do when a pandemic ravages the planet is to borrow money to invest, as most are in survival mode instead. Meanwhile, most consumers put cash aside during a calamity. The law of supply and demand for loans means that bond yields will go lower.

*** It means the discount applied to future profits is lower and, thus, the value of those future profits goes up.

Market Rallying When the Economy is so Bad?" But they were looking in the wrong place. They did not check what was happening in the bond markets.

The power of bond yields was also evident in early 2021, when vaccine programmes were starting to be rolled out and the number of daily COVID-19 infections began to fall in many countries. As economic growth forecasts rose, investors started to worry about inflation for the first time in years. Higher inflation means future payments from bonds would not buy as much – because the price of just about everything will be higher than it is today. When inflation expectations rise, the prices of bonds fall, which pushes up their yield. Bond prices move in the opposite direction of interest rates.

This time, bond yields headed sharply higher and stock markets wobbled. The thinking was that higher discount rates would hurt the future profits of market darlings like the big internet and technology companies, the growth stocks that had long rewarded investors with hefty returns as they expanded their businesses. As a result, boring old "value" companies, the plodders with highly predictable earnings that chug along at a steady pace, came back into fashion after years in the wilderness. This style rotation, as it is known, was the direct result of the movement in bond yields.

In this book, we will often refer to the tug of war between profits and discount rates (bond yields). A real tug of war is a test of strength between two teams pulling on the opposite ends of a rope. Stock markets are similar, with the contest being between profits and discount rates. Generally, if discount rates go up, stocks markets will fall, but if profits increase, stock markets will rise. To understand the small shifts that can take place during this tug of war, it is important to look at the strength of the two teams pulling on the rope.

Before we tackle the last misconception of stocks being too risky, a quick note on valuations. Rather than get bogged down in technical details of how to discount dividends, there is an easier way to value stocks – the price to earnings (PE) ratio.[14] This is calculated by dividing the current share price of a company by its earnings per share in the current year. If the share price is $50 and the earnings per share is $5,

In a tug of war, we don't look at the minuscule movements in the marker in the middle, but look out for which team pulls harder on the rope. So it is with stock markets – do not get too hooked on daily changes in the market but look at the big forces that make these changes, in this case, profits and discount rates (bond yields). Image © Mike McKeever.

the PE ratio is 10x. The higher the PE, the more expensive the stock. Most PEs in Asia range between 10x and 25x, but they can be as low as 3x and as high as 80x. As PEs are easy to use, we will refer to them when discussing the valuation of stock markets and individual stocks.

5 Investing in stocks is risky, but so is driving a car

The final misconception we need to get out of the way is that investing in stocks is too risky. It is true that there is some risk involved, but the same can be said about driving a car or crossing a street. Statistically, the chances of you experiencing a crash or getting knocked down are exceptionally low. It's all about managing the level of risk. With stocks, the simplest way to manage risk is to diversify your investments. If you put all your money into one stock and something goes horribly wrong with that company – remember the early voyages of Dutch spice traders to Asia – you could lose the lot. It still happens. If, however, you invest in a wide range of companies, the level of risk falls sharply.

The easiest way to diversify your investments is through exchange traded funds (ETFs). They are traded on exchanges just like individual stocks and mimic a particular index by investing in a range of companies, rather like the index funds mentioned earlier. It is nearly impossible to lose all your money because, for that to happen, all these companies would have to go bankrupt at the same. In the absence of a nuclear holocaust or an asteroid hitting Mother Earth, that is quite unlikely.

Just as some of the VOC's shareholders were housemaids, ETFs allow everybody to participate in the stock market. They offer convenience, low cost and a minuscule level of risk. Today's ETF investors are avoiding the risk of investing in a single maritime expedition. It's as if they are the modern-day equivalents of the people who first put money into the VOC in Amsterdam to invest in future expeditions. ETFs also allow small investors to diversify their portfolios and reduce risk. That is not to say that the value of an ETF cannot go down. If the share prices of the majority of the stocks bundled together in an ETF fall, so will the price of the ETF. But that should not concern investors who, like the early VOC shareholders, are in it for the long haul. The statistics do not lie – over the long term, most stock markets rise.

The world's first ETF was created in Canada in 1990. By 1993, an ETF was trading on the US stock exchange, mimicking the S&P500, the largest 500 stocks on the US stock market. These days, ETFs come in all sorts of shapes and sizes. Some mimic indices – such as Hong Kong's Hang Seng Index, Mumbai's Sensex or Jakarta's JCI – and others mirror the performance of small companies or a basket of technology companies. There are ETFs for different market segments, too, such as solar panel makers, banks or semiconductors. There is even a slew of interesting, some might even say wacky, ETFs that invest in companies that merge or spin-off parts of their businesses. One even uses forensic accountancy to rate the quality of company earnings.[15] And there are also synthetic ETFs that rely on all manner of financial wizardry to mimic a basket of stocks.[16]

The universal benefit is that ETFs track the performance of a basket of stocks with a single investment. They are similar to mutual funds but are less expensive to buy. There is no cheaper way to get access to a diversified list of stocks. Thanks to ETFs, investing in Asian stock markets has never been easier.

Stock valuations

How do you know what's a reasonable price to pay for a house? Or a car? Or a stock? Bitcoin? Any investment for that matter? For stocks, we need to know why the firm is of any value to anyone in the first place. Most make things cheaper, better or get them to us faster. That is what generates profits and determines the value of a company's shares in the stock market.

In this book, we don't look at stock valuations in detail. Whole forests have disappeared to produce books that describe stock valuations in incredible detail. No need for another one.

There is, however, one valuation that we sometimes refer to. Not because it is the best, but it is the most commonly used one in Asian stock markets. And that is the price to earnings (PE) ratio. And it's dead simple. It takes the price of a stock and divides it by the earnings. If a company made a profit of $120 and has 10 shares outstanding, the profit per share is $12. If the market price is $240, it means that the stock is trading at a PE of 20x. A low PE suggests the stock offers value, and a high PE means it's expensive (often for good reason).

The majority of PEs in Asia's stock markets are somewhere between 5x and 30x, and the average is 16x. But there is a big difference between markets. PE ratios in Korea and Japan are much lower than in Taiwan and India. A lot of this has to do with the swings in earnings from one year to the next – profits are more volatile in Korea than they are in India, so not only is PE is lower but forecasting profits becomes more difficult. Another issue is "governance", or how companies are managed – the structure of Indian companies tends to be straightforward, Korean ones less so. Again, that pegs PE ratios in Korea a notch lower.

It does not take an advanced degree in finance to understand that it is best to buy stocks when PE ratios are low, that is, when they are cheap. In years gone by, when Asia traded at an average PE of 9x, stock markets would sometimes shoot up between 40% and 60% in the following 12 months. But when the average PE rose above 17x, markets could fall as much as 20%.* Watching PEs can make a big difference between making or losing money.

---

* This was, however, when bond yields were substantially higher.

Average index PEs in the past 5 years (2016-2021).
Shenzhen and India are the highest PE markets,
Singapore and Hang Seng the lowest PE markets.

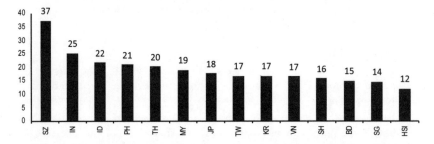

Note : Trailing PE means the PE is calculated based on trailing earnings, The term "trailing" implies earnings calculated on a rolling basis. That is, trailing EPS may describe the most recent 12-month period or four earnings releases. This differs from forecasted earnings. Country codes: SZ = Shenzhen, IN = India's Sensex index, ID - Indoensia's IDX, PH = Philippines' PSEi index, TH = Thailand's SET index, MY = Malaysia's FTSE Bursa index, JP = Japan's Topix index, TW = Taiwan's TSEI index, KR = Korea's Kospi index, VN = Vietnam index, SH = Shanghai's SE Composite index, BD = Bangladesh' BSE index, SG = Singapore' Strait Times index, HSI = Hong Kong's Hang Seng index, HSCEI is Hong Kong's Hang Seng China Enterprises index. Source: Stock exchanges.

Back to 1997 and a collapsed soufflé

My days as a junior analyst in Jakarta were long and hard. Not that it mattered. I loved analysing stocks and writing reports, and I was often in the office until late in the evening. The added advantage was missing the weapons-grade traffic jams, so I could get home in ten minutes rather than an hour. Back home, we sat in our small garden, smoked *kretek* cigarettes, drank refreshing Bintang beer and ordered *satay* or *nasi goreng* from one of the passing vendors. They had their own calling cards. The sound of a wooden stick being hit against a board meant *nasi goreng*, while a high-pitched shriek sounding something like "*s'tay*!" indicated that chicken was on the menu. On Fridays and Saturday evenings, we would invite friends over before heading out into Jakarta's adventurous nightlife.

This was in 1996 and early 1997, and Indonesia's stock market was among the most popular in Asia. Every week, clients flew in from all over the world to meet the companies they were investing in. Once or twice a year, our boss from Hong Kong came to town to meet all the analysts. On one of these trips, he asked if anyone might be open to a transfer to Korea or Taiwan where, apparently, technology companies were starting to make their mark. I remember that one of the analysts suggested that would be a bad idea: "Korea and Taiwan?" he sneered. "Those markets aren't going anywhere." How wrong he would be.

In mid-1997, dark clouds hung over the markets. Currencies across the region were getting jittery, led by swings in the Thai baht. By late 1997, the Indonesian stock market bonanza was over and all across Asia, stock markets imploded like a collapsing soufflé. The Asian Financial Crisis had arrived. We will discuss this event in more detail later, but in the years that followed, many companies across the region went bankrupt, banks failed and governments fell. It was a massive reality check for Asian stock markets and the crisis shaped how they would develop in the next two decades.

Over time, China emerged as the hottest new market in the region. With the help of our "tug of war" analogy, we analyse this large and complex stock market in a later chapter to see why it continues to shape the fortunes of several other stock markets in Asia. As I will explain, this involves returning to my first day in China in 1991, which turned out to be an absolute disaster.

Endnotes

1   The Jakarta Stock Exchange introduced an electronic trading system on 22 May 1995.

2   It is true that wealthier people seem to have more exposure to stocks. In the US, the wealthiest 10% of families own 81% of the stock market in 2010. Wolff 2014, p 374. The top 1% owned 35%. In 2001, the top 10% owned 77%. Data quoted is for 2010.

3   There are quite a few studies that looked at this relationship. Dimson *et al* 2002 is a well-known one. They found that there is only weak evidence of any relationship, and in some cases the relationship between GDP growth and stock market returns was negative. More recent studies are Klement 2015 or Mladani and Germani 2016, which found similar results. The latter also finds no relationship between annual returns in stock markets and annual changes in GDP. When they use stock market returns in one a year and GDP growth changes in the year thereafter, there is moderate positive relationship that is statistically significant, which suggests the stock markets do reflect to a small degree future GDP growth.

4   Schlingemann and Stultz 2020 in the case of the US.

5   That is not to say we should discard economics. It is, for example, to get a feel for what happens with bond yields, something we will discuss later.

6   Just to complicate the matter further, it is sometimes also referred to as "cash equity" because these investments in equities can, these days, be quickly turned into cash.

7   At that meetings, other matters of importance are also discussed, such as who can sit on the board that supervises the company's management or if the company can seek access to loans from banks. These dividends are most often paid every year, although sometimes companies spread the annual payments out over two bi-annual payments or a payment in each quarter.

8   Even for the simple reason that one can invest that dollar now and have more money in ten years' time.

9   Assuming, of course, the dividend payments are the same.

10 There are all sorts of other ways to look valuations too, such as asset-based valuations, the aggregate market value of assets that a company owns, although these are also based on discounted cash flows. And there are issues with companies which don't pay dividends. Of importance here is to set out a framework to look at stock markets in Asia that examines profits and discount rates.

11 All this data is based on the *2020 Capital Markets Fact Book*, issued by Sifma in September 2002.

12 Burgess 2018.

13 In reality, it's a little more complex. Typically, the discount rates are set using government bonds upon which a risk premium is set to deal with risks to invest in a country or in a specific company. But conceptually, here we use government bond yields as our discount rate.

14 Under certain circumstances, a PE can be rewritten as a flow of discounted dividends.

15 This is the Forensic Accounting ETF, the ticker is FLAG US.

16 Synthetic ETFs were first introduced in Europe in 2001 and are generally more common in Europe than in the US. Leveraged ETFs, which seek to double or triple the positive or negative return of the index they mimic, are also considered synthetic ETFs.

Chapter 3

Market Psychology: Greed, Fear and Misplaced Confidence

To truly understand Asian stock markets, we need to go beyond just looking at revenue, profits and interest rates. We also need to understand why certain people make particular investment decisions. Often, it is the mass psychology of greed, fear or misplaced confidence which determines whether a sudden sharp decline in stock prices amounts to a meaningless blip or something much more.

A good starting point is my friend Stephen, who is the first to admit he doesn't know much about stock markets.

In 2020, the coronavirus ravaged the planet and social distancing was compulsory. People worked at home, schools and restaurants closed their doors, business meetings were done by video and holidays were cancelled. In the absence of tourists and business travellers, deserted Hong Kong hotels offered all sorts of staycations, with dinner coupons, spa visits and shopping vouchers thrown in for good measure. They needed the money as much as the residents needed a break.

Stephen, a professor at a local university, loved staycations. Every month or so, he and his wife could be found sunning themselves by the pool with a gin and tonic in hand. One day, after a particular long and sumptuous breakfast buffet, Stephen was digesting a peculiar combination of croissants, smoked salmon and dim sum under a large sun umbrella. His wife, book in hand, was sitting next to him and their young daughter played in the pool. It was a beautiful weekend in late

September, when the hot and humid Hong Kong summer retreats in the face of cooler, drier weather. Stephen was happy.

A few weeks back, he had bought some Chinese stocks and an Asian exchange traded fund (ETF) on something of a whim. After an initial check the day after the purchase, he had been too busy with university lectures and academic papers to follow his new investments. A sudden impulse at the pool made him grab his laptop and check how they were doing. His jaw dropped – everything was down. He had lost the equivalent of many, many staycations. A knot developed in his gut, he started to sweat and then fear set in, followed by abject panic.

In despair, he wondered what to do next. Stephen was worried that he would lose all his money. What would he tell his wife? His initial instinct was to sell the stocks and the ETF, keep his savings in cash and forget the damn stock market altogether. But then he calmed down a bit. Although a novice at this game, he reminded himself that he was a long-term investor, not a day trader, and that stock prices go down as well as up. He closed his laptop, jumped into the pool with his daughter, and then dived into a gripping spy novel while relishing the thought of another sumptuous buffet for dinner. But the realization that he had lost money would not leave him. It gnawed away at his peace of mind and not even a large gin and tonic helped. Stephen's staycation was ruined.

Investing in stocks is an emotional business. Even seemingly trivial things can have a huge influence on the way we make decisions. One psychological study in the Netherlands in 2011 even found that a full bladder helps us make more rational, long-term decisions.[1] *The Economist* reported that two sets of participants were tested. The first was told to drink five cups of water; the second to take just five sips. After 40 minutes, they were tested on their decision-making abilities. The group who were, by now, crossing their legs, were better able to exercise self-control and hold out for larger rewards.

When stock markets fall, fear and anguish set in and, just like Stephen, we question whether making the investment was a good decision. But when stocks fly, say hello to our old friend greed – we don't want to miss the party! The industry term for this is the fear of missing out (FOMO). These panicky reactions, when we follow our gut feeling, is when we are prone to make the biggest mistakes. Benjamin Graham, a famous investor of yesteryear, once stated that "the investor's chief problem – and even his own worst enemy – is likely to be himself."

Investing in stocks – particularly for people like Stephen who have an investment horizon of at least ten years – requires a willingness to live with bear and bull market swings. This is especially the case in Asia, where markets move up and down more than anywhere else. No wonder that research shows that Asian investors are a volatile bunch.[2] But to avoid making the same mistakes over and over again, we need to know how our mind can play tricks on us.

Spend time thinking *slow*

In the 1970s, two psychologists, Daniel Kahneman and his colleague Amos Tversky, began studying how we make decisions. They discovered we are prone to all sorts of errors, biases and flaws, most of which operate at a subconscious level – in other words, intuition. Evolution is at the heart of these mental shortcuts. For humans to survive, dealing with threats was more important to survival than spotting the next opportunity. If there is a deer and a tiger around, you focus on the tiger. It is these impulses that also drive the way we invest in stock markets.

One of the broad conclusions Kahneman and Tversky[3] came to was that we have two types of mental operations nested inside our brain. The first is what they called System 1. This is a kind of reptilian reaction to whatever happens to us – it is automatic, often unconscious, effortless and coherent in that it makes quick comparisons and associations to previous situations stored in our brain. For example, when you are in a rush and grab your usual brand of milk at the store, it does not require a lot of thought. Marketers would love to crack the code to System 1 to make sure that, without spending time thinking about it, you pick their brand of milk, yoghurt, beer or coffee.

But there is another set of mental operations – System 2. This is the controlled, slower, deliberate and logical contemplation of a situation, the weighing of positives and negatives, thinking the situation through and then coming to a decision. Sitting down and planning a road trip or thinking about a job offer both fall in this category. It turns out that our capacity for System 2 thinking is rather limited. We struggle to do two multiplications at the same time, for example. That's why our brain prefers to use System 1. And it is seemingly unrelated matters that make us switch between these two systems, such as the pressure of a full bladder.

Nobel laureate Harry Markowitz, a professor in finance and one of the founders of modern investment theory, once had to fill in a form indicating the split between equities and bonds in his pension fund. If there was anyone who knew how to make such a decision, it was Harry Markowitz. He had dedicated his life to the issue of how we make such decisions and entire forests have been felled in order to provide academics with enough paper to discuss his findings. Asked what he eventually did, he answered: "I should have computed the historic covariances of the asset classes and drawn an efficient frontier. Instead, I split my contributions 50-50 between bonds and equities".[4]

Like Markowitz, we like to make simple System 1 short cuts. When Stephen opened his laptop and noticed that quite a few dollars had disappeared from his retirement savings, the reptilian System 1 kicked in. He started sweating and was overtaken by fear, but moments later, the logical System 2 started to work and he reminded himself that he was in it for the long run (although the reptile returned to ruin his weekend, he didn't sell).

The lesson is clear – when it comes to investing, it pays to think *slow*.

Fear

We humans have a great fear of losing money. Psychologists and behavioural economists have discovered that a loss hurts three times as much as an equivalent gain gives pleasure. This is why some people don't invest in stocks at all. And that's a pity – Asian stock markets have generated an annual average return of 7.3% in the last ten years. A hundred dollars invested on 1 January 2006 would now, some 15 years later, be worth US$348.[5] But markets move down as well as up, resulting in "paper losses" – we don't lose money until we sell the stock. On paper, the numbers can look grim. Between 2006 and 2020, Asian stock markets fell about 20% on five different occasions. Once, in

2008, at the height of the Global Financial Crisis, they lost half their value. Any way you look at it, that's pretty bad. And it is these kinds of experiences which scare the living daylights out of many investors and send them heading for the exits, never to return.

Psychologists have discovered that that the fear of making losses is amplified by how often we check stock prices.[6] The more often we check, the more risk averse we become. Constantly reading financial news does not help either. Newspapers bombard us with news about fears of a recession, unrest in the Middle East, slower growth in China, the latest from North Korea, and the imminent (and yet to happen) end of the Hong Kong dollar peg. And, of course, there is always someone willing to predict an imminent collapse in property prices.

Newspaper editors know this. They play on our fears. Just as we focus on the tiger and not the deer, our nerves jangle when a message includes anything negative. Words like "crash", "slump" and "doom" are used in headlines to attract readers and get more "clicks". No wonder people get scared about putting their money in markets. Anyone who ignores these stories is dismissed as a misguided optimist. For some reason, people like to hear that the world is going down in flames and become scornful when some optimist intrudes on their pleasure.

The more exposure we get to these apocalyptic stories, the more risk averse we become, especially when we are faced with big paper losses. Behaviourists call this phenomenon "myopic loss aversion". It turns out that this is not just an issue for small investors, professional investors get scared, too. When stock markets fall, risk managers at large financial institutions will instruct fund managers to take risk off the table, especially if their customers are withdrawing money from their funds, in fear of a further decline in markets. And when everybody does this, markets can go into a tailspin. By now, what was to be a small blip in stock prices turns into a full-scale crash. Never underestimate the power of herd mentality.

There is an easy way to deal with the fear of further losses. Behavioural economist Richard Thaler, a Nobel prizewinner for his work on these matters, was once asked by the host of an early morning financial news TV programme: "What should you do if you wake up and discover the stock market has fallen by 3%". His message was blunt. "Change channels. Turn the show off."[7] His laid-back investment advice might sound a bit simplistic, but, for many, buying stocks without obsessing about their performance is actually a good strategy.

Greed, confidence and delusions

The history of Asia's stock markets is littered with bull runs and bear markets. The good news is that markets are undeniably higher than they were 20 years ago, but on many occasions greed and overconfidence have gone into overdrive. In later chapters, we will discuss scandals where greed is central to the narrative, such as Harshad Mehta in Mumbai in 1992 and the collapse of Steady Safe, an ambitious taxi company in Indonesia and, more recently, the Luckin Coffee rip-off in China. In all these cases, people deliberately took crazy risks in pursuit of massive rewards. Getting unintentionally sucked into such scandals can happen to the best of us. Isaac Newton, after losing his savings in the South Sea Bubble that ruined many British investors in 1720, bemoaned the fact that: "I can calculate the motions of the heavenly bodies, but not the madness of people."

So far, we have seen how our brain takes short cuts that often result in bad decisions. But when it comes to investing, the biggest problem is actually misplaced confidence. In the 1980s, Swedish psychologist Ola Svenson conducted a study[8] in which she asked American and Swedish students to rank their driving skills. The results showed that the vast majority ranked themselves as above average, something that is not mathematically possible.[9] It's also called the Lake Wobegon effect because, at that time, a popular radio show in the US used to sign off with the line: "Well, that's the news from Lake Wobegon, where all the women are strong, all the men are good-looking, and all the children are above average."

The conclusion is clear: we tend to overestimate our own abilities. Academics call it "illusory superiority"[10] and this is what Bill Gates was referring to when he said: "Success is a lousy teacher. It makes smart people think they can't lose."

A professor named Hyman Minsky put forward the idea that, when markets rally, investors become overconfident and misjudge risks. They start to speculate. Some will borrow to put even more money into the stock market. But if stock prices go into reverse, it is these speculators who will be forced to sell first to avoid gigantic losses. In doing so, they amplify the market sell-off, creating what is now called a "Minsky moment".[11] This is why overconfidence is considered the mother of all behavioural biases;[12] it gives teeth to all the other mistakes we can make.

And this is especially true in Asia. Here, a special variety of overconfidence is at play, something we can call the "big market delusion", and the region, with a population of four billion, is particularly prone to this problem.[13] The very thought of hundreds of millions of Chinese and Indian consumers can turn the brains of rational investors (and equity analysts) to mush. Big market delusions are nothing new – think how trading in VOC shares held Amsterdam in its grip in 1688 – but in Asia, they are in a class of their own.

The big markets arrived in waves. India's opening up in 1992, investing in ASEAN tigers in 1997, Taiwan PC makers in the late 1990s, China steel in 2006, Asian mobile phone operators in 2007, and the run in Chinese consumer companies in 2010 were all based on big market stories. In the past few years, think of Chinese internet names and the boom in electric vehicles (EVs). Nio, a Chinese EV maker, was listed in New York in September 2018. Its stock price hit a low of US$1.20 in late 2019 on sales and cash woes but when the big EV market story moved into high gear, it raced to US$62 in January 2021.

Often, it's the rise of new consumer markets that drives this optimism. In the years after China entered the World Trade Organization (WTO) in 2001, millions of Chinese left their farms to find jobs in factories. Suddenly, these migrant workers had money in their pockets for the first time and they were in the market for anything from mobile handsets, TVs and small motorcycles to sports shoes and beer. Sales of all these products went through the roof and there is nothing more exciting for investors and entrepreneurs than the perceived presence of a big new market for their products and services. It means large profits and high valuations. So, by 2006, Chinese stock markets were booming.

When stocks rally on the back of these big market stories, everybody wants in. FOMO is a powerful force that sucks in new investors. People then borrow money to try to make even more profit and that is when speculation becomes the main force driving the price of a particular stock. As the market rallies, we give more weight to information that confirms our prejudices, when it would be better to analyse data that would call our assumptions into question.[14]

When the big market delusion is in full force, investors generally downplay news about new entrants, failing to factor in the reality that growth will have to be shared with both existing competitors and new rivals. Or they ignore the fact that the companies involved are young, have untested business models and have yet to make any profit.

To make matters worse, when these stocks are rising fast, investors get so excited that the traditional toolbox used for stock analysis tends to get thrown out of the window. Instead, all sorts of disingenuous alternative valuation methods are used – eyeballs, subscribers, website hits – anything to justify the sky-high stock price.

All these factors create a false sense of confidence – the big story must be true otherwise others would not be buying into it. Sceptics are scorned. Chinese stocks rallied hard for more than two years before they popped in late 2007. The growth opportunities appeared limitless. Until they didn't. This does not mean that every company that is part of the big market story is overpriced. On the contrary, a few will succeed and exploit the big market to full effect. Eventually, the pricing delusion corrects itself.

The cause can be linked to anything from new industry regulations, consumer preferences or even self-inflicted wounds. For example, in 2009, a news report suggested that Bawang, a hugely popular Chinese herbal shampoo, contained dioxane, a toxic liquid that could cause cancer. True or not, the company did not get on top of the story on the public relations front and the stock never recovered. Big stories can also lose their fizz slowly, like the air going out of a tyre. China's giant banks were hot in the years after they were listed, but when Beijing removed a number of protective regulations and allowed more competition from internet companies, the stocks underperformed for years.

The changes in investor sentiment that take place during big market stories go through five phases.[15] The first is "displacement", when something happens that puts a stock or a market in a different and very positive light. The first investors to react start to pour money in. This phase is typically grounded in reality and good intentions. This is followed by phase two: "expansion". This is when the narrative takes hold and more and more investors jump in. Stock prices start to rise.

Then comes phase three: "euphoria". By this point, everyone assumes they can get rich quickly and easily. Speculators arrive, risks are taken with abandon, the party is in full swing and nobody worries about the hangover in the morning. This is also when people decide that they can make more money trading stocks than they can from their day job. Euphoria makes people think the good times will last forever. In 1989 in Japan, at the peak of the market, it was generally assumed that nobody, not even the government, would stop the rise in Japanese stocks because "it was in everybody's interest to keep the party going". That is, until the lights went out.

Eventually, we get to phase four: "crisis". This is when insiders and early investors exit. Then a Minsky moment arrives and panic buying turns into panic selling. Everybody wants to get out, amplifying the downturn. Loss aversion kicks in and people sell more than they should. Even professional fund managers who want to buy can't do so because the holders of their funds cash in their investments, or their risk managers want to cut any exposure to falling stocks. It becomes a vicious circle.

Phase five is when "revulsion" kicks in. People think things will never get better again and, just as prices overshoot to the upside as a result of euphoria, they often overshoot to the downside. This is often the best time to pick up stocks on the cheap. In the last 20 years, two of the best performing markets have been Indonesia and Thailand, whose economies and stock markets were in tatters after the Asian Financial Crisis of 1997–1998. By 2000, their stocks markets were at the revulsion stage.

In 2021, China internet stock went from euphoria to revulsion in a period of only six months. In February that year, these stocks were considered market darlings. But after a raft of new regulations issued by Beijing, which had a detrimental impact on the profits of these internet giants, their stocks sold off and reached what can be described as revulsion by August.

Not all of these five phases are as dramatic as described above. Sometimes, the euphoria dies down quickly, or markets do not even reach the "crisis" and "revulsion" phases. Every cycle is different, and these phases can be either short or take years to play out. They are, however, a useful reminder that while there are few constants in stock markets, the mass psychology of greed, fear and overconfidence will always be around.

Getting advice from hairdressers

It is clear that we are often less rational than we like to think, use inaccurate information, jump to conclusions and are prone to becoming overconfident. We are easily fooled, causing us to make emotional decisions that we later regret. In short, we need all the help we can get. It turns out that we often turn to the wrong people for advice.

Jurgen Klopp, the coach of the hugely successful Liverpool football team, gave this answer when asked for his take on the coronavirus:[16]

> What I don't like in life is that with a very serious thing a football manager's opinion is [considered] important. I don't understand that. I really don't understand it. If I asked you, you are in exactly the same role as I am. So, it's not important what famous people say. We have to speak about things in the right manner – not people with no knowledge like me talking about something people with knowledge will talk about it.

He finished by joking that he was just someone with "a baseball cap and a bad shave". He was right about both the shave and the coronavirus. We often ask the wrong people for advice. Football coaches are no experts on pandemics. The same applies to investing, but many people turn to spouses, friends, relatives (beware the sharp-suited brother-in-law bearing hot stock tips) and all sorts of other people, hairdressers included.[17] Word of mouth is a particularly dangerous force in the investment world.

The thing is, financial experts are not always much help either. Many professional advisors tend to throw around lots of jargon – the effect of QE2 on M3, duration effects, synthetic indexation or CDOs and CDSs – that leaves the average human being none the wiser. For anyone willing to put their hard-earned cash into the stock market, making investments should be a simple and straightforward process.

Think *slow* before you wee

As we said at the start of the chapter, to understand Asia's stock markets, we need to understand the people who invest in them. But none of the human traits – greed, overconfidence and panic in the face of losses – tell us anything about which Asian stocks or markets to buy. However, knowing about how we make investment decisions allows us to avoid common pitfalls and traps that our own minds set for us. This allows us to think *slow* instead of making fast (bad) decisions. So, fill up that bladder before you check on your investments, or, as was the case with Stephen when he realised markets had tanked, take a deep breath and remember investments are for the long run.

And mass psychology is particularly important in Asia's volatile stocks markets, where greed, fear and overconfidence are never in short supply.[18] When markets fall, we have to understand that risk aversion sets in, redemptions rise and what initially appeared to be a small blip can turn into something much bigger and nastier. It is nearly impossible to time the peaks and troughs of bull and bear markets. What we do know is that it's often better to be careful when the market is in the euphoria phase and buy stocks when markets are at the "revulsion" stage, abandoned and ignored.

Lastly, if there is one guideline that has worked for me, it is to be optimistic. People like to hear that the world is falling apart but pessimism has consistently been a poor guide to stock markets (or, for that matter, the modern world). We are gigantically richer in wealth, body and spirit compared to even a few decades ago. This, I hope, will also be the case in the future. And buying stocks or an ETF gives investors access to bright people – the ones who run companies – who know how to capitalise on these opportunities. This is, ultimately, why I invest in stocks.

Endnotes

1   Tuk 2010.

2   Chuang *et al* 2014.

3   Kahneman 2013.

4   Quote in Benartzi and Thaler 2007.

5   This uses the widely used MSCI Asia ex-Japan as a benchmark. If we include Japan, it would be US$225. At the same time, global markets – as measured by the MSCI ACWI index – would be worth US$291. See the MSCI website.

6   Benartzi and Thaler 2007.

7   Houlder 2017.

8   Svenson 1981.

9   To put some numbers to this: 88% of the Americans and 77% of the Swedes ranked themselves as above average when it came to driving safely. As for general driving skills, 93% of the Americans rated themselves above average, compared to 69% of the Swedes.

10   See Malmendier 2015.

11   A Minsky moment is when a sudden decline in market sentiment and asset prices inevitably leads to a market crash.

12   Benartzi and Thaler 2007.

13   Cornell and Damodaran 2019.

14   Benartzi and Thaler 2007, p 102.

15   Kindleberger 2005.

16   Chris Chavez, "Jurgen Klopp on Coronavirus Concern: 'It's Not Important What Famous People Think'" *Sports Illustrated*, 4 March 2020 < https://www.si.com/soccer/2020/03/04/jurgen-klopp-coronavirus-question-reporter-liverpool>.

17   Benartzi and Thaler 2007, p 94.

18   Chuang *et al* 2014.

Chapter 4

China's Stock Markets
股市

A robbery, a plane crash and a comforting bowl of noodles
In early September 1991, a year after my first trip to Indonesia, I decided
to explore China. Very few people were travelling there at the time and
most tourists went on package tours that were heavily supervised by the
government-run China International Travel Service. But backpackers on
a shoestring budget like myself were allowed to roam freely around the
country. From Amsterdam, I flew into Hong Kong and landed at the
old Kai Tak airport. You never forget your first time. The descent to
runway 13 involved making a 47-degree right turn above Kowloon Tsai
Park, skimming so close over the rooftops you could almost see what
people in the flats below were watching on TV, before coming to a halt
at the end of a short runway alongside the city's famous harbour. It was
common for passengers to break into a round of applause on landing.
After passing through immigration, I went straight to the Lo Wu border
crossing to get to Shenzhen – then little more than a small but fast-
growing city next to Hong Kong, but today a giant metropolis and tech
hub. From there, the whole of China was open to me.

But first, I needed to change money. In those days, foreigners were
not allowed to buy Chinese currency, the *renminbi* (RMB). They had to
exchange US dollars for what were called "foreign exchange certificates"
(FECs). These could be used in special "Friendship Stores" that, as I soon
discovered, mostly sold stuff that I had no interest in. I did, however,

buy some long underwear which came in very useful on a trek on horseback through eastern Tibet. China was not exactly the shopping mecca that it is today. Most of the Friendship Stores were pretty grim places where customer service was an alien concept. A "no smiles" policy was strictly enforced, except for the time when I asked the price of a hat and mispronounced the Chinese word, *mao*. I made it sound like the Chairman. The staff thought it was hilarious.

I soon discovered that it was easy to get my hands on RMB, which made life much more convenient as I could use the currency anywhere. FECs were also much sought after by Chinese consumers as they were the best way to get access to TVs, radios and all sorts of other useful consumer goods that were hard to buy. This created trading opportunities, especially as FECs, supposedly equal in value, were actually worth 30% more than RMB on the street. I would walk into a bank branch and make my way to the FEC window. It was so unusual for a foreigner to show up that it had to be opened specially by a clerk. News that FECs might be on offer would spread quickly. The moment I walked out of the bank, a swarm of budding entrepreneurs encircle me, asking to trade. The bigger the crowd, the stronger my bargaining power. After a bit of haggling, I identified the best RMB rate being offered and the deal was done. It was easy once you knew how the system worked and had some street smarts.

Things, however, did not always go smoothly, as I discovered on my first day. After getting through immigration at Lo Wu, I spotted a bank close to the railway station in Shenzhen. After exchanging some US dollars for FECs, I sat down on the stairs of the station to sort through the large, unfamiliar bundle of notes and put them in my small waist pouch. Suddenly, someone close to me made a loud noise and I turned to see where it was coming from. I felt a sharp blow on my nose and instinctively closed my eyes. That was when the FECs were ripped from my hands, and before I could react, the thief was gone. I looked sheepishly into a crowd of people who quietly stared back at me. I was a mug who had just been mugged. I lost the equivalent of about US$125, which represented a decent chunk of my meagre budget. I had little choice but to go back into the bank to exchange more dollars. This time,

I walked to a quiet spot far from the crowded station before securing the FECs in my pouch.

Slightly chastened by making such a rookie mistake, I decided to have a look around town. I wasn't impressed. In those days, Shenzhen was expanding rapidly but it appeared little more than a large building site to me, full of dust and noise. I quickly decided to leave and, after buying a ticket at a travel agent with my hard-won FECs, I caught an afternoon flight to Guilin, a city in the south west that was the jumping-off point for Yangshuo, a picturesque backpacker-friendly town famous for its dramatic limestone hills. Here, I would lick my wounds and acclimatise to this new country. Then, disaster struck again.

As we descended into Guilin airport, the engine below the left wing started to sputter and the pilot could not slow the plane down as we came in to land. I vividly remember looking out from my window seat and seeing the plane race past the small airport building against a spectacular backdrop of mountains. A few seconds later, the plane came to a shuddering halt in a paddy field next to the runway. It was mayhem. Adults were screaming, children were wailing and some passengers were pushing others out of the way as they scrambled to get out of the plane. Those that did got stuck in the paddy field and a few fell face down into the mud.

Luckily, nobody was hurt. A bit later, I sat outside Guilin airport and wondered if backpacking around China was such a good idea. At this rate, I was not going to make it to the end of the week. But then my mood lifted. A friendly old man beckoned me to follow him to what appeared to be his noodle shop. He gave me a bowl of soup with pork and pointed me to a bus stop where I could catch an early evening bus to Yangshuo. I thanked him and a few bows and smiles later – my Chinese was pretty basic back then – I began my journey to my final destination of the day without further incident.

I stayed in Yangshuo for a few days to soak up the atmosphere and wondered what would go wrong next, but the rest of the trip turned into a delightful adventure. I made friends in a teahouse in Chengdu, travelled across Tibet on horseback, and took the train to Xi'an and Beijing to see the famous tourist sites. I then travelled down the east coast through Nanjing, Suzhou, Hangzhou, Shanghai and Xiamen, and slowly made my way back to Hong Kong before returning home. It was a fabulous experience, so much so that I would eventually become a tour guide in China. But a few weeks into this first trip, I was given a harsh reminder that air travel in China came with considerable risks. In November 1992, I read in a newspaper that another flight had crashed on approach to Guilin.

Of course, much has changed. The days of exchanging FECs for RMB are long gone and the currency is allowed to trade outside China, but there is still a distinction between the onshore and offshore RMB. Onshore RMB can be traded within mainland China and uses the CNY symbol. Offshore RMB trades outside mainland China and is referred to as CNH.[1] This is very important to stock markets. Remember that movements in stock markets should be seen as a tug of war between profits and dividends on the one hand and the discount rate set in bond markets on the other. Having two types of RMB – onshore and offshore – means that the discount rate within mainland China is different to the rate used outside the country. Having different discount rates for these markets will, as we'll see later, result in all sorts of unique trading patterns in Chinese stocks.

A-shares and H-shares: understanding the different markets

There are four major Chinese stock markets: two onshore and two offshore. Combined, the onshore Shanghai and Shenzhen markets have grown to be the second largest in the world, and this is where the shares of some 4,200 mainland companies are listed.[2] The main offshore market is the Hong Kong Stock Exchange, where a wide range of Chinese stocks are traded alongside domestic Hong Kong companies. There are two categories of these stocks: red chips, Hong Kong companies with large operations in mainland China, and H-shares, Chinese companies listed in Hong Kong.[3] The Hang Seng China Enterprises Index (HSCEI) is the benchmark used to reflect the overall performance of mainland stocks listed in Hong Kong.[4] A few Chinese companies are dual-listed in Shanghai and Hong Kong. Please refer to the "Asian Stock Market Indices" section at the back of the book for further details of the major indices across Asia.

Especially in the early 2000s, Chinese stocks listed in Hong Kong (HSCEI index) performed better than those in Shanghai (SSE index).

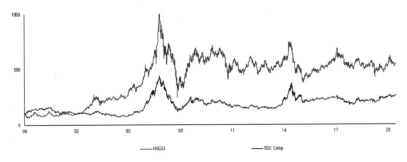

Note: Both indices are set at 100 on 1 January 2000
Source: Factset, author's calculations

To these markets we can add the Chinese stocks listed in the US, mostly via American Depository Receipts (ADRs). These are certificates issued by a US bank that represent shares in foreign stocks, making it easy for US investors to trade them. In 2020, the US made it more difficult for Chinese companies to issue ADRs and many "went home", that is, they withdrew the ADRs and listed their shares in Hong Kong.[5] As a result, the mix of Chinese companies listed in Hong Kong has changed significantly. Other mainland firms are listed on stock exchanges in Singapore, London or Frankfurt but these stocks are a small part of the overall universe of China stocks.

And this universe is now very large indeed. The combined average monthly turnover on the Shanghai and Shenzhen markets is US$2 trillion; for context, the largest market in the US, the New York Stock Exchange, also trades an average of US$2 trillion a month.[6] Remarkably, on some days the value of stocks of individual Chinese companies is greater than the daily turnover of some stock markets in Asia. What makes these markets even more interesting is their volatility – they have bouts of extreme optimism as well as periods of fear, panic and collapse. The result is that Chinese stock markets have seen some pretty wild swings in the past and probably will again.

Shanghai is the largest of the three. It was closed to foreigners until around 2002, when "qualified foreign institutional investors" (QFIIs) were allowed to start buying A-shares in this market. Once they had been

Comparing stock markets – size and trading activity. Taiwan and Korea are smaller than India, but see higher trading activity.

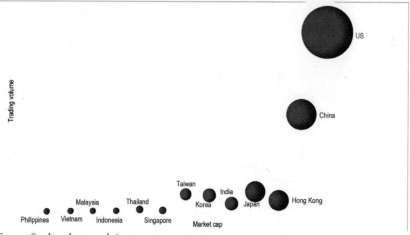

Source: Stock exchange websites

approved by the local financial authorities, interested parties, mostly large investment firms, were granted QFII quotas allowing them to buy a certain amount of shares every year. The scheme was regularly expanded and as of September 2019, when the quotas were finally scrapped, nearly 300 overseas institutions had received QFII quotas totalling US$111.4 billion.[7]

As China continued to open up its financial markets, new channels of investment were created. In 2014, a simple but highly innovative way of buying stocks was introduced.[8] This trading system is called Stock Connect, a unique collaboration between the Hong Kong, Shanghai and Shenzhen stock markets which allows international and mainland Chinese investors, without bureaucratic intervention, to buy or sell a selection of stocks in each other's markets.[9] The scheme was launched in Shanghai with Shenzhen joining in 2016, and has proved to be wildly popular, broadening the connection between China's onshore exchanges and global markets. By 2020, some 2,000 stocks were covered by Stock Connect but that number will probably rise in the next few years.[10] This does not mean that foreigners dominate trading in Shanghai stocks. Far from it. By the end of 2020, only about 10% of the trading on this market was done by overseas investors.

A quick word on Stock Connect jargon: southbound flows refer to mainland Chinese investors buying stocks in Hong Kong; northbound flows refer to overseas investments from Hong Kong in China A-shares.[11] Both flows have risen considerably in the past few years, from a trickle in late 2014 to a wave in 2020, and a torrent in early 2021.

The second big onshore market for Chinese stocks is located in Shenzhen which, like Shanghai, was long closed to foreign investors but is now open through QFII quotas and the Stock Connect program.[12] The Shenzhen exchange took a giant step forward in October 2009 when the ChiNext market was launched to raise capital for innovative and technology companies. ChiNext allows young companies without a long history of making profits to list, something not allowed in Hong Kong or Shanghai.

Shanghai did not want to be left behind. In 2019, it opened the STAR market, an acronym for the Shanghai Stock Exchange Science and Technology Innovation Board. It's been widely touted as Shanghai's equivalent to the tech-heavy NASDAQ in New York and is the only market in China where loss-making firms can list their shares.[13] The addition of STAR market stocks to Stock Connect is another sign of two important developments in China – the growing significance Beijing attaches to the advancement of technology and how the country is opening up its financial markets to encourage greater participation by global investors.

Despite all this progress, up until 2020, the stock market where most international investors bought the most Chinese shares was in Hong Kong. In the early 1990s, when I arrived there as a backpacker, only a handful of mainland Chinese companies were listed in Hong Kong but by 2020, the number of these "red chips" had risen to nearly 160.

The complexity of Chinese markets now starts to become apparent. First, there are three different major exchanges, each with their own characteristics. Second, although the discount rate, which is based on the onshore bond yield, is the same in Shanghai and Shenzhen, the two onshore markets, the nature of the companies listed and the profits they generate and dividends they pay are very different. That means that these two markets can move in different directions at the same

Southbound flows have exceeded Northbound flows in 2020 and 2021.

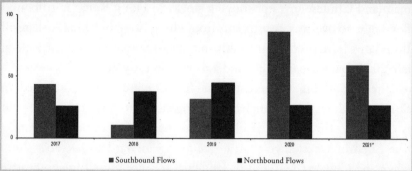

Note: all in USD billions. (*) 2021 data for January-June only.
Source: Hong Kong Stock Exchange

Shenzhen's tech-heavy ChiNext has seen a dramatic rise in the last few years

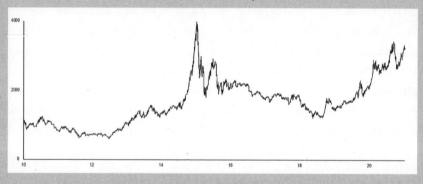

Source: Factset

Shanghai launched its STAR 50 index in 2019

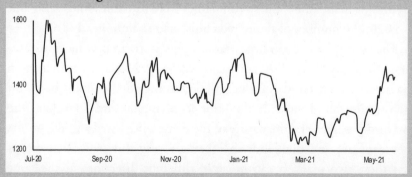

Source: Factset

time. Third, Hong Kong has its own discount rate because it is an offshore market.

This is where things start to get a bit tricky. Some stocks are dual-listed, which means that the A-shares trade in Shanghai and the H-shares in Hong Kong. This means they have different discount rates, which in turn means that the A-shares and H-shares of the same company can simultaneously move in opposite directions.

This can lead to price anomalies – welcome to the world of the A-H share premium. The main thing to remember is that the mainland markets are driven by small retail investors who trade on rumour and speculation, while the Hong Kong market is dominated by much more sober institutional investors such as pension funds and insurance companies. This often leads to situations where the prices of A-shares are detached from the value assigned to H-shares. It is not uncommon for the A-shares of a company to be 30% higher than the price quoted on the H-share market in Hong Kong.

Having come to grips with the peculiarities of the different Chinese stock markets, it is time to look in more detail at how they have evolved – which type of companies are listed and how they make their profits. Many of these companies were listed in "waves" based on the nature of their business, starting from 2000 with the country's giant exporters.

When exporters drove the market

When I backpacked around China in the early 1990s, China was still largely inward looking. In the countryside, many people wore dark blue Mao suits and the major thoroughfares of the big cities were clogged with bicycles, not cars. The streets were lined with large, shady trees and all manner of small mom and pop restaurants, long since replaced by large shopping centres and malls chock-full of luxury goods. But there were also signs that things were changing and that China was starting to open up. The country's first McDonald's opened in Shenzhen, just across the border from Hong Kong, in 1990 and I remember seeing long queues outside the Beijing outlet in the early 1990s.

Beneath the surface, there was a lot more going on than the arrival of Big Macs. Economic reforms were beginning to bear fruit and Chinese

A and H shares for Tsingtao traded very differently in the past, but much less so since the Stock Connect program was put in place in 2014.

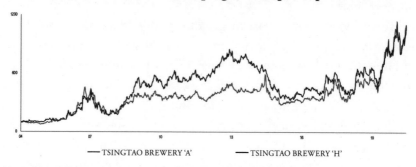

Note: Tsingtao Brewery's stock codes are 168 HK ("H") and 600600 CH ("A")
Source: Yahoo Finance

companies were starting to look for opportunities abroad. They raised billions of dollars in overseas stock markets, mostly in Hong Kong and New York. Telecom operators China Mobile and China Unicom, along with two oil refiners, PetroChina and Sinopec, were among the first large Chinese stocks investors could buy outside China.

But these were baby steps. Everything changed in late 2001 when China became a member of the World Trade Organization (WTO). It was now possible for foreign companies to set up factories in China and export their products all over the planet. The floodgates opened. Within a few years, any CEO of a global company worth his salt needed to have a presence in low-cost China and those that didn't were considered to be way behind the times.

Factories soon dotted the landscape, churning out everything from underwear and toys to shoes and agricultural machinery. People from all over China were more than willing to leave their villages and flock to the cities to work. They could often make more money in a month than they did in a year back on the farm. Even today, these migrant workers are the backbone of the economy, labouring in factories, toiling on building sites and zipping across cities to make e-commerce deliveries. Their lives are tough. They work long hours for low pay, have little job security and receive few welfare benefits. They live in basic housing often shared with other migrant workers and return home only once or twice a year on major holidays to see their wives and children. But it is these hardworking people who were at the centre of China's transformation to an export-led economy in the early 2000s.[14]

These included exporters Li & Fung, a sourcing company which listed in Hong Kong in 1972, Techtronics, a maker of power drills which listed in 1990, and Yue Yuen, a producer of sports shoes for brands such as Nike, which listed in 1992. Big exports meant big profits and in 2000, stock markets in China boomed. At the same time, new reforms allowed the public to take their savings held in bank deposits and invest in mutual funds for the first time.[15] The average market cap of Chinese firms listed in Hong Kong tripled between 2000 and 2005.[16] In 2000 alone, Shanghai was the world's best-performing major stock market, rising more than 50%.

However, what goes up can also go down, and investors were soon given a painful introduction to the other side of stock markets – the sharp correction. While 2000 was a stellar year for the Shanghai market, the party came to an abrupt halt in 2001. The problem was that the government liked what it saw so much that it allowed the Shanghai market to be flooded with fresh share offerings. On 13 June 2001, the index hit a record high of 2,242. That evening, regulators ordered listed firms to sell some state-owned shares and also offer additional shares for sale. The market forces of supply and demand came into effect and many investors, nervous and new to this game, headed for the exits. The Shanghai stock market tumbled and a lot of small investors lost their money and, having been burned once, were reluctant to return for a number of years. It was the start of four lean years and on 11 July 2005, the Shanghai market hit a low of 1,011.

The hottest China stocks were no longer in Shanghai, but in Hong Kong. For example, Techtronics, the exporter of power drills, saw its share price rise from less than HK$1 in January 2000 to over HK$18 by the end of 2005, and Li & Fung, the company that sourced products in China for retailers in the US, also boomed.[17]

But the market's love affair with exporters started to change when the big banks arrived on the scene.

Cashing in on the big banks

Sometimes, it is useful to remind ourselves just how quickly things change in China. It is often all too easy to overlook what has happened in a relatively short space of time. Having taken the plunge to open up the economy by joining the WTO in 2001, China then undertook another huge enterprise, shaking up the country's huge, ailing and spectacularly inefficient state-run companies. These "iron rice bowls" guaranteed jobs for tens of millions of workers, and often came with social benefits such as basic housing and medical care, but the level of productivity was soporific, and the quality of the goods produced generally poor.

With the turmoil of the Asian Financial Crisis 1997–1998 still fresh in the minds of the country's leaders, in the early 2000s, economic reformer Premier Zhu Rongji decided to take a knife to the state sector. Some big state-owned enterprises (SOEs) were closed, others merged, and the better ones were cleaned up and listed on the stock market. Central to these bold reforms were the big commercial banks which were, and to a lesser extent still are, strange hybrids. They generated profits like banks in other countries but were also supposed to support all manner of government projects, irrespective of whether they would ever be repaid. They often provided funds to shore up zombie state enterprises or satisfy the demands of powerful local officials. In the early 2000s, reformers such as Premier Zhu argued that this had to change. The banks' mountainous pile of bad loans were hived off to a new company that would house the bad assets, and the leaner, cleaner banks were prepared for listing on the stock market.

This massive overhaul of the state's banking system coincided with the end of the giant sale of government shares that had spooked the Shanghai market back in 2001.[18] In May 2006, Shanghai registered the biggest monthly rise in nearly four years, building its reputation as a rollercoaster market. Appetite for Chinese stocks grew dramatically and later in 2006, people were lining up in the streets to buy Chinese stocks. At the same time, two of the country's mega banks, Bank of China and Industrial and Commercial Bank of China (ICBC), were listing their shares in Hong Kong, raising a remarkable US$27 billion in a matter of days.[19]

By that time, a whole new story was starting to unfold, one that would add fresh impetus to the growth of the economy and the country's stock markets. China's consumers were beginning to open their wallets for the first time. A white-collar middle class was emerging and migrant workers also had some money in their pockets. Sales of everything from mobile phones and TVs to washing machines, sport shoes and even cars took off. Goods that were regarded as impossible luxuries just a few years ago were now becoming affordable to millions and millions of people. Buying shares in banks, which lent money to this new breed of consumer companies, was one of the best ways to invest in this local story. There is nothing more exciting for stock markets than the arrival of a big, new growth market because it means larger profits and higher stock valuations. This is when "big market" stories are in full swing.

One of the market darlings was Hong Kong-listed China Mobile. By mid-2007, this company had five times as many customers as AT&T, the largest US telecom carrier, and was signing up about five million new users every month. The company's wireless network stretched from Hong Kong to the Himalayas and its signal could be picked up in the Shanghai subways, inside Beijing elevators and deep in Sichuan paddy fields. In rural China, at the time home to two-thirds of the population of 1.3 billion, the company even beamed farmers in remote hamlets advice on how to improve harvests and where to get the best prices for their crops. In short, buying China Mobile stock was like buying into the China growth story, as discussed earlier in Chapter 3 on market psychology.

China Mobile was a "big market story" in 2007, but never got back to its peak afterwards.

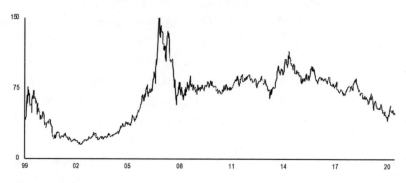

Note: China Mobile stock code is 942 HK
Source: Yahoo Finance

By April 2003, its stock price stood at HK$15 but that was before millions of customers started signing up to its mobile services and sales growth accelerated to over 26% in 2005. The stock rose to HK$35 by the end of 2005 and that's when the party really started. Profits soared[20] and by the end of 2006, it was up to HK$65 and then peaked at nearly HK$155 in October 2007. At the time, the stock traded at a PE of 37x. Looking back, this multiple seems eminently reasonable compared with some of the tech start-ups of today which have been known to break 100x!

Then, suddenly, the share price started to fall even though profit growth was still strong. The problem was that discount rates – the onshore bond yields – rose from around 3% in late 2006 to 4.6% by September 2007. That might not sound a lot but it was actually a pretty big move. And as it was with fresh sushi, higher discount rates (bond yields) pushed share prices lower. Within 12 months, China Mobile's share price had halved.

There are several lessons we can draw from this. First, Asian stock markets can go nuts about a good growth story – it's a theme that resurfaces regularly. Second, the share price can peak before growth peaks. Again, that's because bond markets matter, a lot. In 2007, it was the rise in bond yields that put an end to the party.

With stock prices so high, many companies wanted to list and, as an analyst, I was involved with numerous initial public offerings (IPOs). To prepare a valuation for an IPO, analysts visit factories and property projects, meet management teams, make industry background checks, talk to industry consultants, and write opinions for investors in Hong Kong, Singapore, Frankfurt, London or New York. In 2007, Chinese companies raised over US$100 billion in IPOs, a record year. On 16 October 2007, the Shanghai stock market hit an intraday record high of 6,124, marking the peak of that particular bull market.

But there is a dark side to all of this. In a bull market, when scepticism is in short supply, companies can get greedy and skim money from gullible investors. Sino-Forest was a classic example. A Chinese company listed on the Toronto stock exchange in 1995, it claimed to own large tree plantations in China. With demand for wood from paper industries and furniture makers booming, its stock surged 540% between 2003 and 2011. In June 2011, a report by famed short-seller Carson Block of Muddy Waters Research alleged that Sino-Forest's management owned only a fraction of the forest resources it claimed, and that most of the profits were based on fraudulent transactions. An investigation followed and when it became apparent that it was a scam, Sino-Forest filed for bankruptcy.

Long before Sino-Forest was exposed as a fraud, clouds were forming on the global horizon. This time, the storm came from across the oceans as global equity markets were shattered by a crisis that originated in the western world in 2008 but reverberated across Asia. The Global Financial Crisis (GFC) had begun. At its core was the bursting of a US housing bubble which caused the value of securities tied to US real estate to plummet, taking financial institutions like Lehman Brothers down with them. Stock markets around the world collapsed and Shanghai and Hong Kong were no exception. The Shanghai market fell 70% and bottomed at 1,728 in December 2008. Hong Kong's HSCEI index dropped 75% and bottomed at 4,990.

As governments around the world struggled to stem the economic free fall, Beijing stepped in and announced a massive infrastructure programme across China. This marked the bottom of the market and on 9 September 2008, the Shanghai market soared 9.5%. This helped to prop up the global economy but also planted the seeds of China's huge debt problem as local governments went into overdrive to boost growth, all with borrowed funds. The country was just starting to get a handle on this problem when the coronavirus pandemic struck, setting China and the rest of the world back on their heels.

It is interesting to note that this time around, China's policymakers were far more cautious about the amount of stimulus they provided to support economic growth during the lockdown and subsequent recovery. Meanwhile, the US government, which was criticised after the GFC for not doing enough to help businesses and consumers, was far more aggressive in terms of monetary and fiscal policy. Both countries seem to have learned from their past mistakes.

As we have seen, between 2000 and 2010 the make-up of Chinese markets changed, with the dominance of exporters being replaced by a range of local companies – telecom operators, banks, property developers and retailers. After that, it was the wallets of local consumers and their willingness to spend money that set the pace.

But yet another transformation was taking shape. As Chinese stock markets became bigger, broader and deeper, their dynamics started to change. Moving millions of dollars into Chinese equities became easier, something that did not go unnoticed by global investment funds. While many did not invest in China in the early 2000s, by 2010, these big global players were piling in and the Stock Connect programmes have accelerated this process. Chinese stocks markets were now on the global stage, alongside those in the US, Japan and Europe. As a result, they started to move more and more in tandem with the rest of the world. Today, if US stock markets have a good day, China is likely to have one, too.[21]

But global investment funds are not the only forces that move markets in China. The *dama* army is a force to be reckoned with too.

The *dama* (大妈) army and the empty-nesters

Anyone who has spent a little time in China will have seen them. They practise *tai qi* first thing in the morning, then elbow their way through bustling vegetable markets, escort grandchildren to playgrounds, and sit in the offices of stockbrokers, keeping a close eye on share prices while reading newspapers, gossiping and sipping tea. And in the evenings, they may dash off to enjoy a square dance in a nearby park or square, often accompanied by deafeningly loud music.

They are called *damas* – literally "big mothers" (大妈). The term initially meant something like "aunty", a respectful name for women between 40 and 60 years old, the stereotypical housewives, steeped in Chinese culture and immersed in cooking, sewing and taking care of grandchildren. But over time, the term became a meme for energetic and calculating middle-aged female bargain-hunters with negotiating skills that would put a New York real estate developer to shame.

The *damas* first came to fame in 2013 when they were behind a new gold rush. The price of the precious metal had fallen from US$1,780 in late September 2012 to US$1,220 in mid-2013. Gold was a must-have for this demographic as it had been a key constituent of Chinese dowries for centuries. And when prices dropped sharply, the *damas* pounced. They swept through jewellery stores across the country, buying gold necklaces, earrings, coins and, most sought after of all, gold bars. Special ATM machines that dispensed gold coins were installed to meet the insatiable demand. The frenzied buying spree pushed global gold prices higher.

For these ardent savers, cash stuffed in bank deposits earned paltry returns, and gold was just the start. Nothing was off limits, whether trading in stocks, foreign exchange, real estate or even Bitcoin. They were also among the first to spot the bargains available through *haitao*, the vast cross-border e-commerce market for imported retail goods bought in bulk. *Damas* have an eye for investment opportunities and a proclivity for trading. They keep their well-connected fingers on the pulse of all the latest money-making trends.

Damas are at the forefront of the army of individual retail investors that drive mainland markets. They sit in stockbrokers' offices, monitor their smartphones and gossip online. Rumours about a hot stock can spread like wildfire and lead to intense bursts of speculation that can drive prices to levels not seen in more mature markets (until recently that is, but more of that later). An amazing 80% of turnover on A-share markets is driven by retail investors and 170 million people have individual trading accounts.

Advertisers pay a lot of attention to internet-savvy young Chinese shoppers who, phone in hand and branded bag on the shoulder, are the life blood of luxury stores. While they attract a lot of headlines, the real keys to the Chinese consumer story are their parents, the empty-nesters who have money to spend now that their only child has left home. This is also rich *dama* country. They were born between the late 1950s and early 1970s and watched their parents scrimp, save and struggle to survive the upheaval of the Cultural Revolution. Currency devaluations and inflation made them wary of paper money and, even today, they prefer hard assets such as gold, silver or real estate.

These empty-nesters have had things much easier than their parents. Quite a few of them have a university education and they all benefitted from the multitude of job opportunities that became available after China joined the WTO. They bought property in the late 1990s when the government opened the real estate market and sold off large swathes of its holdings in apartments at a fraction of today's prices. Many also own stocks. By the time 2020 came around, their only child had flown the nest and they had become financially independent.

Unlike in some parts of Asia, it is not uncommon for Chinese women to have a job, so this group includes many "dual income, no kids" (DINKs) households, another consumer force to be reckoned with. In 2019, was estimated that 44% of all adult consumers in urban China were aged between 40 and 64, and that they accounted for 53% of all urban consumer spending.[22] The number of these empty-nesters is staggering, estimated at 290 million in 2032, up from 232m in 2012. In addition, their annual income rises by an average of 5%.[23] In short, it is this generation of middle class *damas* and empty-nesters that drives consumption in China.

Empty-nesters also have distinct characteristics when it comes to spending money. They already have a property (perhaps two or three), a car, and all the latest household goods like flatscreen TVs, fancy personal computers and the latest dishwashers and washing machines. Empty-nesters want experiences, be it travel, a healthy lifestyle, a massage chair or a new kitchen. They buy imported, additive-free groceries and are willing to pay for yoga classes or invest in a good pair of running shoes. When they go out for dinner, they might visit a Michelin-starred restaurant for the first time. Some have become connoisseurs of French wine or prized *pu'er* tea from Yunnan, while others will quaff only expensive *baijiu*, distilled Chinese liquor, when they meet up with friends. These empty-nesters are living the good life.

Their rise has had a big impact on China's stock markets in many ways. They are behind the growth in profits of footwear companies like Anta and Li Ning, and the brisk sales in home improvement companies such as Gree.[24] They visit restaurant chains such as Haidilao, drink Moutai and Wuliangye *baijiu* and use Ctrip to book their holidays. But their investments are as important as their spending patterns. They put their money to work through insurance companies such as Ping An or China Life Insurance and brokers with wealth management arms such as Citic Securities.

ANTA Sports Products is a Chinese sports brand.
Its stock is up over 18x since its listing in 2007.

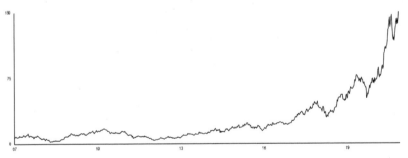

Note: ANTA trades under stock code 2020 HK
Source: Yahoo Finance

The overall pace at which Chinese consumer power has grown is quite extraordinary. In 2010, most urban Chinese had enough money to cover basic needs like food, clothing and housing;[25] by 2020, half were living in relatively well-to-do households with ample funds for perks like regular meals out, beauty products and overseas holidays.[26] All sorts of new, private companies popped up to serve this emerging consumer market in what has become an increasingly digital economy.

However, not all companies have benefitted. State-owned enterprises (SOEs) are still struggling to keep up and the government has launched a fresh round of reforms to streamline these lumbering industrial giants. Some have been closed down and others told to merge. It's not that Beijing has given up on SOEs – far from it, they will remain a key characteristic of China's economy for years to come – but they need to shape up, slim down and compete in the open market.

Many Chinese banks trade at levels where they traded a decade ago.

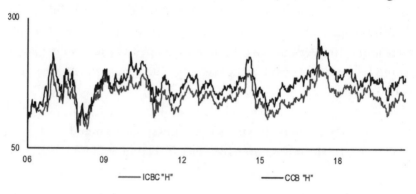

Note: ICBC is Industrial and Commercial Bank of China and its stock code is 1398 HK. CCB is China Construction Bank and its stock code is 939 HK. The share prices are re-set at 100 in 2006 for easy comparsion. Source: Yahoo Finance, author's calculations.

The country's banks have struggled, too. In the early 2000s, they played a crucial role in China's centrally-planned economy. They made sure credit flowed to where Beijing needed it and in return, fees and interest rates were set at levels which guaranteed huge profits. But over the years, this has changed. The days of fat margins are over[27] and some ailing smaller banks, weighed down by bad loans, had to be taken over. It's no surprise that profits have been hit hard. For example, ICBC's profit growth slowed from 15–40% in the early 2000s to near zero after 2015.[28] The share price at the end of 2020 was 10% lower than at the start of the decade.[29]

But while banks and old economy SOEs stumbled, a new group of enterprises emerged to serve the booming consumer market. These internet companies have become the new giants of China's stock markets.

BATs and brickbats

In September 2014, Alibaba listed on the New York Stock Exchange, raising US$25 billion, the largest IPO the world had ever seen.[30] Before that, foreign awareness about China's internet landscape was limited and based on a belief that these companies were copycats – Alibaba was seen as China's Amazon, Baidu its Google and Tencent its Facebook.

But Alibaba's listing helped to hammer home the message that these companies were a force to be reckoned with. The big three, Baidu, Alibaba, and Tencent – soon shortened to BAT – were innovating rapidly, coming up with new ideas to build their platforms to create some of the most valuable businesses on the planet. And how they flourished. In 2016, Tencent's WeChat service handled more mobile transactions over the Chinese New Year – that is, in a single week – than PayPal did in the whole year.[31]

Many commentators have attributed the enormous success of these companies to the blocking of the likes of Google, Facebook and Twitter in China. Without doubt, that has helped. But in South Korea and Japan, where Google and Facebook aren't blocked, home-grown messaging apps such as LINE and KakaoTalk and e-commerce giant Rakuten have outpaced their western competitors. Maybe the BATs are just good at what they do. For example, when Tencent launched WeChat, it was just a chat app. It now supports social media, payments, dating, news, messaging and more. Think Snapchat, Whatsapp, Skype, Instagram, Paypal, Facebook and Apple Pay all rolled into one. You can run your life on WeChat while western counterparts can only dream of giving users so many experiences on a single platform.

Still, being in China comes with several huge advantages. First, the scale of the place: there are more than 720 million mobile internet subscribers. A second advantage is that Chinese consumers are early adopters of all sorts of new technologies, willing to tolerate "beta" products and provide instant feedback.[32] But this market remains fiercely competitive. New ideas, innovations or online features are quickly replicated by competitors within days or weeks. The market leaders can never rest on their laurels. The success of these internet giants has spawned all sorts of new companies, such as Meituan (food delivery), DJI (a drone manufacturer), Kuaishou (a video-based social network), e-commerce platforms JD and group-buying website Pinduoduo (PDD).[33] And Beijing was willing to help these new start-ups, supporting them with generous grants, tax breaks and subsidised technology parks.[34]

Like China Mobile and the banks in 2007, stock markets love nothing more than a big, new growing market. These internet companies are now intertwined with the daily lives of more than a billion people in China. They have also grown their operations in many directions in the past few years, extending their reach into different parts of the economy (for example, Alibaba is now a big player in cloud services). Not surprisingly, they are also extremely profitable.[35] And just like in 2007, when China Mobile was trading at 37x, these internet companies traded at similar high valuations at the end of 2020. What is different this time around is that discount rates (bond yields) are low and falling, while in 2007 they were high and rising.

These giant companies now have a big influence on China's stock markets, tilting the balance from exporters to local businesses. Alibaba sold roughly twice as much as Amazon on its platform in 2020. The top seven largest listed stocks based on market cap – Tencent, CCB (a bank), Ping An (an insurer), Xiaomi (mobile phones), Meituan, Alibaba and Kuaishou – make up 50% of the total market cap of the HSCEI index in Hong Kong.[36] Although the market is now more diversified, over the years, earnings in China have been increasingly driven by local factors such as the wallet of the consumer and online shopping and gaming.

Being big and private does not, however, mean that companies are insulated from Beijing. The regulator remains very powerful. When new rules to crack down on e-cigarettes were announced in March 2021, the share price of RLX, one of the biggest producers, fell 24% overnight. But the bigger story is Alibaba and the internet sector.

Hundreds of millions of people use Alibaba's services every day and, in one way or another, the e-commerce giant has become ingrained in the lifestyle of China's consumers. You can pay for just about anything using the Alipay app, and you can buy just about anything on Taobao, a business-to-consumer platform, a sort of Chinese eBay, or from the brand-name retail site, Tmall. The tentacles of Alibaba's vast business reach pretty much everywhere. And it is huge. In 2020, the sales of Taobao were about double that of Amazon's sales.

That is not all. Millions of Chinese have put their savings into Alibaba's money market funds, run by its fintech arm, Ant Financial. By late 2020, Ant Financial had become China's largest consumer lender and it was preparing for an IPO that would have been the largest in history. But at the very last moment it was cancelled by China's regulators, creating headlines around the world. A few months later, in April 2021, the authorities fined Alibaba a record US$2.8 billion for abusing its market dominance and announced a plan to shrink Ant Financial's business. Beijing's displeasure was clear and Alibaba's share price dropped 25% between November 1 and the last day of 2020.

Alibaba is, of course, the brainchild of Jack Ma, China's most famous entrepreneur. Fluent in English, comfortable rubbing shoulders with politicians and business leaders on the world stage, Mr Ma is a powerful symbol of the success of China's private enterprises, particularly in the realm of the internet. Too powerful, perhaps. For example, China's state-owned banks were growing concerned that Ant represented a threat to their businesses. Mr Ma needed to be taken down a peg or two. For the full story, see the article by Ryan McMorrow and Sun Yu, "The vanishing billionaire: how Jack Ma fell foul of Xi Jinping" published by the *Financial Times* on 15 April 2021.

But a broader story soon emerged. It wasn't just Alibaba that was in the regulators' cross hairs. *The Wall Street Journal* reported on 22 December 2020 that six of China's largest consumer internet businesses – Alibaba, Tencent, food-delivery operator Meituan, e-commerce platforms JD.com and Pinduoduo, and ride-hailing app Didi – had been summoned to a meeting with the State Administration for Market Regulation. The message was clear: you are all getting too big for your boots.

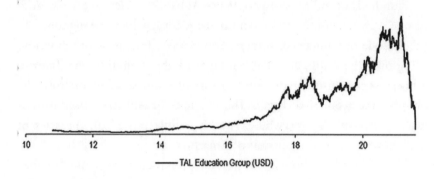

The power of regulations: New rules on online education in China sent education stocks down sharply in July 2021. Source: Yahoo Finance

The newspaper described the meeting as the latest in a string of moves by authorities to rein in China's major consumer internet companies. "Many of them enjoyed relatively unchecked growth over the past decade as China sought to develop its own global technology champions," it said. "But as the companies have grown powerful, armed with massive consumer data, authorities are increasing scrutiny to keep them in check."

Another example of this arrived in late July 2021, when Beijing zeroed in on tutoring start-ups that thrived when schools sent students home. Their concern centred not just on reckless pricing or misleading advertising by some in the online tutoring business, but also on the widening divide between the haves and have-nots – those who can and cannot afford to load up on extra lessons. Officials announced a plethora of restrictions, including limiting after-school tuition fees companies could charge. It sent online education stocks into a tailspin.

In China, investors should never underestimate the power of the country's policymakers. Astute observers will see parallels elsewhere. For example, the US government is considering moves to check the power of Facebook and Amazon.

Self-sufficiency

But there is more to Chinese markets than banks, consumer companies and internet stocks. We also need to understand what drives profits in the technology, power and energy sectors. The major factor here is the government's drive towards self-sufficiency.

Take energy. China is the world's second largest consumer of oil and gas, much of which has to be imported. Some 70% of its oil and 40% of its natural gas is shipped by tanker from the Middle East through the South China Sea; more will soon be delivered by a pipeline running through Pakistan.[37] But China's relationship with the US has become increasingly tense and this means that the shipping lanes through the South China Sea and the Malacca Straits, the stretch of water between Malaysia and the Indonesian island of Sumatra, are of great geopolitical importance.

To reduce its dependency on oil and also address the growing problems of pollution and climate change, China is betting heavily on gas and alternative energy sources such as wind and solar. In 2018, they accounted for 14% of China's energy consumption[38] but Beijing wants this to rise to 20% by 2030 and 50% by 2050.[39] This is very good news for those in the business of making solar panels, gas storage equipment and wind turbines. Chinese companies are already very strong in green energy. Xinyi Glass and Tongwei are big in solar equipment, Goldwind is a leading producer of wind turbines, ENN Energy specialises in gas storage, while Jereh and COSL make different kinds of energy equipment. And a well-functioning power grid needs ultra-high voltage (UHV) power lines and grid metres to distribute solar or wind power to the places where it is needed most, the big cities. Xuji and Nari Tech are both specialists in this area.

China wants to be self-sufficient in other technologies too, especially those that it considers to be strategically important. It is here that China's transition from a manufacturer of low-cost goods to a technological powerhouse is most visible. In some cases, Chinese companies have emerged as global leaders, sometimes to the wrath of their competitors. For example, Huawei was in the headlines after the US attempted to freeze the telecom company out of the global supply chain. Elsewhere, progress has been smoother. Hengli Hydraulic is now a leader in hydraulic equipment, Sany Heavy is a large producer of construction machinery that is giving Caterpillar stiff competition. In robotics, while Japan's

Fanuc is the global No 1, China's Hongfa and Shanghai Mechanical & Electric Corp are breathing down its neck.

There are, however, two sides to this coin. In other industries, Chinese companies have struggled to narrow the technology gap. There are not yet global Chinese auto brands that can compete with the European, Japanese and US car makers (although, in electric vehicles, companies such as BYD are making rapid progress). In semiconductors, China is also trailing. SMIC is the domestic leader but it is still several years behind the leading Taiwan, Korean and US producers. We will pick up this theme again in later chapters.

How China's stock markets work

We have seen how Chinese stock markets have grown from small, obscure bit players into the giants of the Asian capital markets. In the early 2000s, they were driven by a single theme – exports – but by the end of 2020 a wide variety of domestic companies, sectors and themes were setting the pace. This diversity has created greater breadth and depth, reducing volatility. If some sectors crash, others can rally and the two will cancel each other out. This was apparent in 2020, when the internet giants benefitted from work from home trends and the boom in online shopping during the coronavirus pandemic, a time when large parts of the economy went into lockdown for several months. This helped to drive the market higher.

This resilience in the face of adversity has been tested before. The trade war between the US and China, which started in 2018, led to tariffs being imposed on a wide range of Chinese goods. Many thought China's stock markets would suffer, but by late 2020, the Shanghai, Shenzhen and Hong Kong markets were all trading higher than they were in January 2018.[40] One reason for this was that the trade war had little impact on the profits of the large internet companies, which were generated locally. Another was that discount rates (bond yields) fell. And a third was that China's efforts to become self-sufficient in strategically important sectors helped some tech and power companies to grow rapidly.

But Chinese stock markets are not just driven by local issues. Their size means that they are now in the major leagues, alongside the US,

Japan and London. This was not the case in 2000. Overseas investors now realise that A-shares are an asset class that is simply too big to ignore. China's markets are deep and multifaceted, which means that over the years, they have moved more in tandem with trends in global stock markets. For example, if Wall Street finishes on a high note, the markets in China are likely to open in positive territory the next day.

All this means that there is plenty to keep different types of investors interested. A keen student of the Chinese economy and profit growth? Try jumping from sector to sector. Eager to invest in straightforward trading patterns? Check bond yields and look at A-H share discounts. Have a good feel for new emerging technologies? Look at listings on Shanghai's STAR market and the ChiNext in Shenzhen. Long-term investor? There are plenty of investment trends – from self-sufficiency to energy transition and Chinese empty-nesters – that can be linked to baskets of stocks.

The simplest and cheapest way to buy exposure to Chinese stocks is through an ETF. These products provide instant diversification and there is no need to monitor markets every day, perfect for the long-term buy and hold investor.

It goes without saying that China is a radically different place than when I first crossed the border in 1991 to start what turned out to be a fabulous journey, despite the disasters of the first day. The bicycles and Mao suits are long gone but the stock markets have flourished and reflect the progress China has made in so many different areas. They now cast a long shadow and have become a sort of regional anchor; movements in Chinese stocks spill over into the rest of Asia and determine the pulse of markets across the whole region.

It's now time to take a closer look at these other markets.

Endnotes

1   The "H" in CNH stands for Hong Kong, which was the first market where offshore *renminbi* was traded.

2   By the end of April 2020, there were 1,872 companies listed in Shanghai and 2,415 in Shenzhen, with 1,474 on the main board and 941 on ChiNext. Shanghai Stock Exchange's stock index, the SSE 50 Index, which was published in January 2004, includes 50 of the largest, most liquid and most representative Shanghai-listed stocks.

3   Technically, red chips are Chinese companies where the Chinese government owns at least 35% of the company, the majority of sales are generated in China, and they are incorporated outside mainland China and listed in Hong Kong. If the company is incorporated in China, it's a H-share.

4   This index was launched in August 1994 at an index level of 2,000 and it has 50 constituents, such as Tencent, China Mobile and Sinopec. See also Hang Seng indices: <https://www.hsi.com.hk/static/uploads/contents/en/dl_centre/factsheets/hsceie.pdf>.

5   It was an accumulation of events. In early May 2020, the US administration announced a policy to restrict the Federal Retirement Thrift Investment Board from investing in Chinese equities. This was followed by further restrictions on Huawei's access to products based on US technology. Then, a new shot across the bows came with the introduction of the "Holding Foreign Companies Accountable Act" that could lead to Chinese companies being barred from listing on US stock exchanges.

6   This data is from the World Federation of Exchanges for February 2021. The NASDAQ traded US\$2.2 trillion in February 2021, the NYSE US\$1.9 trillion. Shenzhen traded the equivalent of US\$1.1 trillion and Shanghai US\$925 billion.

7   Source: Investopedia.

8   The QFII system was still in place but has become largely obsolete.

9   The trading takes place in their "home" market, so the actual money that's invested does not leave their "home" market.

10 This was the situation as at the end of 2020.

11 All the trades are settled in their "home" currency.

12 Since 1992, it has traded so-called B-shares, which were Chinese shares listed in Shenzhen but traded in Hong Kong dollars. Other B-shares were USD listed shares in Shanghai. A-shares, conversely, are traded in RMB. But when China entered the WTO, domestic investors were also allowed to invest in B-shares using foreign currencies.

13 Only under specific conditions, though. For details, see <http://star.sse.com.cn/en/gettingstarted/features/offering/>.

14 According to an official survey, they numbered 291 million in 2019 and their numbers grow every year. More than 65% of the country's migrant workforce is male, 40 years old on average and earning a monthly salary of RMB3,962 (about USD600). Millions of people were pulled out of poverty, got a job in a factory and by the end of 2005, exports were twice as large a share of China's economy as they were in 2000. Source: China Labour Bulletin 2020.

15 This is important. Chinese bonds move on their own, unfazed by what happens in global bond markets. The low foreign ownership of Chinese financial assets means that Chinese bonds had limited exposure to the global financial cycle and the correlation of bond index returns between China and G7 bond markets was low, even in 2020. Also note that the Chinese government bond market shows low correlation, overall, with both the US Treasury market and the US equity market.

16 The HSCEI index rose from around 1,450 in early 2000 to nearly 5,000 at the start of 2005.

17 Li & Fung's earnings per share (EPS) grew from HK\$27.3 in 2001 to HK\$60.7 in 2005. That implied an average annual compound rate in earnings per share of circa 22%.

18 To be specific, the statement was made by the stock market regulator, the China Securities Regulatory Commission (CSRC).

19 Bank of China's IPO in Hong Kong took place on 1 June 2006. This was its H-share listing. On 5 July 2006, the A-shares of Bank of China were listed on the Shanghai Stock Exchange. Industrial and Commercial Bank of China (ICBC) followed in October that year. It was the first time a company had listed simultaneously in Hong Kong and mainland China.

20 China Mobile's EPS grew 26% in 2006, 29% in 2007 and 29% in 2008.

21 For example, the correlation between the Shanghai stock market index and the S&P500 has risen from no correlation at all – that is, 0.0 – in 2000 to 0.2 in 2010 and 0.5 in 2020. For the HSCEI, it's been less dramatic. It was 0.4 in the early 2000s, 0.5 by 2010 and 0.61 in 2020.

22 Laurent 2013.

23 Laurent 2013.

24 In 2019, records fell on Singles Day, referred to as Double 11 as it fell on 11 November. Total sales reached RMB410 billion (US$58 billion), far more than the Cyber Monday and Black Friday online sales in the US combined.

25 At the time, 92% had annual household disposable incomes of RMB140,000 or less.

26 Ho *et al* 2019.

27 Interest rates were liberalised and allowed to be set by markets, which meant that interest margins contracted.

28 ICBC, for example, saw its return on assets (ROA) fall from 1.45% in 2012 and 1.44% in 2013 to 1.11% in 2018 and 1.08% in 2019.

29 Early in January 2010, ICBC traded at HK$5.8/share, by December 2020, it traded at HK$5.1/share.

30 It exceeded that of the previous record holder – the 2010 offering from the Agricultural Bank of China which raised US$22 billion in Hong Kong. Alibaba was able to sell more shares due to its so-called "greenshoe" option, which allowed banks organising the sale to get more shares from the company at the IPO price in case demand was strong. And it was. The initial plan was to raise US$21 billion but this rose to US$25 billion to meet demand.

31 PwC Experience Centre 2016.

32 PwC Experience Centre 2016, p 7.

33 By sharing Pinduoduo's product information on social networks such as WeChat, users can invite their contacts to form a shopping team to get a lower price for their purchases.

34 PwC Experience Centre 2016, p 8.

35 Tencent's EBITDA margin was 42.5% in 2014, 45.5% in 2017 and 41.5% in H1 2020. Earnings per share grew from HK$2.58 for the full year 2014 to HK$12.88 in September 2020. That is an average annual compound growth rate (CAGR) of 32%. In the same period, Alibaba's EPS rose at a CAGR of 28%.

36 To compare, the most concentrated market in Asia is Indonesia, where the top five stocks account for over 60% of the total market; the least concentrated is India, where it's 35%.

37 Part of the China Pakistan Economic Corridor (CPEC), the pipeline that was still under construction in 2021.

38 This is the so-called primary energy consumption (PEC) and includes coal, oil and gas.

39 Solar, wind, water and nuclear energy are the prime sources of this. Another option is to generate power from water. The mountains and rivers of China provide many opportunities for hydroelectric power. The best potential for hydroelectric power lies in southwest China, providing power in an area lacking in coal resources. The Three Gorges Project on the Yangtze River reached full capacity in 2012, with 32 turbine generators and two additional generators. Hydroelectric power could, potentially, generate 378 million kilowatts for China (IHA website). Source: Five-year plans and China National Renewable Energy Centre.

40 On 22 January 2018, President Trump announced tariffs on solar panels and washing machines.

Chapter 5

A Tale of Two Cities:
Hong Kong and Singapore

Hong Kong

When I arrived in Hong Kong in 1990, the place was way too expensive for my backpacker budget, so I decided to head straight for the border. Later, as a tour guide, I would pick up groups of tourists in Hong Kong and shepherd them around China. While waiting for them to arrive, I stayed in a cheap hostel in Reclamation Street in Kowloon – it's still there – and explore the city on foot. At ground level, the city's energy assaults all the major senses. Noise is all around, the hammering, the shouting, the impatient car horns. It has its own smells too, from fried bean curd and petrol, to the whiff of an overripe drain. Your eyes are constantly shifting from the forest of skyscrapers to the harbour and, after dark, the neon frenzy of a million electric billboards in multicoloured Chinese characters. Boring, it isn't.

The late Jan Morris, a long-time observer of the city, put it beautifully in *Hong Kong: Epilogue to an Empire*, a book she wrote just before the 1997 handover:[1]

> It is like a cauldron, seething, hissing, hooting, arguing, enmeshed in a labyrinth of tunnels and flyovers, with those skyscrapers erupting everywhere into view, with ferries churning and hoverfoils splashing and great jets flying in, with fleets of ships lying always offshore, with double-

decker buses and clanging tram-cars, with a car it seems for every square foot of roadway, with a pedestrian for every square inch of sidewalk ... all in all, with a pace of life so unremitting, a sense of movement and enterprise so challenging, that one's senses are overwhelmed by the sheer glory of human animation.

Hong Kong has also long been an electrifying city in another way, by plugging international financiers into the massive economic socket that is China. Here, bankers have more in common with their counterparts in London or New York than those in Beijing or Shanghai. They flog shares to Californian hedge funds and pretty much anyone else who is interested, help raise capital for thrusting companies seeking to list or expand and make loans to support trade and mergers and acquisitions on both sides of the border. Meanwhile, the Chinese state-run banks are busy funding projects across the region and corporate lawyers make a fat pile of cash from the whole throbbing, pulsing maelstrom of contracts and deal-making. After working in finance in Indonesia, South Africa and Taiwan, it's been my home for more than 15 years. And the stock market, like the city, never stands still.

Less than four hours away by air sits Singapore, another extraordinary creation that is sometimes a rival, sometimes a friend, and shares many of the same historical roots – British colonialism, city states, trade and, of course, very large amounts of money. Outside Japan, which we will discuss later, Hong Kong and Singapore are regarded as having the most developed stock markets in Asia. They have a lot in common. Real estate is part of the DNA of both cities, but they have also created interesting niches that set them apart from each other. Understand one market, and you will have a firm grasp of the other. First, let's revisit Hong Kong in the summer of 1969.

The summer of '69

Even by Hong Kong standards, the summer of 1969 was particularly hot and sticky. As ever, Stanley Kwan was working diligently as the head of the research department of the Hang Seng Bank in Central, the commercial centre of Hong Kong. For many years, he was the research department as he was the only financial analyst employed by the bank. He had been hired because of his excellent command of English and over the years had moved up the ranks, publishing the popular weekly *Hang Seng Newsletter* along the way. His office contained a small desk, a wooden chair, a Smith Corona typewriter and some stationery. His first assignment of the day was to translate the research reports of the foreign banks into Chinese for the chairman, Ho Sin Hang, more commonly known as SH Ho.

The man was a true latter-day Li Ka-shing. Born in poverty in southern China, Mr Ho had little education but went on to become an entrepreneur, financier and philanthropist. Hang Seng started life as a small currency exchange booth in Sheung Wan, a rundown district adjoining Central. Ho fled to Macau after the Japanese invaded Hong Kong in 1941 and revived the business after the war. Hang Seng became one of the leading Chinese-owned banks and went public in 1960. Ho also co-founded New World Development, one of Hong Kong's first big property developers, in 1970. He didn't get everything right – in 1965, HSBC took a majority stake in the business after a run on the bank depleted Hang Seng's reserves.

Hong Kong was a turbulent place in the 1960s. In the early part of the decade, thousands of refugees had poured across the border to escape the famine caused by the disastrous Great Leap Forward, a campaign to modernise China's economy that had gone horribly wrong. Then, in 1966, Chairman Mao launched the Cultural Revolution, setting in motion a period of turmoil that saw another torrent of people flood into Hong Kong. Riots broke out the same year after the government raised the fare of the iconic Star Ferry, and in 1967, there were major disturbances linked to the political upheavals that were taking place in China (near the border at Sha Tau Kok).

Bank runs added to the febrile atmosphere. In 1961, malicious rumours circulated that the Liu Chong Hing Bank[2] was in trouble, causing a brief panic until confidence was restored. On 27 January 1965, the *South China Morning Post* (SCMP) reported: "There was a run on the Ming Tak Bank at the junction of Pedder Street and Queen's Road Central and its branch in Nathan Road, Tsimshatsui, Kowloon, yesterday." The following day, the government took control of the bank and, as rumours spread, the SCMP reported "heavy runs on other Chinese banks". British pounds had to be flown into the city to restore stability to the banking system.

Despite all these dramas, Stanley Kwan was a very busy man. Companies were queuing up to list on the Hong Kong stock market and by 1969, the shares of 100 firms were being traded, up from 50 in 1954. Mr Kwan was no longer a one-man show and the research department had increased to seven analysts. Then he got a call telling him that the chairman wanted to see him. SH Ho had an idea. He thought it was time for Hong Kong to have its own stock market index, a kind of "Dow Jones Industrial Average of Hong Kong,"[3] figuring that it would be good publicity for the bank.

Fully briefed but daunted by the size of the task, Kwan and his team set about creating the Hang Seng Index from scratch. First, they studied how other indices were compiled. This involved analysing all manner of technical issues, from how to treat dividends and bonus shares and dealing with new listings on the market.[4] In the end, the hardest part was selecting the stocks that would be included in the index. It was a political minefield. The last thing the Hang Seng Bank wanted was to alienate clients by leaving them out. Presumably, the chairman got involved and smoothed the way; 33 of the 100 stocks were selected for the first edition of the Hang Seng Index, which debuted at 158 on 24 November 1969.

It was an instant success. Over the next 12 months, the index rose 33%. The fact that the Hang Seng Bank had cleverly tiptoed around the sensitivities involved by including all its major clients in the index did not go unnoticed by local journalists, who sarcastically named it the "Old Pal Index".[5] These days, the Hang Seng Index is part of everyday life in Hong Kong and its movements are recorded in elevators, on digital billboards, hourly news bulletins and countless financial websites. And unlike New York and London, the stock codes of the leading companies are known by everyone from office workers, taxi drivers and hotel doormen, to housewives and bartenders. SH Ho's dream has become reality. As of 17 February 2021, the Hang Seng Index stood at 31,085 and comprised 52 companies.[6]

The Hang Seng index since its launch in 1969, when it started trading at an index level of 158.

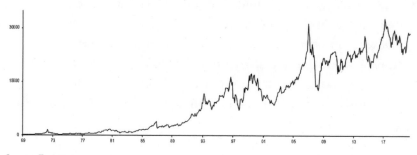

Source: Factset

The Hang Seng Index was created in the days of typewriters and pencils. To update the index, the analysts on Kwan's team had to make their way to the stock exchange and copy down the closing stock prices and trading volumes that were displayed on a large blackboard on the floor of the exchange. After a short walk back to their desks, they calculated the index, on paper, to be published in the morning. It was not until July 1981 that computers were used.[7]

The launch of the Hang Seng Index was a big moment for the Hong Kong stock market, which had been around since 1891, approximately the same time the Shanghai market opened.[8] It had a better track record than its Shanghai cousin, generating average annual returns of nearly 9% between 1896 and 1930, far superior to the 6% offered by Shanghai stocks in the same period.[9] But even in the 1950s and late 1960s, the Hong Kong stock exchange was still considered a backwater and only a handful of rich locals dabbled in the market.[10]

That started to change in the 1970s, when some of what were to become bellwether stocks listed – property developers Sun Hung Kai and Cheung Kong Holdings in 1972, followed by Cathay Pacific in 1986, Dah Sing Financial Group in 1987 and sourcing expert Li & Fung in 1992. Of course, this being Hong Kong, this evolution was not a universally smooth process and scandals came and went. One of the most famous followed the "Black Monday" global stock market crash of 19 October 1987, when US markets fell more than 20% in a day.

Ronald Li, the chairman of the Hong Kong Stock Exchange, came up with a plan to dodge this nasty bullet. His solution was simple: close the market for four days in the hope that the storm would pass. Of course, the opposite happened and as soon as it reopened, prices went into free fall. Mr Li made things much worse by holding a live televised press conference to defend his actions. When pressed by an Australian reporter about his authority to close the exchange, Li exploded. Pointing his finger at his tormenter in full view of the cameras, he shouted: "Arrest that man," threatened to sue him for slander and then had the foreign correspondent frogmarched out of the press conference.

The Hong Kong market recovered, but Li never did. Earlier, he had been lauded for helping to give small investors access to the market, boosting the city's brokerages, but his reputation was now severely damaged. It did not end well. Li was later sent to jail for accepting bribes in exchange for approving stock market listings.

By the time I first visited the city in the early 1990s, on my way to start that disastrous first day in China, the Hong Kong market was no longer a backwater. It was bigger, broader and rising up the global stock market ranks, populated by large local banks and local property developers. Mainland Chinese companies were now eyeing the market, too. On 15 July 1993, Tsingtao Brewery became the first H-share to be listed in Hong Kong.[11]

The 1997 factor and the dollar peg

As in all markets, Hong Kong experienced its fair share of booms and busts, and the bull and bear markets that followed. But for many years, there was one issue that was front and centre for Hong Kong investors – what would happen after 1997, when the territory returned to Chinese sovereignty? Concerns began to emerge as early as 1982, when the problem of land leases was raised by local businessmen. In September that year, British Prime Minister Margaret Thatcher visited Beijing to discuss the matter with Deng Xiaoping, who despite her objections insisted that China would resume both sovereignty and administration over Hong Kong. Investors were already on edge but things were about to get a whole lot worse. On leaving the meeting, Mrs Thatcher slipped on the steps of the Great Hall of the People and fell to her knees. The moment was captured on film and played repeatedly on global news channels.

To many in Hong Kong, an extremely superstitious place at the best of times, this was clearly the worst possible omen. Hong Kong went into full panic mode. Queues formed at supermarkets, and shops refused to accept Hong Kong dollars and started to quote prices in US dollars. The Hong Kong dollar fell 14% between June and November 1982[12] and fresh rumours that banks might collapse didn't help.

Faced with public unrest and wavering confidence in Hong Kong's banks, a rather unusual solution was found. On 24 September 1983, it was announced that the Hong Kong dollar would be tied – or pegged – to the US dollar at a fixed rate, as of 17 October 1983. At any time, all Hong Kong dollars could be exchanged for US dollars. The whole idea of a peg was that there were always sufficient US dollars available to meet demand for Hong Kong dollars.[13] This novel approach did the trick. The Hong Kong dollar stabilised and confidence in the banks returned. The following year, China and Britain signed the 1984 Sino-British Joint Declaration and investors started to breathe easy once again.

However, as a result of the peg, the local currency was now a proxy for the US dollar and this had major implications for how the Hong Kong stock market behaved. To understand why, we need to go back to the tug of war in stock markets between profits and interest rates. At the time, Hong Kong's stock market was dominated by banks and property companies (as we will see later, this has changed). Real estate is such a big deal in Hong Kong that it dominates dinner conversations, newspaper headlines and career choices. The city is one of the few places where local taxi drivers can quote property prices down to the nearest dollar per square foot. These companies are sensitive to what is happening in the domestic economy, especially when it comes to interest rates, for the simple reason that banks extend loans and mortgages to buyers of apartments and office towers.

What makes this even more relevant is that exchange rates and interest rates act as financial shock absorbers in an economy. If something happens – say a trade war, a recession or a rise in inflation – these two factors help to soften the blow. Weak exports? The exchange rate will fall to make exports cheaper, making it easier to export them. Is the economy growing too fast? Rising interest rates will slow things down. Strong imports? The exchange rate will rise to make imports a bit more expensive.[14] But just as with cars, if one shock absorber is not working, the other one will have to work overtime to compensate. So, if the exchange rate is forced to follow the US dollar – which is what happened when the Hong Kong dollar peg was introduced – one of the shock absorbers essentially disappears, putting pressure on the other moving parts. This is the reason that local interest rates and stock prices became more volatile.

Going back to our tug of war analogy, it is as if "team interest rates" was now pulling even harder at the rope, just when "team profits" was weaker because banks and property companies don't enjoy brisk sales when interest rates are rising fast. In short, stock markets amplify any movement in interest rates, especially in Hong Kong.[15] And that's exactly what happened in 1997–1998 during the Asian Financial Crisis, and again in 2003–2004 when the SARS outbreak hit parts of Asia. Interest rates soared, property prices fell, and the share prices of banks and property companies followed them down. The stock market tanked.

Of course, Hong Kong was not the only market in the region to go off the rails during the Asian Financial Crisis. They all pretty much did. Politicians looked on in disbelief and tried all sorts of different measures to stop their economies from haemorrhaging. They introduced new laws, made policy statements and asked people not to take money out of the country. Quite often, this made things even worse, scaring the living daylights out of investors, who headed for the exits.[16]

Again, as with the peg, Hong Kong found its own solution. Rather than imposing capital controls, the government started to buy Hong Kong stocks in huge quantities in order to prop up confidence.[17] It worked. The next problem was to decide what to do with the billions of dollars of stocks it now owned. Eventually, someone came up with the brilliant idea of creating a tracker fund, an ETF that investors could buy to track the Hang Seng Index.[18] On listing, the ETF was the largest IPO Asia had ever seen at the time and it is still one of the biggest ETFs available on the Hong Kong market (its ticker is 2800 HK).

Hong Kong hongs *and Macau high rollers*

Hong Kong is often considered to be a champion of free markets, and in many ways it is, but there is no disguising the fact that large parts of the economy are run by conglomerates. These companies are involved in property, retail, telecoms, supermarkets and airlines. The most prominent are Jardine Matheson (Mandarin hotels, Dairy Farm supermarkets, Hong Kong Land) and the Swire Group (Cathay Pacific, real estate, retail).[19] The *Financial Times* puts it rather nicely in a 2021 feature about the two companies that started by describing the movements of a business traveller arriving in Hong Kong:[20]

> Our hypothetical business traveller is just halfway into her day and most minutes passed, footsteps taken, elevators ridden, calories consumed and Hong Kong dollars spent have been under the umbrella of two family-run empires: Jardine Matheson and the Swire Group.

Hutchison Whampoa, founded in the 19th century, was another conglomerate with considerable clout. It made its name as a shipbuilder and an importer of consumer products, but after getting into financial trouble in the later 1970s, the company was acquired by Li Ka-shing. Mr Li requires little introduction. Starting in the 1950s at age 21 with a few thousand dollars in savings and loans from relatives, he built a global business empire that now runs the Hong Kong port, health and beauty chain Watsons and has stakes in telecom, property, energy and infrastructure businesses. Often ranked the richest man in Hong Kong, he is known locally as "superman" for his ability to make money and clever investments. He has retired and his son Victor is in charge of what is now known as CK Hutchison Holdings, which operates in more than 50 countries.

Jardine and Swire were the two most prominent foreign trading houses or *hongs*. Jardine was involved in the opium trade in the 1830s, leading to wars with Britain and the start of a long period of foreign interference in China, referred to today by the Communist Party as the "century of shame". Swire began trading tea, silk, cotton and wool with

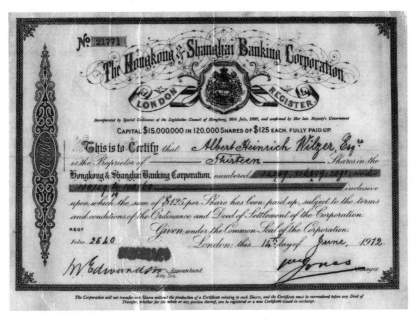

A 1912 share certificate for 13 shares in The Hongkong and Shanghai Banking Corporation (HSBC), owned by Alberty Heinrich Wilzer, Esquire, issued on 14 June 1912. Each share was HKD125 at the time. Source: HSBC Archives, HSBC Reference Number HQ HSBCEB 0008-0003-0001.

China in the 1860s. The *hongs* are a holdover from Asia's colonial age and even today, the top boss is called *taipan*.[21] For most of their history, these family-run companies have had a fraught relationship with China.

Like many Hong Kong companies, Jardine's businesses on the mainland disintegrated after the Communist Party came to power in 1949. The group began to diversify across Asia and in 1994 moved its Hong Kong listing to Singapore. It also expanded into ASEAN and in 2000, Jardine Cycle gradually took control of Astra International, an Indonesian conglomerate that was hit hard by the Asian Financial Crisis. But while Jardine moved its listing out of Hong Kong, new types of companies were moving in. And they came from Macau.

A Portuguese territory until 1999, Macau is now, like Hong Kong, a Special Administrative Region of China. But it always had the reputation of being the more "edgy" of the two. Before the handover, Macau was gripped by a gang war that led to 20 murders in 1997 alone. Centre stage was a man called Wan Kuok-koi, aka "Broken Tooth". A powerful triad leader, he lost nine teeth in a fight and had limited use of his fingers following a meat cleaver attack. His first fortune was reputedly made through controlling VIP gambling rooms in casinos, but he expanded into a wide range of criminal activities – protection, people smuggling and the arms trade.

He defended his turf with bullets, bombs and death threats. In 1998, a bomb exploded under a vehicle belonging to the Macau police chief, António Marques Baptista, who was fortunately not in the car at the time. Broken Tooth's involvement was never proved but he was arrested later that year and jailed for 15 years. He was freed in 2012 and has been busy since. According to an article in the SCMP, in December 2020, Broken Tooth was placed on a list of individuals sanctioned by the US Treasury Department, which designated him "a leader of the 14K Triad, one of the largest Chinese organised crime organisations in the world". His current whereabouts are unknown.

The triads are still around but these days, Macau is a much more peaceful place. It's also a lot more international. For years, a company called Sociedade de Turismo e Diversões de Macau (STDM) had a monopoly on the casino business. This was the domain of Stanley Ho, the colourful and much-married businessman who dominated the town. In the 1990s, half of the city's tax received came from STDM.[22]

Then, in 2002, casino licences were awarded to several foreign multinational firms and joint ventures, including big casino players like Las Vegas Sands, MGM, Galaxy and Wynn Resorts. They raised money on the Hong Kong stock market to fund their new, large casino projects and a few years later, Macau became China's answer to Las Vegas. In 2010, Macau overtook Vegas as the world's casino capital and before COVID-19 struck in 2020, it generated three times more gambling receipts than its rival in Nevada.[23]

While all sorts of punters are welcome in Macau, the real focus is on wealthy mainland Chinese businessmen. They are flown in on private jets, stay at luxury hotel suites and are pampered in private gambling rooms that come with all sorts of perks and privileges. Playing baccarat is their thing. As the saying goes, the house nearly always wins and the casinos have raked in huge profits. As the high rollers poured in, so-called junket operators sprung up to provide lines of credit and any hospitality that might be required.[24]

Macao casino stocks rallied in 2012 but fell sharply after 2013 when an anti-corruption drive was underway in China. The recovery in 2016 onwards was later interrupted by COVID-19 and travel restrictions.

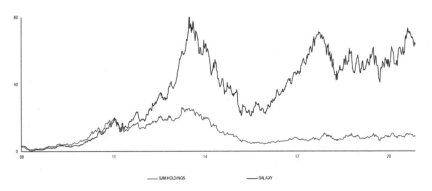

Note: SJM Holdings stock code is 880 HK and Galaxy is 27 HK
Source: Yahoo Finance

The Macau stocks quickly turned into the new darlings of the Hong Kong market. There was a blip in 2014 when China launched a corruption crackdown. No government officials and few businessmen wanted to be seen at a roulette table throwing tens of thousands of US dollars around. The high rollers beat a hasty retreat and it took the industry about two years to recover. Normal service resumed until the casinos had to close temporarily because of the pandemic. Fear not, they will be quickly back on their feet after the coronavirus threat has passed.

The Macau casinos added a whole new dimension to the Hong Kong stock market. In the early 1990s, the Hong Kong market was dominated by banks and property developers, but by 2010, a wide range of mainland Chinese companies were making their presence felt. Hong Kong was going through yet another change, with mainland elements playing an increasingly important role. These stocks often featured in the Hang Seng China Enterprises Index (HSCEI), a barometer of the mainland China companies listed in Hong Kong.[25]

The NASDAQ of the East?

Tsingtao, the 110-year-old mainland brewer, entered the history books in 1993 when it became Hong Kong's first H-share listing. At its listing ceremony, stock exchange executives used beer to make the toast rather than the traditional champagne. Many other Chinese companies followed but others decided to take a different route and went to the US to list in New York, often through American Depository Receipts (ADRs), certificates issued by US banks that represents shares in foreign stock, allowing that company's shares to trade in the US financial markets.

By mid-2020, the total market cap of this select group of Chinese companies was US$1.6 trillion, or about 35% of the whole H-share market in Hong Kong. They included established internet giants such as Alibaba, Tencent, Baidu and JD.com, as well as relative newcomers like Pinduoduo and Bilibili, and restaurant giants like Yum China, whose two largest brands are KFC and Pizza Hut. However, superpower politics then took a turn for the worse. In 2020, the administration of US President Donald Trump decided to put the brakes on Chinese companies raising money in US stock markets. New regulations made it more difficult for them to list or remain listed in the US and many chose to move out. Their preferred destination was Hong Kong.[26]

The first to make the journey were Alibaba, JD.com and Netease. Encouraged by policymakers in Beijing, the caravan of companies that followed became known as "the homecoming". Most are tech companies and if the trend continues in the next few years, the Hong Kong market will be on course to become a tech-heavy "NASDAQ of the East". As of early 2021, five of the top ten traded stocks were tech companies. The days of banks and property setting the tone in Hong Kong are fading. As mentioned at the start of this chapter, this market is always evolving and reinventing itself.

But while Hong Kong is celebrating the arrival of powerful new players and an injection of financial muscle, the opposite is happening in Singapore, its long-running competitor. The number of listed companies on the Singapore Exchange Limited (SGX) has fallen in the last few years.[27] The authorities are trying to reverse this trend and there are proposals to make it easier for smaller companies to list on the SGX. While Hong Kong has a lot in common with Singapore – they are both huge Asian financial centres with lots of listed banks and property companies – Singapore has several unique features that make it different.

The Lion City

Singapore, also known as the "Lion City"[28] – from the Sanskrit "simha" (lion) and "pura" (city) – sits at the strategically important southern tip of the Malaysian peninsula and has long been an important port and a place to do business in Asia. This is reflected in the insane amount of delicious food available, from Chinese Hainanese chicken rice to Indian curries, Indonesian *rendang* and Malay sweets. As soon as the city secured independence in 1965, it put together all the ingredients needed to create a vibrant financial centre – state of the art architecture, low taxes, little corruption and a highly educated labour force. Over the years, the city state with some of its home-grown companies such as DBS, CapitaLand, Keppel Corporation and Fraser & Neave, emerged as a gateway to Southeast Asia and the rest of the region.

While Hong Kong's stock market has been around for a long time, the Singapore market is a relatively late addition. It started in 1973 with a few separate stock markets which eventually merged in 1999 into what is now called Singapore Exchanges.[29] The index that covers the Singapore market is the Straits Times Index, put together by a finance professor in 1998.[30]

The Singapore market can't match Hong Kong for drama and scandal, but it has had its moments. In early 1995, it was the epicentre of the collapse of Barings, a venerable British investment bank. Barings, founded in 1762, was the world's second oldest merchant bank but the man who caused its downfall was of a rather younger vintage, a 28-year-old trader called Nick Leeson. Lightly supervised in the Singapore office but with a great deal of confidence in his own ability, Nick racked up losses of US$1.3 billion in unauthorised trades in a very short space of time. As head of derivatives trading, he had been making bets on the rise of Japanese stocks, and he was making large profits until disaster struck.

On 17 January 1995, an earthquake hit the city of Kobe in Japan and Asian markets plummeted, as did Leeson's positions. Instead of cutting his losses, he decided to double down, hoping markets would bounce back so he could recoup his losses. They didn't. Investopedia, an excellent website that is a go-to place for clarity and simplicity in all things financial, takes up the story:[31]

> At the time of the loss, he was assigned to an arbitrage trade, buying and selling Nikkei 225 futures contract in both the Osaka Securities Exchange in Japan and the Singapore International Monetary Exchange, in Singapore. However, instead of initiating simultaneous trades to exploit small differences in pricing between the two markets, he held his contracts, hoping to make a larger profit by betting on directional moves of the underlying index.
>
> Making matters worse, Leeson hid his losses with accounting tricks. Had the bank discovered this earlier, it would have taken large but not devastating losses and remained solvent.

Leeson fled but was arrested in Frankfurt, extradited back to Singapore, sentenced to six and a half years in prison, and released in July 1999. After being in business for 233 years, Barings ceased operations on 26 February 1995, after being unable to meet its cash requirements following all the unauthorised trades. Leeson later wrote an autobiography, *Rogue Trader*,[32] which was made into a film of the same name in 1999 starring Ewan McGregor. From 2005 to 2011, he held management roles at a football club in Ireland and these days, he is a regular guest on the after-dinner and keynote speaking circuit.

The Singapore authorities were not amused by the scandal. To prevent a similar incident, the Futures Trading Act was amended to allow the Monetary Authority of Singapore to monitor the activities of traders selling futures contracts more closely. Normal service soon resumed until a bigger problem buffeted the market – the fallout from the Asian Financial Crisis that swept the region in 1997 and 1998. By 2000, it was clear that the Singapore market was in serious need of a confidence boost to persuade people to invest in stocks again. In November 2000, the Singapore stock exchange listed on its own market and CapitaLand, one of the island state's biggest property companies, debuted that same year on 21 November. It grew to become one of the largest listed property companies in Asia.

No tech, S-REITs and agri

While the Hong Kong market is on the way to transforming itself into a kind of Asian NASDAQ, this is not the case in Singapore. Tech IPOs are still rare, as they are in the rest of Southeast Asia. A handful of companies have gone all the way from start-ups to listing in Singapore, but they are the exceptions. One is Sea Ltd, an internet company founded in Singapore that runs Shopee, the largest pan-ASEAN e-commerce platform, and SeaMoney, a leader in digital payments in Southeast Asia. Another is the listing of Bukalapak, an Indonesian e-commerce player, in Jakarta. But at a time when global stock markets are enthralled by tech stocks because of their growth potential, the Singapore stock market and its Southeast Asian peers are largely spectators.[33] Having said that, Singapore has developed niches that have attracted a large following. Two could not be more different, one is stable and predictable, the other is anything but – they are Singapore's S-REITs and its agri-businesses.

Let's look at the volatile agri-businesses first. They are dominated by three players: Golden Agri Resources, Wilmar and Olam. Golden Agri was set up by Eka Tjipta Widjaja, who became yet another of Asia's rags-to-riches stories. Born in China, he emigrated to the Indonesian island of Sulawesi and after selling biscuits and sweets from a bicycle rickshaw, he founded Sinar Mas in 1938 and gradually turned it into a trading business. This evolved into a sprawling conglomerate, led by Golden Agri, the world's second largest producer of palm oil, and Asia Pulp & Paper, one of the world's biggest paper manufacturers.[34] One of the wealthiest men in the region in the mid-1990s, he was hit hard by the Asian crisis of 1997–1998. Unlike many others, he survived and Golden Agri was listed in Singapore in 1999.[35] The Sinar Mas portfolio now spans energy, real estate, financial services, telecommunications and mining. The founding father died in 2019 and the business is run by the second and third generations of the family.

Wilmar, which was founded in 1991, was also set up by entrepreneurial Chinese immigrants. Kuok Khoon Hong, born in Johor, Malaysia, ran a thriving food distribution business before he co-founded Wilmar and built it into one of the world's largest palm oil producers. His father had arrived from China at the age of 18 in what was then British Malaya. He was a cousin of Robert Kuok, who went on to turn a tiny flour shop into a billion-dollar Asian conglomerate, which includes the Shangri-La hotel group. In 2007, Kuok Khoon Hong and his uncle, Robert, agreed to merge the Kuok Group's edible oil, trading and oil palm plantation assets into Wilmar. In December 2015, Robert made headlines when he sold his stake in Hong Kong's venerable English language newspaper, the *South China Morning Post*, to Alibaba, then run by Jack Ma.[36]

Olam has rather different origins. It was established in 1989 by the Kewalram Chanrai Group (KC Group), one of the oldest international companies in Africa and Asia, which has more than 150 years of trading history. Olam started as an agricultural commodities trader in Nigeria dealing in cashew nuts, and by the early 1990s, it was sourcing a wide range of nuts for food companies such as Kraft and Nestle. It is now among the world's largest suppliers of cocoa beans, coffee, cotton and rice. The company listed in Singapore in 2005 but it has not all been plain sailing. In 2012, Olam came under attack from short-seller Muddy Waters, which criticised its accounting practices. Olam denied the claims but the stock sold off rapidly until Temasek, Singapore's state investment fund, scooped up shares at rock bottom prices. Temasek has been the majority shareholder since 2014. Olam's business is more volatile than that of Golden Agri and Wilmar, but it has also grown rapidly in the last decade.

Olam's share price fell when it allegations of accounting malfeasance were issued by Muddy Waters in late 2012.

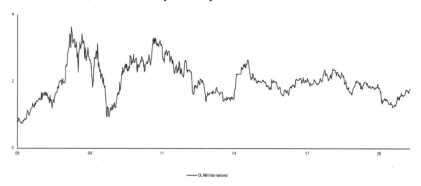

Note: OLAM stock code is Olam SP
Source: Yahoo Finance

While Singapore's agri-businesses can be volatile, the market's other niche is a hallmark of stability and serenity: Real Estate Investment Trusts or REITs (with S-REITs referring to Singapore-REITs). REITs are nothing new, they have been around since the 1960s.[37] In essence, they are simple: REITs pool investors' money to invest, own and operate properties. It's a low-risk and easy way to buy and sell property, even for those who only have a few dollars and cannot buy an apartment, condo or house themselves. In fact, it is the easiest and possibly the cheapest way to buy into property.

What makes them special is that they are required to pay out at least 90% of their profits in dividends, generating a steady stream of income for investors. They have become very popular for the simple reason that if bank deposits pay low interest, REITs offer an alternative place to park your money and make a decent return.[38] Singapore has all sorts of interesting REITS. Some focus on industrial property (Ascendas, Mapletree), some on hotels and hospitality properties (CDL Hospitality Trust) or residential property (Ascott), while others cover the whole real estate industry (CapitaLand, Suntec). Hong Kong, however, has the largest REIT – Link REIT – which manages an array of real estate assets, from retail facilities to car parks and offices.

Ascendas REIT is sensitive to changes in bond yields (lower yields is a positive to the stock).

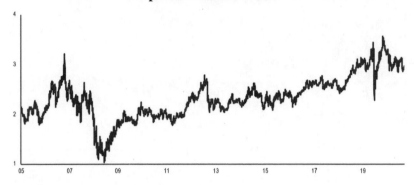

Note: Ascendas REIT's stock code is AREIT SP
Source: Yahoo Finance

Understanding these markets

While Singapore is still a highly concentrated market dominated by banks, property and S-REITs, Hong Kong is going through a makeover thanks to the raft of new listings of large tech companies. This has made the Hong Kong market more concentrated, with the top ten stocks accounting for 61% of market cap and 45% of turnover in May 2021.[39] But it is still not as concentrated as Singapore which, after Indonesia and the Philippines, is the third most concentrated market in the region, with a small number of large cap stocks setting the pace.

In terms of valuations, the financial companies listed in Hong Kong and Singapore are quite similar and that is reflected in their PE valuations, which don't differ much. Hong Kong's tech companies and Singapore's agri-businesses are a far more diverse bunch and their PE ratios vary greatly.

Both markets continue to be among the most sensitive to swings in interest rates. In Singapore, it's because of the banks and property companies. In Hong Kong, it is because the currency shock absorber disappeared when the Hong Kong dollar was pegged to the US dollar. As a result, interest rates and stock prices amplify every bump in the economy. This is also why profits in Hong Kong have been much more volatile than in Singapore (its super-stable REITs add to Singapore's relative calm). Hong Kong is definitely the more impulsive and capricious of the two.[40]

This sensitivity to interest rates also strengthens their connection to global markets, but to different degrees. Singapore is more sensitive to what happens in markets around the world,[41] while in Hong Kong, China's influence on stocks and businesses is much more noticeable. The reason is simple: many Chinese companies are listed in Hong Kong[42] and a number of large Hong Kong companies do big business in mainland China.

From Hong Kong and Singapore, we move to another large Asian stock exchange with its own history and unique dynamics. Welcome to India's bustling city of Mumbai.

Endnotes

1   Morris 1997, p 44.

2   The bank run started on 14 June 1961.

3   The Hang Seng index is a free float-adjusted market-capitalisation-weighted stock market index. The Dow Jones Industrial Index is a price-weighted index that tracks 30 large, publicly-owned companies trading on the New York Stock Exchange and the NASDAQ. It would have been better to call the Hang Seng Index Hong Kong's S&P500 as they use the same methodology.

4   They decided on a base "day" from which the index would be calculated, so there could be a comparative basis. This was 31 July 1964, a day when the market was stable.

5   Kwan 2011, p 129.

6   The Hang Seng Index (HSI) started with only 33 constituents, rising to 38 in 2007 when it began to include H-shares companies. The HSI then gradually expanded and reached 50 constituents in 2012, when there were around 1,380 listed companies in Hong Kong and the HSI covered roughly 60% of the aggregate market capitalisation at that time. The number remained at 50 until December 2020, when this rose to 52. In 2021, there were proposals to increase the number again.

7   Initially, this was only provided on a minute by minute basis. See Kwan 2011, p 130.

8   This is when the Association of Stockbrokers in Hong Kong, the first formal stock exchange in Hong Kong, was formed. This association was renamed the Hong Kong Stock Exchange in 1914. In fact, there were more stock exchanges at different times. In 1973, the Far East Exchange, the Hong Kong Stock Exchange, the Kam Ngan Stock Exchange and the Kowloon Stock Exchange agreed to standardise their trading sessions, and they were incorporated into the Hong Kong Stock Exchange in 1980. These four exchanges ceased trading on 27 March 1986. Source: "Hong Kong Stock Market Historical Events" on hkex.com.hk.

9   These are total returns, meaning increases in share prices and dividends. Source: Taylor 2019.

10   Kwan 2011, p 127.

11   Technically, Tsingtao was not the first. Some Chinese companies bought small, Hong Kong listed firms – "shells" – so instead of listing their company, they acquired a listing on the Hong Kong Stock Exchange. These can be considered the very first Chinese listed companies. There were 19 such deals in 1992–1993 and some US$1.84 billion was raised. Source: Chan 1995, p 945.

12   It fell from HK$5.86 to HK$6.67 against the US dollar.

13   Technically, this is a currency board. The Hong Kong dollar was originally set at a rate of 7.8 per US dollar, although it has been allowed to trade between 7.75 and 7.85 per US dollar since 2005. If capital flows out of Hong Kong result in a weakening of the local currency to 7.85 per dollar, the lower end of the trading band, the Hong Kong Monetary Authority (HKMA) will buy Hong Kong dollars held in reserve by banks, causing a reduction in banking liquidity that pushes market interest rates up to a level that attracts money back into the city. Conversely, if money flows into the city and the exchange rate strengthens to 7.75 per dollar, the upper end of the band, the HKMA will sell Hong Kong dollars to banks, causing an increase in bank liquidity and putting downward pressure on local interest rates that discourage capital inflows. See Greenwood 2016, especially Chapter 7.

14   It's not the government that sets exchange rates, but markets. Weaker demand from, say, the US for Singapore's exports also means less demand for the Singapore dollar because the US is not buying Singapore goods. The weaker Singapore dollar will make Singapore goods cheaper for US consumers. The reverse is true when import demand is strong.

15   In economics, this is called the "impossible trinity" which states that it is not possible to have all three of the following at the same time: (1) a fixed foreign exchange rate; (2) free movement of money – an absence of capital controls; and (3) setting interest rates independently. At best, countries can have only two of three at the same time.

16   All sorts of ideas were tried to stop the haemorrhage. Malaysia and Thailand put controls on money flows and Indonesia toyed with the idea of fixing its currency to the US dollar, as that had worked in Hong Kong.

17   Hong Kong bought and put it in what is called the Exchange Fund. These actions directly penalised speculators that were "short" the market.

18   Greenwood 2016, pp 278–279. With an issue size of HK$33.3 billion (approximately US$4.3 billion), the tracker fund's IPO in 1999 was the largest IPO in Asia ex-Japan at the time.

19   Swire also own properties and has been a Coca-Cola franchisee since the mid-1960; soft drink production and distribution is one of the group's core activities.

20   Leo Lewis, Primrose Riordan, Alice Woodhouse, Nicholle Liu & Stefania Palma, "Hong Kong's historic businesses face an uncertain future" *Financial Times*, 18 February 2021 <https://www.ft.com/content/3ab1091c-8ebc-47a9-b57c-0264ab75e677>.

21   The Keswick family that married into the Jardine family now runs the Jardine group, while the Swire family manages Swire.

22   He passed away in 2020, leaving behind 14 surviving children fathered with four wives. During his later years, his extended family engaged in high-profile squabbles over his empire.

23   In 2019, before the coronavirus crisis, Macau generated revenue of US$36 billion and Nevada US$12 billion. Source: Inside Asian Gaming <https://www.asgam.com/index.php/2021/02/03/macau-and-las-vegas-2019-vs-2020-gaming-revenues/>.

24   In the early 2000s, China only allowed RMB20,000 to be moved out of the mainland during any single visit. To circumvent this, high rollers deposited money with junkets in the mainland and used the money in Macau. They could also borrow from junket agents. Once they're done gambling, they can take their winnings in US or Hong Kong dollars and invest it in property or offshore tax havens.

25   Source: Hang Seng indices <https://www.hsi.com.hk/eng>. To make the HSCEI more representative, its constituent universe was expanded in 2018. Apart from H-shares and red chips, P chips – private sector Chinese companies incorporated in places such as the Cayman Islands – are also eligible for selection. The distinction between what exactly was a Hong Kong or a Chinese company has started to blur. Hong Kong companies such as jeweller Chow Tai Fook started to do more business in China. By 2012, 57% of its profits came from China and by H1 2020, this had grown to 68% (source: Chow Tai Fook 2020).

26   There were pretty good reasons for this: the Hong Kong stock market was vibrant and ranked No 1 in the world for IPOs. By 2020, it had been ranked No 1 in seven out of 11 years. Source: Wang, Levin, 2020.

27 By December 2018, there were 741 companies listed, down from a 2010 high of 78 (Schmidt 2019).

28 It gets its name from the Malay words *singa*, which means "lion," and *pura*, which means "city." Lions have never lived there, although tigers have.

29 The company was formed in 1999 through a consolidation of three Singaporean companies that ran exchanges and clearing services: the Stock Exchange of Singapore (SES), Singapore International Monetary Exchange (Simex) and Securities Clearing and Computer Services (SCCS).

30 The index has a history dating back to 1966, when another index, the Straits Times Industrials Index (STII), was in use before being replaced by the current Strait Times Index. It began trading on 31 August 1998 at 885.26 points.

31 James Chen, "Barings Bank" Investopedia, 31 October 2020 <https://www.investopedia.com/terms/b/baringsbank.asp>.

32 Nick Leeson, *Rogue Trader: How I Brought Down Barings Bank and Shook the Financial World* (Little, Brown & Co, 1996).

33 The tech and communication sectors account for just about 11% of the Singapore stock markets versus a weighting of more than a third in the S&P500 Index and about a fourth in the whole of Asia. At the end of 2020, financials and real estate made up about 42% of the index.

34 Nikkei Asia, December 2019.

35 Golden Agri Resources, Olam and Wilmar (and other Singapore businesses) are described in detail in Vijayaraghavan 2017.

36 For US$265 million.

37 REITs have been around since the 1960s in the US, Australia had its first in 1971, Japan in 2000 and Singapore soon thereafter.

38 Singapore's Ascendas REIT correlation with the US 10-year bond yield is negative 0.37 over the last five years, meaning the total return of the stock, that is price movements and dividend paymnents, tend to go in the reverse direction of the bond yield, or discount rates. If rates fall, the total return of this REIT goes up. The correlation for all Singapoire REITs is a bit lower but also negative. The S-REIT index has a -0.36 correlation over 2015–2020.

39 In Hong Kong, the top ten made up 40% of the total market in 2010, and by end 2020, this had risen to 61%. In Singapore, this went from 62% in 2010 to 70% in 2020.

40 The standard deviation in the FTSE Hong Kong index is 6% measured on monthly returns from 1 January 2002 to end 2020. That is amongst the highest in Asia, while Singapore is 5%, in line with the average across the region.

41 Its five-year correlation with the US S&P500 index is 0.77 measured over 2015–2020, one of the highest in the region. In Hong Kong, it stands at 0.64.

42 The five-year (2015–2020) correlation with the Shanghai index stands at 0.66, while in Singapore it is lower at 0.49.

Chapter 6

India's Stock Markets
शेयर बाजार

Dalal Street – a walk down memory lane

Rakesh Jhunjhunwala,[1] the teenage son of a Mumbai income tax officer, tucked himself away in a corner of the living room. There, he listened to his father and his friends as they discussed the local stock market while sipping milk tea and eating crunchy snacks, *khatta dokla* with green chutney and an assortment of Britannia's biscuits, that his mother had prepared. Newspapers were stacked on a nearby table. He heard them talk about profits and margins, taxes and governments, stock valuations and interest rates. To young Rakesh, it was mesmerising.

For him, it appeared that his father and his friends were engaged in a verbal battle in which facts and erudition were used, like swords and knives, to win the argument or wear the opponent down. While one was making a case, others would listen carefully. When they disagreed with the point being made or the wording was poorly chosen, heads were shaken, hands were thrown in the air, voices were raised and fingers pointed. A verbal assault on the logic soon followed. The intense heat of the debate made it appear to young Rakesh as if the very future of the nation were at stake. But then, later in the afternoon, after they had swapped their best investment ideas and insights, and the milk tea and snacks were long finished, they would all part amicably and head back home. For an impressionable teenager in the 1970s, it was mighty good theatre.

However, Rakesh had little clue about what was actually being debated. Interest rates and equities were new to his vocabulary, but he had seen that share prices quoted in the newspapers changed every day. A few years later, Rakesh asked his father what all the excitement was about – why did share prices move around so much? His father told him that it was all about news flow: "If there is an item on Gwalior Rayon (a leading pulp and fibre company) in the newspaper, Gwalior Rayon's price will fluctuate the next day".[2] Rakesh found it all fascinating and, just like his father, he was hooked.

When Rakesh qualified as a chartered accountant, instead of looking for a junior position at a respectable company, he told his parents that he wanted to try his luck in the stock market. His mother disliked the idea. To her, stock markets were gambling dens, but his father told him to go ahead, as long as he agreed to two conditions: first, to read the newspapers regularly, and second, not to borrow money from friends. And, as if to put the young man at ease, he also told Rakesh to stay with them in Mumbai. His father added further reassurance – after all, what was there to lose? If his investments went sour, he could always find a job as a chartered accountant.

He probably didn't realise it at the time, but Rakesh was following in the footsteps of the stock traders who used to sit under shady banyan trees in central Mumbai as far back as 1875. Those early Indian investors and brokers later gathered in nearby Dalal Street – *dalal* being the Marathi word for "broker" – which has since become synonymous with all matters finance and known as India's Wall Street.

Rakesh started to pour through financial statements and began to make his first investments. He bought some Tata Tea shares in early 1986 and the price promptly rose threefold in a few months. This was exciting! Having skin in the game came with a certain thrill. Rakesh decided to keep his stock selection simple – find good, profitable companies that had something special to offer and had impeccable management. And buy when they were down and looked cheap. He also made a habit of separating stock trading – looking for short-term gains when the market fluctuated – from buy and hold investments that he would put away for the long-term, irrespective of the ups and downs of the market.

Elphinstone Circle in 1879, where people gathered to trade stocks. Following independence, it was renamed Horniman Circle, after Benjamin Horniman, the editor of *The Bombay Chronicle*, who was known for his advocacy of Indian independence. It is one of the very few landmarks named after a British citizen in post-independence India. This view shows the gardens and fountain in the centre, with the banyan tree a little further up, left of centre. Source: Wikimedia Commons <https://commons.wikimedia.org/wiki/File:Elphinstone_Circle,_Bombay_in_the_1870s_(2).jpg>.

In 1986, the same year that Rakesh started investing, the Mumbai market – abbreviated to BSE for Bombay Stock Exchange, using the old colonial name for the city – announced the launch of the Sensex Index, comprising 30 leading stocks.[3] Then, in 1992, in addition to the BSE, a new electronic stock market was established, the National Stock Exchange (NSE). This market started to use its own stock market index in 1996, the Nifty 50. So there are two stock markets in India, and although most companies are listed on both, for investors it makes little difference where the stocks are bought or sold.[4]

India's Sensex and Nifty indices move in a very similar fashion.

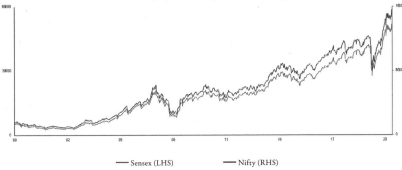

Note: RHS stands for right hand scale. So the Nifty index is measured on the right, Sensex on the left hand scale. Source: Factset.

When Rakesh started out, life as a stock trader was not easy. Since independence from Britain in 1947, India had been stuck in the slow lane, unlike the Asian Tigers of Hong Kong, Singapore, Taiwan and South Korea, the economies that had started to roar in the 1960s and had not looked back. Economists dubbed this the "Hindu growth rate", which had nothing to do with religion but more with the government policies that discouraged international trade and foreign investment.[5] Domestic private sector companies needed approval from scores of government agencies before they could start to operate. A Bloomberg columnist put it this way: "Imagine Soviet style central planning run by the British civil service."

This all changed in 1991. The government,[6] dismayed by decades of slow growth, decided to try a completely new approach by opening the door to private investments and deregulating industries. Domestic and foreign investors were invited to establish new industries – two of these, pharma and software, will be discussed later – and this excited investors. The tortoise became the hare. Entrepreneurs thrived as India moved into the fast lane and one of the best ways to make money was to invest in the stock market. The Mumbai stock market was off to the races, with a frenzied Dalal Street resembling a well-shaken beehive. In mid-1990, just before the old policies were discarded, the Sensex had crossed the 1,000 mark for the first time. By January 1992, it had doubled to 2,000 and two months later, it hit 4,000.

Now everybody wanted a piece of the action. Sweaty touts and tipsters crowded the exchange's gloomy hallways where, pushing and shouting, they offered advice to anyone with a fistful of money. What could possibly go wrong? A lot, as it happened. In April 1992, news began to spread that some brokers were skating beyond even the fuzzy edges of Indian securities laws in order to gain control of large amounts of shares. About the same time, it became clear that several banks had provided hundreds of millions of dollars to brokers to finance speculative bets on stocks, and a lot of the money could not be accounted for.

In a matter of days, a massive stock market scandal erupted. At the heart of it was a flamboyant broker named Harshad Mehta, who was caught manipulating stocks and conniving with investors, politicians and banks. Mehta ended up behind bars, the chairmen of several banks were forced to resign and one committed suicide. Stock prices plummeted, dropping 72% at one point, and the bear market lasted for about two years. It would take another decade before the market hit the 5,000 mark.[7]

But Rakesh, who had been in the market early, took advantage of the crash and continued to put his money to work. Over the course of the following decade, the value of his investments skyrocketed as did his status as a local investment celebrity. The young boy who listened to his father and his friends argue is now better known as the *Badshah of Dalal Street* – stock market mogul or the Big Bull. By 2009, Rakesh Jhunjhunwala was one of the richest men in India.[8]

Opposites attract

My own introduction to India came in 1990 when I picked up a novel in an Amsterdam bookstore, *India: A Million Mutinies Now* by VS Naipaul. It was filled with gripping tales about people the writer had met on his journey through India. He painted a beautiful picture of how they were affected by innumerable small forces and frictions – the decisions of parents, compromises of faith, the whim of random political forces – that determined their path through life. Rakesh would have fitted comfortably into Naipaul's narrative.

My first journey to India came about a decade later, when I went on a business trip in 2001 to attend an investor conference. There were plenty of these conferences back then. Money was needed to build roads, bridges and businesses, and companies (and the government) were turning to the bond markets in order to borrow from foreign investors. As in many other Asian nations at the time, these projects could not be funded domestically. But this reliance on foreign capital also came with a risk – as soon as dark clouds gathered on the horizon, many foreigners sold their rupees and dashed for the door marked "exit". Even today, the Indian rupee is one of the more volatile currencies in the region.

As my flight came in to land in Mumbai, I could see a million pinpricks of light shining in the darkness, conjuring up images of a vast LED circuit board. I wasn't sure what to expect. I carried with me a soft copy of VS Naipaul's novel that had gripped me ten years earlier, and in the evenings after work, I would dip in and out of the book at random to remind myself what I had found so enthralling.

I stayed at the famed Taj Mahal Palace hotel (the Taj) at the Gateway of India, in Fort, in the very southern tip of the city. I kicked off the day with a killer breakfast: *uthappam*, a savoury pancake, crisp at the bottom, soft and fluffy at the top, followed by a stroll to the conference venue. That took about 30 minutes, but that brief experience became the highlight of the day – the smell of fishy waters, the hustle and bustle of shops opening, policemen in khaki uniforms blowing whistles, cars honking their way through the traffic, children sleeping on the pavement and brown smoke from a million exhaust pipes. There were huge movie billboards showcasing glamorous film stars and storylines that seemed completely at odds with the hard life on the teeming streets. The brief snapshot of Mumbai that I observed assailed the senses, a maelstrom of sight, sound, smell and colour that I found mesmerising.

New Oriental Bank and share market, from *The Illustrated London News,* 14 October 1865. This was years before Asia's stock exchange would formally open and presumably, share trading took place in the square in front of the New Oriental Bank. © Illustrated London News Ltd/Mary Evans.

Joan Robinson, the famous Cambridge economist, is widely credited with the famous quip that "whatever you can rightly say about India, the opposite is also true". I know what she means. At the conference, the Indian businessmen making their pitches and presentations were among the richest people in the country. On my way to and from the hotel in the morning and late afternoon, I saw some of the poorest. While newspapers were full of stories about gruesome murders, what struck me about India was not how violent it was, but how peaceful. Even today, in terms of schooling,[9] some parts of the country are ranked below sub-Saharan Africa, while some of its universities are among the world's best. Even the weather is extreme: in winter, Delhi shivers when the temperature falls close to freezing and swelters in summer when it can approach 50°C. Somehow, India blends all its opposites and extremes effortlessly into one.

And so it is with the country's stock markets. They comprise a motley crew of companies which manage all sorts of different businesses: local retailers and manufacturers, internationally renowned pharmaceuticals, hotels, airlines, software engineers, banks and makers of traditional ayurvedic oils and balms. This makes Mumbai the most diverse stock market in the region. To come to grips with how it works, we need to look at some of the big stocks that set the pace. First up are two groups of companies that have made their mark in international markets: India's celebrated pharma companies and its illustrious software developers.

Reverse engineering

After India opened its doors to investors in 1991, it quickly became clear that the nation had two important assets. First, it was home to the world's second biggest pool of English speakers, and second, some of its universities offered world-class education. From this, two industries emerged, literally from the paddy fields, that would eventually become a global force – pharmaceuticals and IT.

India's approach to patent protection was always patchy.[10] This allowed a handful of clever lab technicians to reverse engineer western medicines in order to make low-cost "generic" copies. Indeed, by the early 2000s, the country's pharma companies were providing so many low-cost drugs that the humanitarian organisation Médecins Sans Frontières called India the "pharmacy to the developing world".[11] One of these new companies, Cipla, announced in 2001 that it would provide a year's supply of anti-retroviral medicines for one person for US$350 – a fraction of the US$10,000 American and European companies were asking.[12]

Making pharmaceuticals involves two key processes: the blending of active pharmaceutical ingredients (APIs) that treat or prevent diseases, followed by a complex chemical process which hammers these ingredients into tablets, creams and pills. For more than a decade, China has dominated the production of APIs, while India led the way making the pills and tablets. One out of every five tablets, pills or creams manufactured around the globe originated in India.[13] But with geo-political tensions between India and China rising, India has moved into the API business.

Most of the big pharma companies which have emerged in the past few decades – Sun Pharma, Lupin, Cipla, Dr Reddy's and Aurobindo, amongst others – are listed in Mumbai. As they continue to grow, it is not beyond the realms of possibility that the "copycat" business model will be discarded as they move into original pharma research and develop their own medicines. But for now, the share prices of these companies are largely determined by their ability to get regulatory approval for drugs in the markets where they sell their products. As exporters, the rupee exchange rate is also important. They charge overseas clients in US dollars so if the Indian rupee weakens, their profits go up in rupee terms, as do their share prices.

India's pharma stocks have seen a spectacular rise in the last two decades.

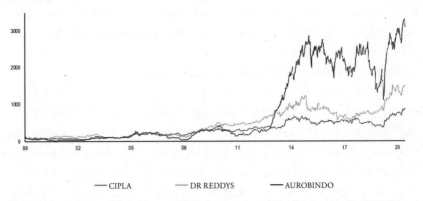

Note: Stock prices set at 100 on 1 January 2000. Stocks codes: CIPLA IN, Aurobind is ARBP IN and Dr Reddy's is DRRD IN. Source: Yahoo Finance

The same skill-set that has nourished the pharma industry – an excellent command of English and advanced levels of higher education – has also supported the extraordinary growth in software engineering. In the 1990s, as the internet started to emerge, the world was in need of coders and software engineers, and India was happy to oblige. The origins of this success story can be traced back to a decision taken in 1985 by US tech company Texas Instruments. Attracted by the country's engineering talent, it established an R&D centre in the city of Bangalore, then something of a backwater. It was the first global technology company to set up such a facility in India and the centre remains an important R&D site to this day. Bangalore is now known as the Silicon Valley of Asia and is home to a host of multinational software companies, hundreds of start-ups and tech companies.

Bangalore also perfectly captures the Indian ability to blend opposites and extremes into one, as mentioned earlier. For the visitor arriving in the city for the first time, the calm of the air-conditioned hotel lobby disappears in the rear-view mirror of the taxi taking him or her to the office, which is only a kilometre or two away. Within minutes, gridlocked buses, cars and trucks, marooned in a sea of motorcycles, grind to a complete halt, flanked by broken pavements and grim roadside poverty. The taxi finally pulls into a huge, gleaming IT park, one of the scores that dot the city. Infosys, Oracle, Wipro – all the big names are here, employing thousands upon thousands of people. And there you have it. World class information technology and Third World poverty rubbing shoulders, every minute of every day.

Demand for software expertise switched into high gear at the end of the 1990s, thanks to a global panic about what became known as the Y2K bug. Y2K was tech speak for the year 2000 and it was feared that this bug would create havoc in computers and computer networks around the world at the start of the new millennium, affecting everything from banks and power stations to airports and traffic lights. The problem was that when software engineers started programming computers in the 1960s, storage and memory were expensive so they used the last two digits of the date to represent the year. This meant that 2000 and 1900 would both be represented as 00. To avoid a digital apocalypse, armies of computer programmers, led by Indian software engineers, were employed to solve the problem, and after more than a year of international alarm and programming corrections, nothing much actually happened when the clocks struck midnight.

The timing was perfect. Having proved their mettle with Y2K, Indian programmers were hired in their thousands to handle the explosion in digital technology. They helped to set up new e-commerce websites and create management information systems for banks, retailers and factories. Business for Indian software companies flourished and the share prices of companies like Tata Consultancy and Infosys boomed.[14] And ingenious investors such as Rakesh were keen to jump on the bandwagon.

India's IT stocks such as Tata Consultancy Services have performed very strongly in the last two decades.

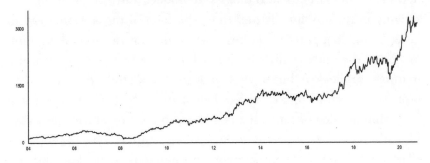

Note: The stock code is TCS IN
Source: Yahoo Finance

But while it's true that pharma and software businesses have gone from strength to strength in export markets, a large part of the Mumbai stock market is populated by very different types of companies. They sell their wares in India's vast hinterland and to understand what makes them tick, we need to take a step back and look at life in the country's legion of smaller cities, towns and villages.

Village life

India is expected to overtake China to become the world's most populous nation by 2025. This event will no doubt be heralded by some as proof that India is a global force to be reckoned with, while others will consider it a sign of pending doom: too many mouths to feed, too big a burden to support. The truth lies somewhere in between.

Away from the bright lights of giant metropolises like Mumbai, Delhi and other major cities, the reality is that India remains a largely rural economy and many still work as farmers or sharecroppers in paddy fields. The move from farm to city, from paddy field to factory, has proceeded at a much slower pace in India than in Indonesia, China and parts of Africa. This may be something to do with language and education. While some universities are top-notch and spawn globally competitive businesses, most Indians have to settle for much less.[15]

India does not have one universally spoken language. All Indonesians speak Bahasa Indonesia and the vast majority of Chinese can converse in *Putonghua* or Mandarin. That means that a migrant worker in these two countries would find it easy to find a job, while a man from Tamil Nadu in the south of India would struggle to find work in Gujarat in the west. There, Hindi, English or Gujarati is spoken, not Tamil. For many, learning another language is too high a hurdle and they stay within the confines of their village.

This means India is a much more rural place than China or Indonesia. But it is not as simple as that. Depending on the state or region, there are huge differences in climate, cuisine, marriage traditions, income levels and even road networks. India is like a gigantic rural quilt, a colourful assembly of people, habits, traditions, languages, rules and regulations. However, one common truth regardless of geography is that Indian households are big: an average of 4.5 people per household compared to only 3.0 in China. This means that there are many more mouths to feed,[16] so most household income goes on food, rent and basic necessities, unlike in China where many families enjoy the luxury of being able to splurge on extravagances.

It's important to understand that life in an Indian village has its own gentle rhythms. Houses of bamboo, clay and mud are surrounded by cows and hens, while villagers comb nearby forests to collect wood and herbs or plough the nearby fields – deep green rice paddies in Kerala and Tamil Nadu in south India, and wheat, sugarcane and mustard in the north. Geography also determines what's for breakfast – *idli* (small cake-like dumplings) with *sambar* (a lentil-based vegetable stew) and *dosa* (a large, flat savoury pancake) in the south, or *roti* (flat bread made of wheat dough) and vegetable curry in the north.

Women wear traditional sarees while they tend to their vegetable gardens or collect water from a common well. Men in the north wear dhotis (loose trousers) and turbans. Many are employed as blacksmiths, carpenters or potters. Electricity is still a luxury in many villages, as is internet connectivity or proper cell reception. There is not much traffic, so the days are calm and peaceful, interrupted by large, loud regional festivals. The Indian village is generally a convivial, friendly and inviting place, but life is far from easy.

Commercial activity centres around the village store. Here, people buy everything from grain, groceries and soap to household goods, tobacco and fertiliser. The shopkeeper often provides credit when needed. Given the scattered geography and differences in tastes and cultures, local knowledge is of paramount importance for the consumer companies that supply this giant if fragmented market. They need to know what sells where and how to get it there.

Tamil Nadu is richer and older than Kashmir, which influences consumer trends; healthcare is bigger in Tamil Nadu, motorbikes in Kashmir. In the south, microwaves come with a kit to make *idli* for breakfast and Asia Paints has special products for the humid regions in the south where wall cracks and algae flourish. It's the same story when running a business. It is different everywhere. To get hooked up to the electricity grid to run a factory takes 32 days in Gujarat in the west and 95 days (or longer) in Odisha (formerly Orissa) in the east. The message is clear, you need a strategy for each state. Hindustan Unilever knows all about this and has devised a "wimi" strategy – "winning in many Indias".[17]

The same is true for the country's auto industry, which in 2019 was the fourth largest on the planet.[18] Indians like small and mid-sized cars, not the big sports utility vehicles (SUVs) Chinese consumers prefer. And while you would think cars would sell like hot cakes in this fast-growing economy, the truth is that domestic sales have been sluggish.[19] That's not the case with motorbikes, which make up 80% of all vehicles sold in India every year. Two-wheelers are more affordable and perfect for navigating the alleys and lanes in villages or weaving in and out of gridlocked traffic in Mumbai, Bangalore or Delhi. Most of the demand is rural and billboards advertising Hero MotoCorp, the dominant market leader in motorcycles,[20] are all over small towns and villages.

Horses for courses

"Can India replace China as the world's factory?" ran a headline in *Mint*, a leading Indian newspaper.[21] The logic is simple. China's success was built on factories and exports, so India should be able to go down the same economic path. But the comparison is fraught with difficulties because the way businesses and officials operate in India is rather different from China.[22] It also helps to explain why some Indian businesses are among the most profitable in Asia.

To say that India's bureaucracy is not known for its efficiency is something of an understatement. According to the government's own estimates,[23] most of the money it distributes to improve the livelihoods and wellbeing of the hundreds of millions of Indians who live in villages and townships fails to reach its intended recipients. Instead, it is sponged up or siphoned off by a vast bureaucracy. Not only do vast amounts of money simply disappear, the wheels of bureaucracy also turn very slowly indeed, if at all. For example, when the central government in Delhi signs off on new rules and regulations, how they should be interpreted is left to bureaucrats in individual states or towns. Approval to build a cement plant or a steel factory obtained in Delhi can soon be tangled in red tape deep in the countryside where local officials may demand additional paperwork and permits. These different layers of bureaucracy often act wholly independent of each other. During COVID-19, on the very day that Haryana, a state that borders Delhi, reopened its border with the capital, Delhi closed its border with Haryana.

This can be a seemingly hopeless, hair-pulling experience for ordinary citizens and companies alike. In 2005, a Korean company, Posco, the world's fourth largest steelmaker, signed a deal to set up a massive steel project in the state of Odisha in eastern India. It was billed as the project that would set Odisha – at the bottom of several development scorecards – on a high-growth trajectory and make India a global steel superpower. Twelve years and countless twists and turns later – largely in the form of endless discussions and regulatory hurdles – the Koreans officially withdrew and flew back home. The plant was never built.

There is, however, a flip side to this. Canny corporate executives who know how to navigate the all but impenetrable maze of the civil service can use this skill to great effect. And large companies can lobby the government to make sure they have a say in the drafting of new industry rules and regulations, giving themselves a huge competitive advantage. Red tape is also a very effective way of keeping new entrants out of lucrative markets, as getting all the licences required can be a nightmare for the uninitiated. It can take years, if not decades, for newcomers to jump through all the regulatory hoops before they can even think about starting to compete on a level playing field.

Hindustan Unilever Limited (HUL) is a good example of how to dominate a market. A subsidiary of Unilever, the Anglo-Dutch consumer giant, HUL was established in 1931 as Hindustan Vanaspati Manufacturing Co and as of 2019 had 35 brands in 20 different categories. It has built a gigantic network of shops and outlets through which it sells everything from Lipton iced tea to Lux soaps and Lakme cosmetics. HUL's products are sold in glitzy malls in huge cities and the humble mom and pop *kirana* shops which populate villages across the country. The company has almost no competition when it comes to serving hundreds of millions of consumers in rural India and that explains why it has one of the highest profit margins in the whole of Asia, surpassing Chinese giants such as Tencent and global brands such as Korea's Samsung.[24]

The same can be said for Titan, which sells watches and jewellery through a network of 1,400 stores, led by its flagship brand Tanishq.[25] For many Indians, jewels are statements of power, prosperity and prestige. In addition, they are a handy store of value which will, it is believed, always appreciate in value. Gifts of gold are deeply ingrained in marriage rituals in Indian society and weddings generate approximately 50% of annual national gold demand. Titan is the go-to place for brides and grooms. It is a highly profitable business as few can replicate its network of outlets across the nation.[26]

Titan is part of Tata, another name that is ubiquitous in India. The Tata Group originated in 1877, when Jamsetji Tata bought a mill and began producing textiles. It was the first company to offer pensions and accident insurance, unheard of at the time. The profits allowed Jamsetji to settle in Mumbai where he acquired property and expanded the business in all directions. He was a pioneer of the steel and power industries and is regarded as the father of Indian industry. The hydro plant he opened grew into what is now known as Tata Power, the largest power generation company in India. A nephew, JRD Tata,[27] continued to grow the business[28] and by the time his successor, Ratan, took over in

1991, India had opened its doors to foreign investors.[29] Tata, already an enormously powerful local brand, flexed its financial muscles by going overseas and making big bang purchases such as Jaguar-Land Rover and Corus Steel.

There are plenty more of these domestic market leaders, from engineering companies such as Larsen & Toubro to Asian Paints, dental care provider Colgate India (part of US giant Colgate-Palmolive) and consumer company Nestlé India (a subsidiary of Nestlé, a Swiss multinational company). All have hugely profitable businesses that throw off lots of cash. If an investor is looking for profitable, cash-generating investments in Asia, India's big local companies are a good place to start.

While some have been around since colonial times, the biggest of them all is a relative newcomer. The small textile and polyester start-up in 1977 had only a table, a chair and 1,000 rupees to its name when Dhirubhai Ambani entered the world of business. He renamed the company Reliance Industries in 1985, and by that time it was starting to expand into petrochemicals, power generation and telecoms. It is now India's largest company. But when Dhirubhai died in 2002, a bitter feud broke out between the two sons, Mukesh and Anil Ambani, often spilling into public view. Eventually their mother, Kokilaben, stepped in to broker a truce. The family business was split into two: Mukesh got control of the oil, gas, petrochemicals, refining and manufacturing operations, while Anil was given the electricity, telecoms and financial services businesses. Anil became entangled in debt and eventually his flagship company, Reliance Communication, had to file for bankruptcy. Mukesh bailed out his brother and, as we will see later, turned the whole telecom industry upside down in 2016 when he launched a new telco company called Jio and started a price war.

But before that, some new telco players were also making their mark in the market, as well as some of the country's largest banks.

Tap an app

Picture the scene. An Indian TV commercial starts with a wide shot of three students, one clearly senior to the other two, chatting in a grocery store as they buy ice cream. One of the younger students insists on paying but the senior won't have it; while he is rummaging through his wallet for cash, the younger student steps forward and scans a Paytm QR through his Paytm App. Baffled, the older student looks at the shopkeeper, who tells him that this is the new way to pay. The commercial ends with a frown on the face of the senior student and the message from the sponsor: "Scan any QR and pay directly from your bank account".

If the holy grail in Indian business is the ability to distribute merchandise across the whole of the country, the internet and new payment systems have revolutionised how companies can get access to the lucrative rural market. Most Indians had little access to basic bank services[30] but that is now changing. In 2014, India embarked on what was to become perhaps the most ambitious financial inclusion initiative of all time. The Pradhan Mantri Jan Dhan Yojna (JDY) programme, designed to give all Indians access to a bank, offered special saving accounts, debit cards and mobile banking apps to entice people to participate.

It worked. People signed up in droves, giving many households access to a bank account for the first time. The secret to success was India's Aadhaar card, an identification system that stores the fingerprints and irises of more than a billion Indians on its database. Take your Aadhaar card to a bank, set up an account and from there it is a small step to sending and receiving funds instantly from anywhere in India using the apps of banks or other payment services. In the first two years of the JDY programme, a staggering 255 million new bank accounts were opened.[31]

These days, millions of mom and pop *kirana* stores accept digital payments using QR codes. Even humble street food is available with a tap on an app.[32] This mobilisation of local savings has also been a big boon for stock markets. Suddenly, investing in mutual funds or buying stocks on online platforms was only a click away, and small-time domestic punters became a force to reckon with.

Some banks were quicker to jump on this lucrative new bandwagon than others. Young private sector banks such as HDFC and ICICI are tiny compared to the State Bank of India (SBI)[33] but their slick websites and consumer-oriented approach meant they soon gained market share. Many of the large state-owned banks, chock-full of bad loans and traditional thinking, were stuck in the slow lane.

The share prices of private banks such as HDFC Bank and ICICI Bank have done better than state-owned banks such as SBI in the last two decades.

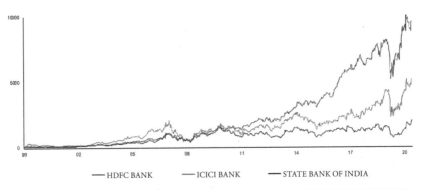

——— HDFC BANK ——— ICICI BANK ——— STATE BANK OF INDIA

Note: Stock prices based at 100 on 1 January 2000. The stock codes are HDFCB IN, ICICIBC IN and SBIN IN. Source: Yahoo Finance.

Just as the mobile phone leapfrogged traditional telecom networks to take affordable communication services deep into rural India, new players such as Paytm and other telcos took digital banking to the unbanked. Millions of Indians in rural areas got their first formal banking experience with these companies. The cunning Indian telecom companies, with a much larger customer base, soon entered the electronic payment business and started to play the banks at their own game.[34]

As in other parts of Asia, Indians rushed to buy the latest mobile phone, starting with 2G and slowly working their way up to 3G and 4G contracts. Everyone was connected and the telecom industry boomed. Until 2016. That was when cash-rich Reliance Industries, run by Mukesh Ambani, launched a new telecom venture called Jio. Reliance took a big gamble by building a high speed 4G network across the entire country and offering mobile phone contracts at prices so low that few Indians could ignore them. In other countries, officials in charge of competition laws might have looked into the matter, but not in India. Rival telecom players had to cut their tariffs by as much as 66% in order to retain their customers. Profits tumbled, and so did share prices.

Some companies crumbled, while others decided to exit the business as profits evaporated. Only three survived: Reliance's Jio, Bharti Airtel and Idea, and they now have this vast market to themselves.[35]

Profits recovered quickly and investors soon returned. After all, investing in industries where a handful of companies have carved up the whole market between themselves is a sound basis for generating strong returns.

India's telecom industry has seen a very wide divergence in share price performance in the last years.

Note: The stock codes are BHARTI IN and IDEA IN. Bharti's share price is displayed on the left hand scale (LHS). Source: Yahoo Finance.

Zomata, a an Indian food delivery player, benefitted too and it listed its shares in July 2020. This IPO was India's first steps to grow a internet sector in the local stock market. But here too, India is different from China or the West – for Indian families, non-home cooked food is often seen as unhealthy and undesirable and seen more as something as recreation, for example when visiting malls in the weekend. This is why take-away is almost non existent in India.

How the Indian stock market works

The India of 2030 and 2040 will be vastly different from the India of today. There will be many more Indians, many of whom will be young and flocking to cities to look for jobs, following in the footsteps of China's army of migrant workers, even if at a much slower pace. Selling products to millions of people, spread across giant cities, big and small towns and countless villages with different linguistic and economic footprints – and understanding what they really want and need – will remain central to generating profits. At the same time, the country's pharmaceutical companies will increase their global economic clout, as will the legions of software engineers.

But this growth story also has vulnerabilities. First up, there's money. Huge amounts of investment will be needed to improve schools and build better roads and railways. And as one of the world's largest energy users, the price of oil will always weigh on economic growth. Foreign investment is the answer. On the other side of this debate lurks a bureaucracy that can entangle a herd of elephants before breakfast. Climate change may yet prove to be another important factor. The monsoon dictates the success or failure of the vast agricultural sector on which the livelihoods of millions of rural households depend.

And investors, beware. A common fallacy is that where India's economic growth goes, so goes the stock market. But that's not always the case, partly because of the economy's structure (or lack of it). There's a large informal sector which employs a vast majority of the workforce and many enterprises are tiny. Many bigger businesses are unlisted. In other words, as in other parts of Asia, the stock market can be a poor proxy for the state of the economy. To understand it properly, we need to look at it from the ground up.

There is a lot going on in this *masala* of sectors and companies. The international pharma players jostle with computer programmers, banks, car and motorcycle manufacturers, telecom operators and swarms of local retailers and industrial companies. India has some of the least profitable companies in Asia – the telecom industry is now still in that category – as well as some of the most profitable, notably the retailers which have built vast distribution networks across rural India, ringfencing their businesses from newcomers.

But there's plenty of dynamism, too. The crossover between telecoms and banking heralded India's entry to the world of fintech. Start-ups have launched new payment systems which have eaten the lunch of many a large bank, especially in the clunky, debt-laden state sector. Younger, more nimble banks have brought their own new payment apps to the market. Meanwhile, the telecom industry is returning to its profitable ways after Jio shook up the market.

In short, there is never a dull moment and this market, like the country, is an incredibly diverse cocktail, unmatched in Asia. And unlike elsewhere in the region, none of the large companies dominate the Indian stock market: the top five make up just over 30% of the total market cap. This is quite low – in China, it's 40% and in Indonesia, the most concentrated market in Asia, it is over 60%.

This has huge implications for how the market behaves. If one big business is struggling in a particular year, another might have a bumper harvest. If local companies are finding life difficult, exporters could be on a roll. As a result, aggregate profit growth is remarkably stable. Across Asia, only Singapore has a more stable earnings profile.[36] This stability in earnings growth is completely at odds with the fact that India is one of the most volatile markets in the region.[37] A lot of this has to do with the rupee. India needs money to grow, and companies and the government turn to the bond markets to borrow from foreign investors. This comes with risks: as soon as dark clouds gather on the horizon, foreigners exit the market and sell their rupees. It is, therefore, no surprise that it is one of the most volatile currencies in Asia.[38]

To make things even more volatile, India imports most of its oil, and rapid movements in oil prices can quickly unsettle investors. Swings in the rupee are transferred and amplified in the stock market – a weaker currency benefits exporters such as software and pharma companies, but is negative for local businesses. The result is a stock market where the volatility in stock prices is in sharp contrast with the stability of earnings.

There are also some useful direction finders. India tends to take a strong lead from US stock markets[39] as many of its pharma exporters and IT players have large businesses there. Meanwhile, the influence of the Chinese stock market, so strong in north Asia, is hardly felt in Mumbai. This makes sense too, as few Indian companies do much business in China.

To sum up, India offers immense opportunities but faces equally immense challenges. The country's economic transformation is likely to be accompanied by disruptions in the form of new business models, regulations and red tape, and other forces like climate change. This calls for a smart playbook – investors need to look for companies that are able to navigate the various cycles to maximise the opportunities. This requires a keen eye, strong nerves and a willingness to look long term. Just as Rakesh Jhunjhunwala did that day in 1985, when he put his first few rupees into Indian stocks which, three decades later, turned him into a local celebrity and multi-billionaire.

Endnotes

1   This story is loosely based on interviews given by Rakesh Jhunjhunwala, the veteran Indian investor.

2   *The Economic Times*, 23 October 2009.

3   From 1 January 1986 onwards, the Sensex was published daily in the newspapers. The Sensex base year is 1978–1979, when it was set at 100.

4   The National Stock Exchange (NSE) kicked off in 1992 and brought with it an electronic exchange system. The NSE is the biggest stock exchange in India, while the Bombay Stock Exchange (BSE) is the oldest. The benchmark index for the NSE is the Nifty, while for the BSE it is the Sensex. Most companies are listed on both markets but if you buy a stock in on one market, you have to sell it in that market.

5   The term "Hindu rate of growth" was coined by Professor Rajkrishna, an Indian economist, in 1978.

6   The finance minister at the time was Manmohan Singh. He would much later become India's prime minister.

7   On 15 January 1992, the Sensex crossed the 2,000 mark and on 30 March 1992, reached the 4,000 mark, closing at 4,091. Only in 1999 did the Sensex break the 5,000 mark.

8   Forbes 2009 <https://www.forbes.com/profile/rakesh-jhunjhunwala/?sh=61cde14a174b>.

9   Programme for International Student Assessment (PISA) tests from the OECD. OECD (PISA) 2019.

10   India's Patent Act 1970 excluded pharmaceuticals and agrochemical products from patent protection, with the aim of breaking India's dependence on imports for bulk drugs and formulations, and provide for development of a local pharmaceutical industry.

11   Horner 2020.

12   Horner 2020.

13   In the US, it is estimated that India supplies 40% of all generic pills and capsules. India has the largest number of FDA-approved plants outside the US. China and India are the source of up to 80% of the APIs imported to the US.

14   Take Tata Consultancy, for example. Its share price rose from 35 rupees in January 2002 to 111 rupees by October that year. The stock traded at 3,230 rupees by the end of 2020. That is a staggering 29x increase.

15   In India, about 29% of children drop out before completing five years of primary school, and 43% before finishing upper primary school. High school completion is only 42%. This puts India among the top five nations for out-of-school children of primary school age, with 1.4 million six to 11-year-olds not attending school. In many ways, schools are not equipped to handle the full population – there is a shortage of teachers and school facilities. Shahni 2005.

16   Also, in India, women often do not work or, at least, much less so than in, for example, Indonesia or China. That means they don't bring in cash to support the household.

17   Hindustan Unilever has divided the country into 14 clusters and tailors its marketing and distribution around this structure.

18 "Automobile Industry in India", IBEF 2020 <https://www.ibef.org/industry/india-automobiles.aspx>.

19 Indian car sales increased at an average rate of only 1.29% between 2016 and 2020.

20 This company, a joint venture with Honda, had a market share of over 50% in 2019.

21 Kwatra 2020.

22 There are many answers to this question. We look here at barriers to entry to Indian industry. Another issue is the lack of leading companies, an issue researched by Saon Ray and Smita Miglani in an ICRIER working paper (Ray and Miglani 2020).

23 Mohanty 2018.

24 Hindustan Lever's return on capital employed, a measure of profitability, was a staggering 129% in 2019, 131% in 2018 and 139% in 2017. That is over ten times the average in Asia, which is about 12%. Source: Hindustan Lever annual report 2019–2020.

25 Titan is the fifth largest integrated own-brand watch manufacturer in the world. Note that not all of its stores carry the Tanishq brand.

26 Titan's return on invested capital, another measure of profitability, stood at 35% in 2018 and 2019, and 32% in 2020, when COVID-19 slowed its business down. Source: Titan presentation, 28 October 2020.

27 Jehangir Ratanji Dadabhoy (JRD).

28 The number of individual companies in the group grew from 14 in 1938 to 95 in 1991, when JRD Tata stepped down.

29 Ratan Tata retired in 2012 and Cyrus Mistry became the new chairman. A few years later, there was a row over some trust funds. Mistry was ousted and Ratan Tata returned. In 2017, current chairman Natarajan Chandrasekaran took over.

30 In 2017, only 20% of adults in India saved money with a financial institution. Of those that had an account, nearly half were inactive.

31 That is, at the end of 2016.

32 As of 2019, Paytm has over 400 million users (Agarwal 2017).

33 For example, in 2020, HDFC had over 5,000 branches and nearly 15,000 ATMs spread across nearly 3,000 cities and towns. ICICI Bank had a network of 5,324 branches and 15,688 ATMs. Compare that with India's largest bank, SBI, which had 22,141 branches and 58,555 ATMs.

34 At the start of 2020, nearly 1.3 billion electronic payments were made each month, more than those using plastic. They accounted for 19% of banking transactions in the year to March 2019. Source: *The Economist*, 9 May 2020.

35 In 2019, these three accounted for over 90% of all revenue.

36 The standard deviation of the earnings of the top ten companies listed in the market is, on an annual basis, 20%. In Asia, only Singapore is lower at 19%. China stands at 24% and Korea 42%.

37 The standard deviation in monthly returns for the FTSE India stands at 6.6% in the period 2002–2020. For the FTSE Asia ex-Japan, Australia and New Zealand, it is 5.0%. On this measure, India is far more volatile.

38 In the Asia Pacific region, the Australian, Indonesian, Korean, New Zealand and Philippine currencies show relatively high sensitivities to changes in global volatility. See, for example, Mccauley *et al* 2007.

39 The five-year correlation, measured from 2016 to end 2020, between India's Sensex Index and the US S&P500, is 0.66. That is only a little higher than the correlations seen in ASEAN, although much lower than in Taiwan and Korea. The correlation with the Shanghai market is much lower at 0.38.

Chapter 7

Taiwan and Korea
주식 시장

Taiwan: mechanics and macchiatos

The city of Taipei grew out of expediency. At the end of China's civil war in 1949, the arrival of about two million mainland Chinese on the island created an immediate housing shortage. The basin in which the city sits, surrounded by the Yangming mountains, was promptly transformed into a cauldron of activity as the new arrivals settled down and constructed houses and workshops for what they initially believed would be a temporary retreat to Taiwan, a few years at most. Expediency, not beauty, was the priority in those early days and well into the last decade of the 20th century, travel guides regularly called Taipei "the ugly duckling of Asia".

A forest of apartment buildings – concrete boxes, rain-washed and greyish, all of about equal dimensions – met our eyes when I arrived in 2002 with my wife and young son for a three-year stint as the head of research at an international bank. It felt as if there were more car repair shops than coffee shops. And then there were the workshops. Small and dimly lit, most had big, bright signboards outside, and were brimming with all manner of gadgets, multicoloured wires, measuring equipment and electrical parts, the work of men who valued mechanics over macchiatos.

Even back then, Taipei was evolving rapidly. The workshops and factories turned out products which were in demand all over the world and as a result, the island was growing wealthier every year. In the process, a self-confident identity was forged, embodied in the audacious statement that is the capital's most famous landmark, Taipei 101. Even today, this giant, towering bamboo stalk, sitting in the middle of a basin regularly hit by earthquakes and typhoons, stands out like a beacon. Taipei's architecture shifted from the practical to the aspirational, from expediency to experimental, slowly turning the city for mechanics into one for macchiato fans.

But some of our first impressions were off the mark. It soon became evident that Taipei was so much more than tower blocks and industrial grit. We became regular visitors to the host of night markets, bustling places full of sights, sounds and smells which assaulted the senses, especially those of new arrivals. Now, just as it did back then, the aroma of grilled chicken blends with that of pineapple and stinky tofu, fermented beancurd which gourmets have described as "smelling like old socks" and "blue cheese gone bad" or quite simply "rotting garbage". This local delicacy is an acquired taste, and one that I'm unlikely to ever get on first-name terms with.

Throngs of people wind their way slowly through these night markets, stopping to sample a seemingly endless array of different foods from carts and stalls – congealed pig's blood, salted duck eggs packed in charcoal and beef noodles. And it is not just food. All manner of wares – shoes, bags, clothes toys and games – are on display. These markets are woven into the social fabric of the city's nightlife, providing a spark of energy that is unique to the island.

My work was just as fascinating. Taiwan has always been a tech-heavy stock market, but those were the days after the collapse in global tech stocks in 2002. Suddenly, investors were eager to discover more traditional companies which had long been overlooked. It was decided that I, together with Kang Ho, a bright young analyst from Singapore who had just joined our Taiwan team, would identify these investment opportunities. Off we went criss-crossing the island, from Taipei in the north to Kaohsiung in the south, visiting factories, plants and retail stores.

This was when it started to dawn on me that Taiwan was a one-off, a one of a kind. The further we travelled out of Taipei, the more we saw a sight that was unique to Taiwan – the mightily odd betel nut trade. "Binlang girls" sat in neon-lit fishbowls alongside the road, dressed in strikingly seductive clothes, selling betel nuts (*binlang*) to tired truck drivers. The nuts are said to lift the mood and boost the energy levels of the drivers and are also, apparently, an effective hangover cure. The trade was so popular that swathes of land were converted to plant betel nuts. The presence of these sensual young girls has been deliberated by sociology professors and was the centre of debate in parliament, and even warranted investigations by the police for fear that these girls might reveal too much for their own, and the country's, good.

On these road trips, we talked to all sorts of firms that had rarely been visited by the investment community. One company specialised in making high-quality rubber rings for NASA's space shuttle. Another was a global leader in bolts, which, not surprisingly, had decided to expand into nuts. But one of the first companies we spoke to turned out to be one of Taiwan's enduring successes. This was the bicycle maker, Giant.

Giant's headquarters were, and still are, concealed between paddy fields and vegetable farms near the east coast, about an hour's drive from Taichung in the centre of the island. A small road gave access to its facilities and upon arrival, a security guard guided us across the parking lot to the main loading area where racks of bicycle frames were waiting to be exported. We were given a tour but were also told that parts of the factory were off-limits. It was all very hush-hush.

Giant started making steel frames in 1972[1] and assembled bicycles for some of the world's top brands in the 1970s and 1980s, including Schwinn, a leading US company. In the 1980s, Giant made the big decision to produce its own bicycles under its own brand name and compete with its clients head-on. Within a few years, this humble frame maker was recognised worldwide by cycling enthusiasts, much to the chagrin of some of its major customers.[2]

Giant knew that to survive in the cut-throat bike market, it had to come up with bold new ideas. In 1987, the company was the first to mass produce carbon frames, the cutting-edge bicycle technology of the day.[3] Much later, it was one of the first to market mountain bikes and in 2008, the company designed bicycles for female riders. Later, it jumped onto the e-bike craze. Giant is now considered one of the top global bicycle brands, competing with Specialized,[4] Trek and Cannondale. Selling bicycles might not have the sex appeal that is associated with computer chips, robots or even betel nuts, but Giant proved that clever marketing and bold innovations can translate into steady growth. Over the years, the share price of this bicycle maker has done better than many tech companies.

Giant's share price is up over 16x since the visit to its factory in 2003.

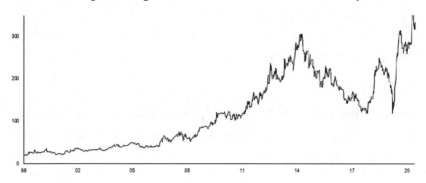

Note: Giant's stock code is 9921 TT
Source: Yahoo Finance

Chips with everything

Taiwan is a relative newcomer to the Asian stock market family, opening on 9 February 1962. Despite success stories like Giant, technology has long been the dominant force, thanks largely to the pioneering work of one extraordinary individual. This story can be traced back to 1986, when a young man named Morris Chang was appointed head of the government's Industrial Technology Research Institute (ITRI), a body which has played a major role in transforming Taiwan's industrial landscape. Mr Chang was the perfect man for the job. He studied at Harvard University, the Massachusetts Institute of Technology and Stanford University, and had also landed a job at Texas Instruments.

With Mr Chang at the helm, the ITRI set up Taiwan's first semiconductor wafer fabrication plant. In 1987, this plant was turned into a company and Taiwan Semiconductor Manufacturing, known around the world as TSMC, was born. Initially, a joint venture between the Taiwan government, Dutch electronics giant Philips and other private investors, TSMC is now the largest company on the Taiwan stock exchange and the biggest contract chipmaker in the world. Its products are used in everything from smartphones to TVs and cars and aeroplanes, and annual shareholder meetings have turned into hallowed pilgrimages for technology analysts around the globe.

TSMC has created its own distinct semiconductor foundry business model. It leaves the design of chips to others and focuses solely on manufacturing made-to-order wafers containing thousands of electronic components which are placed on a tiny chip of silicon.[5] TSMC produces chips for tech giants such as Apple, Google and Qualcomm and has, for decades, been the undisputed global market leader in advanced semiconductors, followed by United Microelectronics Corporation (UMC), another Taiwan company which also started life as part of Morris Chang's ITRI.

TSMC has led the way forward in semiconductors and in the Taiwanese stock market.

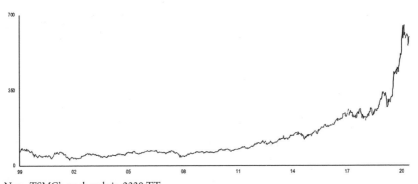

Note: TSMC's stock code is 2330 TT
Source: Yahoo Finance

Another big global tech player that has its origins in Taiwan is Foxconn, formally known as Hon Hai Precision Industry, which is one of the largest electronics contract manufacturers in the world and a top assembler of Apple's iPhones. It was founded by Terry Gou, who borrowed

US$7,500 from his mother in 1974 to start the business. Foxconn was an early mover to mainland China, where its massive factories employ more than a million workers. Other Taiwan companies run by entrepreneurs soon followed, including Pegatron, another assembler and developer of computer products for US brands.

Most of these companies decided to huddle around Kunshan, a city located between Shanghai and Suzhou on China's eastern seaboard. It is also known as Little Taipei, given that more than a million Taiwanese are reckoned to live and work there. These companies have flourished on the mainland and many made sure that politics – China views the island of Taiwan as part of its territory – did not get in the way of growing their businesses.

While companies around the world are willing to pay very high prices for the latest chips made by TSMC, Foxconn and Pegatron have taken the opposite approach. They charge low prices for their services, such as the assembly of iPhones, and their businesses are in effect workshops that churn out large volumes of products.[6] Foxconn does a lot of business with Apple, as do many other Taiwan tech players such as Merry, a producer of earphones, headsets, speakers and microphones, and Largan, a global leader in making lenses for smartphones and laptops. The sprawling Apple supply chain, as we will see later, has a significant impact on how the local stock market behaves.

Nurseries

Taiwan tech giants such as TSMC and UMC have acted as nurseries for many a new tech venture. One was Chroma ATE, which Kang Ho and I visited on a hot, sunny day in 2003. One of the managers and founders, a Mr Ming, patiently explained that they custom-made testing equipment for tech companies which produced everything from batteries and power systems to LCD screens.

He was the perfect host. After showing us around the factory, Ming ushered us into a brightly-lit meeting room. A young lady poured steaming hot water over oolong tea leaves in a clay pot, which was then poured into small teacups a few minutes later. This was Ming's favourite daytime drink, although I later discovered that, by night, he preferred to quaff French wine of a rather expensive variety. The formalities over, we started to chat. Our visit had surprised him as no foreign investors had arrived on their doorstep. At the time, the major shareholders of the company were the founders, a few friends and a small bunch of local investors. Over the years, that would change as more and more foreign investors discovered this hugely profitable company.

As we sipped our tea, Ming told us about how the founders of the company once all worked at UMC. In the early 1980s, they decided to leave and set up their own company in a garage. They worked day and night to perfect the test products and there was just about enough money to survive for a few months, by which time the first orders had arrived and kept the young company going. It was a risky business. They had borrowed money from friends and family that, left unpaid, would be a stain on everyone's reputation. Ming joked that he had already thought about Plan B, which was to become a farmer. However, the young company survived and then thrived, listing on the Taiwan stock exchange in 1996. Twenty-five years on, Ming is probably a prized target for private bankers and brokers of insanely expensive Burgundy wines.

Just like Taipei's original architecture, which was grounded in expedience and practicality, Taiwan tech companies have tended to focus on engineering excellence in a wider range of tech components. Take Delta Electronics, for example, a global leader in energy-saving gadgets that are widely used in power electronics and automation, or Airtec, a big player in pneumatic equipment used in robots. Hiwin is another producer of components used in robots and automated factories. Taiwan is an island full of engineers and mechanics (and Binlang girls).

But very few of them have shown any ambition to expand and grow into broad business empires with powerful international brands. They like to stay close to their roots. It's a completely different story in Korea, the other tech dominated stock market in Asia. To understand why, we need to go back to the end of the Korean war in 1953.

Korea: catastrophe, *chaebol* and computers

The country received its geographical adjective "South" after the armistice was signed in 1953, when the Korean peninsula was officially divided.[7] At the time, the country was extremely poor and heavily dependent on the US for protection and security. The devastating conflict had left many cities in ruins and plans were drawn up to rebuild the economy by creating a strong industrial base. New factories started making everything from machinery and plastics to washing machines and televisions. The aim was to create a domestic consumer market as well as export goods to US and European customers. Foreign companies were encouraged to invest, and they were given the freedom to run their businesses as they wished as long as they set up technical training programmes for local employees. To help things along, the government started a number of research institutes and a national R&D programme was launched in 1982.[8]

The first local stock market was the Daehan Stock Exchange but it was forced to closed during the war years. As the country recovered, it was decided to start all over again and the Korea Stock Exchange (KSE) opened its doors on 1 April 1962 – 360 years to the day after the first shares were traded in Amsterdam. The KSE was populated with large, established companies and the "Kospi 200" became the best-known index to gauge the overall performance of the market. In 1996, another market, the Kosdaq, was opened to cater to start-ups in search of funds, with an index of the same name. The Kosdaq is considered to be much riskier and more volatile than the Kospi and is often compared to the NASDAQ in the US.

The efforts to revive the economy gave rise to giant business groups called *chaebol*, which received strong support from the government and were instrumental in pulling South Korea out of poverty. The *chaebol* were influenced by Japan's *zaibatsu* – the two words are even spelled the same in Chinese. Many *chaebol* trace their origins back to the period of Japanese occupation, which lasted from 1910 to 1945. The name is a combination of the characters for "rich" and "clan", hammering home the message that it is all about the wealthy families which dominate these business empires. To this day, key managerial posts are almost always given to the relatives of the chairman, the patriarch. The best-known *chaebol* are Samsung, Hyundai and LG, and others include Hanjin, Kumho, Lotte and the SK Group.

In the 1960s and 1970s, these conglomerates had easy access to money and were involved in everything from cars, shipbuilding and steel, to oil, chemical industries and life insurance.[9] Initially, Korean products were met with considerable scepticism abroad. I remember watching Dutch TV shows in the 1980s when Korean cars were given away free in a desperate effort to get people to drive them. How times have changed. Many Korean brands are now hugely popular all over the planet and this has great significance for the stock market, a topic we will return to later.

The biggest of these industrial powerhouses is Samsung or three stars. In Korean, three represents something big and powerful, and stars are something everlasting, like stars in the sky. Like so many Asian success stories, the company's origins were extremely humble. Founder Lee Byung-chul opened a small trading company in 1938, selling vegetables, dried fish and noodles. After the war, he built a sugar refinery before expanding first into textiles and then retail, insurance and finance. Samsung made the leap into consumer electronics in the late 1960s.

Mr Lee died in in 1987 and his son, Lee Kun-hee, inherited the company. He built Samsung into a global corporation, famously calling on his employees in 1993 to "change everything but your wife and children" in the pursuit of leading the company into a new era, one in which quality trumped quantity. Two years later, he ordered a mass burning of Samsung products which he considered to be defective. Samsung is now one of the most recognisable names in global technology and telecoms, with a brand more valuable than Pepsi, Nike and American Express.

The company produces about a fifth of South Korea's exports and is seen as the centrepiece of what is called the Miracle on the River Han, the transformation from one of the world's poorest countries to the economic giant it is today. The phrase, a reference to the river that flows through the capital, Seoul, was coined by Prime Minister Chang Myon in 1961 and was a nod to the "Miracle on the Rhine," the economic resurgence of West Germany after the Second World War.

Samsung Electronics has led the way forward in the Korean stock market.

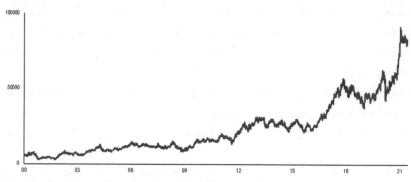

Note: Samsung Electronic's stock code is 005930 SK
Source: Yahoo Finance

Another *chaebol*, LG, originally called Lucky-Goldstar, went through a similar evolution. It was originally the country's major toothpaste manufacturer before moving into electronics by making cheap radios, TVs, refrigerators, washing machines and air conditioners in the 1960s. In 1995, the company changed its name to LG and went on to become one of the world's largest consumer electronics firms. LG Chemical, another part of the group, is now a major producer of batteries for electric vehicles.

Hynix, a part of the Hyundai *chaebol* in the 1980s, went out on its own to produce electrical components, communication equipment, semiconductors and memory devices. Initially, these chips were only used in PCs and laptops but with the electrification of everything from fridges to cars, its memory chips are now in demand everywhere. It is now the world's second-largest memory chipmaker after Samsung Electronics and the third-largest semiconductor company.[10] Hynix's main product is dynamic random access memory (DRAM), which is used in computer processors. DRAM prices can swing wildly and this is reflected in Hynix's earnings and stock price, which both yo-yo depending on the balance between supply and demand.

But there was a flip side to fostering these large, family-run empires. They tended to crowd out small businesses, came with big egos and many aspired to have a finger in every pie, no matter whether the business made economic sense or was even viable. They also had an enormous appetite for debt. This proved to be a toxic combination when the 1997 Asian crisis shook the region and the Korean won crashed. Overnight, a number of these business empires discovered that they did not have the cash to repay their loans and they collapsed like sandcastles.

Take Haitai, for example. This producer of lollipops, biscuits and soft drinks that also launched "Supermint", Korea's first bubble gum, had ambitions to move into electronics and construction. In order to expand, the company borrowed large amounts of money at just the wrong time and went bankrupt in 1997. It was acquired by another Korean company, Crown Confectionery, in 2004 and its famed confectionary brand has survived. Haitai's Oh Yes! chocolate cake remains one of South Korea's most popular snacks.

After the dust settled, the five biggest *chaebol* – Samsung, Hyundai, Daewoo, LG and SK – were still standing but 11 others had to shut their doors. The costs to ordinary Koreans were massive. Many lost their jobs and the number of suicides skyrocketed. Seoul's city officials even applied grease to the railings of a bridge to reduce the number of people who tried to jump to their deaths.

Koreans, however, have an unmatched ability to see opportunity in crisis. A new breed of entrepreneurs started their own businesses, creating a wave of start-up companies. Many listed on the Kosdaq market where it was easier to raise money. By 2000, these new ventures outnumbered the listings of ordinary businesses by a wide margin.[11]

The support these enterprises needed came from Koreans who were sitting on a large pile of savings. Many started to return to the stock market, which had been largely abandoned by foreign investors after the crash. These small retail investors piled into Kosdaq stocks,[12] in effect funding this wave of start-ups. It proved to be a shrewd investment. Some mushroomed into large domestic companies, such as Naver, an internet search engine that is known as the Google of South Korea, and Daum, which initially sold insurance online but reinvented itself as a web portal with its own news feeds and messaging apps.

But, to the careful observer, the scars of the Asian crisis are still visible. To protect themselves from takeovers, Korean companies are built like fortresses and some have the most convoluted ownership structures in Asia. Take the Samsung empire, for example. Its ownership structure looks like a bowl of Korean *japchae* noodles.[13] This allows the ruling families to have maximum control with as little investment outlay as possible, their ownership hidden behind layer upon layer of companies. Outside investors have little influence – it's all about the family.

But these complex crossholdings represent a poor use of capital. Money is locked up in investments in their own companies instead of being used to construct plants, invest in new technology or pay dividends.[14] This is why Korean companies are among the least profitable companies in the region. As a result, Korean stocks on average trade at a discount to their Asian peers. It is also one reason why Korea is typically the cheapest market in Asia (having a northern neighbour with a bad attitude – and a nuclear habit to support – does not help, either).

This is changing, though. Some Korean business empires have lowered the drawbridge and made their stocks more attractive to overseas investors. Lotte Group, Nonghyup, Hyundai Department Store and Daelim are among those which have raised the standard of their corporate governance, and even the Samsung Group has reduced its cross shareholdings, as has Hyundai Heavy Industries. This is a big step forward, but myriad crossholdings still exist and remain a distinctive feature in Korea (and Japan, too). The Korean discount will be with us for a while longer.

Yo-yos

When China joined the WTO in 2001, the Koreans were among the first to open factories on the mainland. Attracted by low wages and improving infrastructure, they produced smartphones, cars, TV screens and cosmetics. Over time, China and the US became Korea's two most important export markets. It is, therefore, no surprise that the Korean stock market is super sensitive to what happens on the Chinese and US stock exchanges.[15] Only Taiwan and Hong Kong have a higher correlation with China than Korea.

The tech-focused *chaebol* empires and the tech start-ups which grew into local giants now dominate the Kospi and this has implications for how the Korean stock market behaves. Tech businesses tend to see more swings in profits than, say, ice cream vendors or companies that sell cookies. And that is not just because demand (and profit margins) for tech gadgets can swing wildly from one year to the next, but also because huge investments are required to make sure these companies don't fall behind in the technology race. Aside from massive annual R&D budgets, building a new semiconductor plant comes with a price tag of US$4 to 5 billion.

It's one of the main reasons why Korea's stock market tends to experience more ups and down than a yo-yo and is among the most volatile in Asia. To some investors, this is hard to stomach but for others it offers opportunities. Stocks that overshoot and snap back quickly are of great interest to investors with a keen eye and a cool head.

Hooray for hallyu

Like Taiwan, the Korean market is far more than just a bunch of tech companies and it, too, has a plethora of other interesting stocks. Many have benefitted from the "Korean wave" or *hallyu* that has swept over Asia and some western countries. Long gone are the days when poorly-made cars were handed out for free on Dutch TV shows. Today, most things associated with Korean culture are considered to be modern, chic, edgy and cool.

This wave started with Korean TV dramas and soap operas, and went on to engulf music, food, movies, online gaming, cosmetics and even cosmetic surgery. It all began with a drama with an unusual storyline. *My Love from the Star*, which aired between 2013 and 2014, told the story of an incredibly good-looking alien who landed on earth 400 years ago and subsequently fell in love with a leading actress in modern-day Korea. It was massively popular all over Asia and there was even talk of a Hollywood remake. At around the same time, Psy's *Gangnam Style* became the first music video to reach one billion views on YouTube.

These days, boy band BTS rules the roost, performing to huge crowds in the US, the UK and other parts of Europe. In 2019, they had to add a second date to their concert at London's Wembley Stadium after their first show sold out in 90 minutes. A tweet by one of the band members once got one million views in ten minutes and five million in just over one hour. In 2020, the management company behind the band listed on the Korea stock exchange and its shares doubled on their first day of trading.

The wave continues to spread. In 2020, *Parasite* became the first non-English film and first South Korean film to win the Oscar for best picture at the Academy Awards. Online gaming has been added to the list, especially MOBAS, or Multiplayer Online Battle Arenas. This phenomenon has turned leading Korean players into global superstars. It is not uncommon for more than 100 million viewers to watch live broadcasts of blockbuster games such as *League of Legends*.[16] As a result, Korea's Lee "Faker" Sang-hyeok has become the Lionel Messi of e-sports.

Korea's exceptional ability to export its "coolness" has turned the country, and its capital Seoul in particular, into a must-see tourist destination. Before the pandemic, millions of Asians, most of them Chinese but also including a small band of my wife's closest Indonesian friends, made regular trips there. They visited sights made famous by the soap operas and bought the cosmetics used by their favourite actresses or pop stars (preferably at duty free prices). And while they were at it, they would indulge in Korean snacks, visit barbeque restaurants and gamble at popular casinos on Jeju, a resort island off the south coast. The bolder among them would also book a visit to a plastic surgeon. The most popular procedures are Botox injections to reduce wrinkles and double eyelid surgery, which makes the eyes look bigger and rounder.

The number of Chinese arrivals jumped from just below five million in 2004 to over 17 million in 2019, before collapsing in 2020 when the COVID-19 pandemic put a cap on international travel. Before that, operators of malls and duty free stores such as Shinsegae benefitted greatly from these throngs of visitors, as did Korean cosmetic brands such as Sulwasoo, which is owned by a listed company called AmorePacific. But expect these travellers to be back soon.

Ageing and singletons

Aside from tech companies and great food, Taiwan and Korea have something else in common: both societies are ageing rapidly. The generation responsible for their economic miracles – the engineers and mechanics who built all the TVs, fridges, ships, cars and semiconductors in the 1980s and 1990s – are now in their 60s and 70s. And thanks to the rise in living standards, they are living longer and healthier lives than their parents and grandparents. At 65, they can expect to be around for another 25 years, and this will soon rise to 30 years.[17] This means they need money to support a long and comfortable retirement.

The problem is that not enough of them have the benefit of big pensions. They were only introduced in Korea in 1987 and the National Pension Service, the world's third largest pension fund, was established in 2007.[18] That was too late for many who now draw only a basic monthly old age pension from the government. After paying for food and electricity, very little is left. Small groups gather in Seoul's historic Pagoda Park, also known as Tapgol Park, to receive bowls of cow blood soup and food boxes handed out by charities. These old people were hit particularly hard by the coronavirus outbreak, which curtailed many charitable activities.

The next generation, however, is better prepared. For one, they are working for much longer: although the official retirement age is 62, the average Korean man stops work at the age of 72, a world "best" (in Japan it's 71). Many have also saved hard and accumulated considerable wealth. This has been a boon for the local finance industry which manages these funds, and the National Pension Service now owns about 13% of the Korean stock market. In Taiwan, life insurers such as Cathay Life and Fubon Life witnessed massive inflows as people poured their money into their savings products to ensure a comfortable retirement. Over time, these companies have become some of Asia's largest investors in stock markets.

Aside from ageing, another demographic trend shared by Taiwan and Korea is that more and more people are living on their own. When I landed in Taipei in 2002, my job was to head a research team of about 12 analysts. Most were single women in their early 30s. Evelyn was one of them. She was a cool-headed investment analyst who specialised in drilling down into the capital strength and profits of Taiwan banks, which made her a valued stock picker. Evelyn owned her own apartment and went on fancy holidays with close friends. One thing was clear:

she had no intention of getting married. I once asked her why. "It's the men," she said with a smile. "We do not want to pass our salaries over to husbands. And that is what most men would expect."

There has been a sharp rise in these single-person households[19] in Taiwan and Korea, and this trend is also starting to become visible elsewhere in Asia. In China, the notion of "three generations living under one roof" has become far less common and in 2019, nearly one in five Chinese households were classified as single-person.[20]

This has spawned all sorts of opportunities. A farmer in Taiwan started to produce a new variant of papaya that weighs only about half as much as those commonly found in markets, the big ones being too large for a single person. Cookbooks for people living alone have become popular, as have books on solo travel (about 80% of buyers are women).[21] Convenience store operators such as President Chain Stores in Taiwan and GS Retail in Korea sell a wide range of items popular with single-person households, such as the Korean *dosirak* – single-serving lunch meals. And small is also beautiful for retailers, whether it's furniture, wardrobes or rice cookers. Korea's Hyundai Motor got in on the act with the "Venue", a very compact sports utility vehicle that targets those in their 20s and 30s pursuing a singleton lifestyle.

How Taiwan and Korean stock markets work

If you are into all the latest consumer electronics gadgets, know the difference between DRAM and NAND, follow developments in nanotechnology and get excited about Apple product launches, you will love Korean and Taiwan tech companies. And if you have a knack for trading and spotting trends in share price movements, these two stock markets are made for you.

But they also have something for every type of investor – day traders in tech, long-term investors with a keen eye for the slower moving trends, and those looking for dominant global brands or smaller, more nimble but highly profitable companies. The two markets are also big and diversified enough to cater to the needs of large players who move billions of dollars every day, as well small investors with a few thousand dollars to play with.

In Taiwan, much of the tech world orbits around Apple. Many of the components which go into iPhones, iPads, Macs, iPods and the Apple Watch are produced under contract by local companies. For some, Apple is their biggest customer, so it is no surprise that Taiwan's stock market is highly sensitive to Apple's supply chain, product launches and sales growth. This is not the case in Korea.

What the two do share is that they, more so than anywhere else in Asia, take their lead from the US and China,[22] their two biggest trading partners. And don't forget US bond yields. They tend to be most sensitive to the ups and downs in US bond markets. If bond yields go higher because there are expectations that the US economy is switching into higher gear, it is these two markets that tend to benefit the most. This is why they often move in the same direction, although Taiwan is the mellower of the two. Swings in Taiwan stocks tend to be less wild than those in Korea, where stocks can sell off and bounce back rapidly. Part of the reason is that Korean earnings tend to be far more volatile.

Add this to the mix of the ungainly *chaebol* empires and lower annual dividend payments and it is easy to understand why Korean stocks have for decades traded at much lower valuations than their Taiwan peers. Taiwan's laser-focus on profitability and dividends makes this market a happy hunting ground for stock pickers looking for high-quality companies with straightforward business models.

But, as explained earlier, both have more to offer than just tech, from bicycle makers in Taiwan to boy bands in Korea.[23] The dynamics of these non-tech companies are often very different from those that drive the tech stocks. They often benefit from demographic shifts that, like tectonic plates, slowly change the shape of Asian consumer markets. While these shifts are often predictable, they take time to materialise.

As these societies have aged, so has the nature of the stock markets. Domestic Korean and Taiwan investors are now the dominant forces, which was not the case in the 1990s. They have also started to spread their wings and invest other Asian stock markets. Yes, a lot of this is institutional money run by asset managers, pension funds and insurance companies, but we are also witnessing the rise of the retail investor. In

2020, when the coronavirus struck, local retail investors drove as much as 80% of all stock trading in Korea. Taiwan was not far behind.

This is good news for regional wealth managers, insurance companies, stock exchanges and brokers. And these smaller, local investors are much more willing to go beyond the big tech names and dabble in retailers, duty free shops and cosmetic brands. This is because they know these products and buy them every day. Over time, this should help to broaden these markets, leading to more trading in smaller stocks.

Despite all the similarities, there are stark differences, too. The big Korean companies are often family-run empires which are heavily invested in the global market. They own big brands – Samsung, Hyundai, Kia, LG and so forth – which showcase products available from Amsterdam to Rio de Janeiro. This is not the case in Taiwan. Most people would struggle to name more than three or four consumer brands that originated from the island.[24]

Nonetheless, we are surrounded by products that are made in Taiwan under contract. These components, widgets, chips and lenses allow our computers and smartphones to function smoothly. It is this emphasis on expediency over beauty, of engineering over brand building, of mechanics over macchiatos, that is mirrored in the make-up of Taiwan's stock market. I don't think this will change any time soon.

We now turn our attention to Jakarta, Bangkok and Manila, markets which are a far cry from those in Taipei and Seoul. Here, it is local buyers rather than global brands and high-end technology that are the centre of attention.

Endnotes

1 Giant website < https://www.giant-bicycles.com/int/about-us/our-history/giant-manufacturing-founded>.

2 Quite a few realised that Giant's excellence in bicycle engineering meant they were better off ordering bicycles from the company, and still do today.

3 For bicycle aficionados, this was the Cadex 980 C.

4 This company is now 49% owned by Merida, another Taiwan bicycle maker.

5 A key issue with semiconductors is how closely microelectronic devices can be packed together on a wafer. Historically, this was measured in nodes but the number itself has lost the exact meaning it once held. Recent technology nodes such as 22nm, 16nm, 14nm and 10nm refer purely to a specific generation of chips made using a particular technology. The latest cutting edge semiconductors are the so-called 5nm ones made by TSMC.

6 This is visible in margins and return on invested capital (RoIC). TSMC's earnings before interest, taxes, depreciation and amortisation (EBITDA) margin, a measure of a company's overall financial performance, was 62% in 2019 and RoIC 29%. For Hon Hai, the EBITDA margin was only 3.4% in 2019 and RoIC 12%.

7 While an armistice was agreed in 1953, a peace treaty was never signed, so technically the Korean War never ended.

8 A national R&D programme was launched in 1982 that included subsidies and tax credits in order to get research projects off the drawing board and into factories.

9 Chung 2007.

10 Typically, a distinction is made between memory chips that need power to dynamic random access memory (DRAM) and flash memory (NAND) chips. DRAM needs power to maintain its content. NAND chips will eventually wear out and lose content and a limiting factor is that there are only so many times you can write data on it and erase it. After a while, it needs to be replaced. Generally speaking, DRAM is more expensive than NAND flash.

11 To be precise, 137 to 14. What distinguishes the growth in new listings after 1998 from that in the early 1990s is the type of companies. In the earlier period, most newly-listed companies were ordinary businesses. But in 2000, "new venture" businesses (lots of tech starts-ups) claimed 116 new listings versus 62 for ordinary businesses; in 2001, these new ventures outnumbered ordinary businesses in new listings by 137 to 14. See Shin 2002.

12 They owned as much as 58% of the market in 2000, followed by local institutional investors who held 37%.

13 The largest shareholder in Samsung Electronics is Samsung Life Insurance, but Cheil Industries, the top shareholder of Samsung Life Insurance, is considered to be the de facto holding company of the group.

14 On average, Taiwan companies pay much more of their profits in dividends than their Korean peers do.

15 This is why across Asia, the Korean stock market has the highest correlation with both Chinese and US stock indices. The five-year correlation (2015–2020) between the KOSPI and the US S&P500 index is as high as 80%. Correlations with China are lower at 42% in the past five years.

16 Custodio 2020.

17 OECD (Pensions) 2017.

18 A national pension scheme covering workers in establishments with ten or more employees was implemented in 1988. In 1992, the compulsory coverage was expanded to those firms with five or more employees. It was expanded in 1995 to cover farmers, fishermen and the self-employed who reside in rural areas and, finally in April 1999, to the self-employed in urban areas. After 2003, coverage gradually expanded to corporations and workplaces with less than five full-time employees. The National Pension Service (NPS), which manages all these pension funds, was established in 2007.

19   In Taiwan, 40% of people between the ages of 30 and 39 were unmarried in 2015 and three out of 10 families in South Korea were single-person households.

20   Rude 2020. Globally, one in ten households is forecast to be both Asian and single-person in 2040.

21   "Single households new market for businesses" *Taipei Times*, 4 April 2017 <https://www. taipeitimes.com/News/taiwan/archives/2017/04/04/2003668047>.

22   In technical terms, Taiwan stocks have a high correlation with Chinese and US stock indices. The five-year correlation between the Taiex and the US S&P500 index is as high as 77%, almost as high as Korea's 80%. Taiwan's correlation with China is 57% in the past five years, one of the highest in Asia (Hong Kong is a little higher).

23   In Taiwan, tech accounted for 54% of the market in December 2020 and banks 13%. The rest were consumer, industrials and chemicals companies. In Korea, tech represented 36% of the market, financials 8% and the rest were a plethora of different retailers and industrials.

24   Here are a few: Giant bicycles, computer makers Acer and Asus, small but recognisable makers of hard drives and routers Gigabyte and D-Link, and software maker CyberLink.

Chapter 8

Southeast Asia's Stock Markets

ตลาดหลักทรัพย์

Dangdut, labyrinths and a paradox

Java casts a spell over visitors, with its ancient traditions, captivating street scenes, spectacular views, and cities inhabited by warm and inviting people. It is an incredibly fertile place: banana trees grow out of the bare earth and the island is covered with frangipani, coconut and mango trees, and deep green rice paddy fields. And it's *busy* – more people live in Java than in Mexico or Japan.

I fell under its spell in 1990 when backpacking across the island as a student. I stayed in *losmen* (cheap guesthouses) and criss-crossed the island by bus and train. The roads were narrow, single lane, and part of a spider's web that spanned the island. Small houses dotted the landscape, set back a little distance from the road, with front yards scraped clean. Java was, and still is, an endless array of smallness, a random string of farms, villages, restaurants, mosques and towns that are hard to associate with the might of the old kingdoms and empires that once ruled. But look closer and signs of Java's pre-Islamic past are everywhere – trucks named *Arjuna* or *Bima* and shops named *Sinta*, all from Sanskrit epics written thousands of years ago in India.

As a young backpacker from a small town in Holland, I was awestruck. The temples had wide views of conical volcanos, and at street level I delighted in sitting on the curb, *kretek* cigarette in hand, watching people go about their business – children walking to school in crisply-ironed uniforms, women selling ice cream, snacks or fried rice, and *wayang* puppets, and men randomly helping to direct the chaotic traffic. As the sun set, the call to *mahgrib* prayer, the *azan*, could be heard as boys passed by in their sarongs and white head caps, on their way to a small nearby mosque.

The Javanese are an open people and I soon made friends. A group of students lodging at a boarding house in Yogyakarta, the city in central Java where they studied, invited me to stay in one of their empty rooms. They took me in with an authentic hospitality that I believe is unique to Indonesians. The two I became closest to were Idham and Cacep who, like me, were in their last year at university. Idham studied engineering but nobody really knew what Cacep was up to – it was a closely guarded secret – although years later I heard he had received his business degree.

During the day, while they were attending classes, I explored the city or went to visit temples. In the evenings, we would meet, smoke *kretek* cigarettes and eat in makeshift restaurants, which were often nothing more than a mobile kitchen below a sheet of canvas, from which the exotic fragrances of spices and roasted meats wafted across the street. Afterwards, we would walk the labyrinth of streets and small alleys that knit Yogyakarta together. Idham and Cacep taught me their language, explained their customs, introduced me to the local cuisine, and told me about their beliefs, worries and hopes. Slowly, Java opened up to me and, in the process, I came to love the place and its tolerant, welcoming people.

One day, my student friends introduced me to *dangdut*, Indonesia's answer to India's I-pop. The sound is like a cross between techno, Bollywood and Middle Eastern pop music, with an odd rhythm that appears to be completely off-beat but somehow isn't. It turns out that *dangdut* is about much more than music and dance, and holds lessons about the whole of Southeast Asia.

Male *dangdut* performers wear open shirts, tight jeans, long neck chains and strut around in rubber thong sandals. But it is the female performers who are the real showstoppers. By slender Javanese standards, they are all voluptuous with incredibly flexible waists, allowing them to gyrate their bodies while wearing high heels and skirts and tops that leave very little to the imagination. Their extraordinary hip movements have been the centre of debates in parliament, deliberated on by Islamic councils and even warranted investigations by the National Security Council for fear they might set off mass riots. *Dangdut* is never far from the headlines.

In 1982, *dangdut* star Elvie Sukaesih was invited to perform at an election rally. It proved to be a political masterstroke. Ten of thousands of people showed up and their response was so enthusiastic that local security forces feared the crowd would go on a rampage. In 2003, a young woman called Inul Daratista appeared on national television and her pulsating hips and erotic screams sent the more conservative segment of society into meltdown. Doctors warned women not to try these moves at home, the Indonesian Muslim Council called for a ban and members of parliament tried to draft laws against such obscenities. Five years later, an American academic wrote a whole paper based on the controversy, describing how "a woman's body became the focal point for public debates about religious authority, freedom of expression, women's rights, and the future of Indonesia's political leadership".[1]

Java, I learned, was a complex place. *Dangdut*, hugely popular but rejected by members of the Muslim clergy, reflects the struggle between defining morality and what is acceptable behaviour in a conservative society. It mirrors the contradictions that characterise Java in particular and Southeast Asia in general. The whole region is in a constant struggle between the old and the new, the religious and the secular, the extremist and the moderate, the city and the village.

I was soon to get a first-hand taste of this. While people I met in Java were open and friendly, back in those days, immigration officers across the region were a different breed. Hordes of western backpackers were roaming Southeast Asia and not all were welcome, especially those with long hair, baggy trousers and who smelled like they had not been near a shower in a week. I passed the test when I showed up in Penang, the lovely island off the west coast of Malaysia, despite having an Indonesian batik sarong wrapped around my rucksack. Many others didn't. Instead, they got a large stamp in their passport: "SHIT" (Suspected Hippie In

Transit), and had three days to leave the country, just enough time to make it to Thailand.

Undeterred, I continued my travels in a region I had come to love. Later, as a stock analyst, I scrutinised small stocks listed across ASEAN (Association of Southeast Asian Nations) – the loose political affiliation of countries wrapped across the equator, comprising Indonesia, Thailand, Singapore, Malaysia, the Philippines, Vietnam, Brunei, Cambodia, Myanmar and Laos. It's a diverse grouping, with Singapore being one of the richest nations on the planet and Cambodia one of the poorest.

But large parts of Southeast Asia have a lot in common, for example, a growing number of middle-income families who live in the labyrinths of single-lane streets in thousands of small towns and villages, just like the ones I had visited as a backpacker. Together, these countries form a massive consumer market of about 600 million people, which in terms of value matches the size of India, Russia or Brazil. The problem in ASEAN is often getting the products to where you want them, but more about that later.

The largest stock markets in this corner of the world are Indonesia, Thailand and Singapore, followed by Malaysia, Vietnam and the Philippines. Laos and Cambodia have very small markets – only a few companies are traded there – while those in Brunei and Myanmar are still at the planning stage. In the mid-1990s, Thailand, Malaysia and Indonesia were the centre of attention, while China was considered a sideshow. This changed after the Asian Financial Crisis struck in 1997 and when China joined the WTO in 2001. These days, it's the other way round. China leads the way and investment funds that move billions of dollars around the region often find Southeast Asia's markets too small.

However, those who ignore them risk missing out on something rather special. To really understand their characteristics, we need to take a step back in time to the sweltering summer's day that dawned in Bangkok on Wednesday, 2 July 1997.

A taxi for Peregrine and an inspirational sandwich man

The origins of the Asian Financial Crisis bring to mind an exchange in Ernest Hemingway's 1926 novel, *The Sun Also Rises*. "How did you go bankrupt?" Bill asked. "Two ways," Mike said. "Gradually and then suddenly." This dialogue has also been attributed to Mark Twain and F Scott Fitzgerald, but its origins is not the point.

Up until that fateful day in early July 1997, Thai and Indonesian companies were often at the top of everyone's investment wish list. This was a growth story that would run and run, a bull market that had already lasted for most of the decade. And it was a two-way street. To soak up all the money that was floating around the region, many Southeast Asian companies went on a borrowing spree or rushed to list their stocks on local exchanges. The problem was that not all of that borrowed money was invested wisely.[2]

The huge pile of US dollar debts that companies in Thailand and Indonesia (and Korea) had acquired over the years suddenly turned toxic when the Thai government devalued the baht. The currency sank like a stone and Thai companies woke up to the reality that the mountain of baht needed to repay those US dollar loans was far beyond their means. Overnight, swarms of businesses went bankrupt, starting a chain reaction that spread across borders. The Indonesian rupiah and Korean won were caught in the vortex and followed the Thai baht down the drain. The consequences were disastrous.

A deal between Peregrine, a brash young Hong Kong investment bank, and an Indonesian taxi company named Steady Safe – which turned out to be an anything but steady or safe – became a microcosm of all that went wrong in the region. Peregrine was founded by a former British racing car driver named Philip Tose, who, with the support of an array of Hong Kong tycoons including Li Ka-shing, grew the business into the largest investment bank in Asia outside of Japan. If there was a big deal in Southeast Asia – a merger, an acquisition or a new company listing its shares – Peregrine was all over it, regardless of who the client was.

The company – named after the swiftest and deadliest member of the falcon family – was not everyone's cup of tea. In November 1997, an article in *The Economist* put it this way:[3] "Peregrine's swashbuckling style and its willingness to cosy up to even the least pleasant governments – notably Myanmar's military junta and North Korea's communists – have left it with plenty of detractors."

Peregrine's downfall was sealed by Steady Safe, an obscure Indonesian taxi company run by one of the country's flamboyant wheeler-dealers, Jopie Widjaya. His dream was to turn his profitable but humdrum Jakarta cab business, with a fleet of 4,000 cars, into a construction conglomerate involved in rail projects, ferries, real estate and toll roads. To win contracts, Widjaya rubbed shoulders with those in power and he was close to Siti Hardiyanti Rukmana, the eldest daughter of President Suharto. His taxi earnings looked rock solid and, to Peregrine's cavalier bankers, it appeared that nothing could go wrong.

To finance the expansion of its business, Steady Safe borrowed US$260 million in cash from Peregrine in the form of an unsecured bridging loan. When the value of the Indonesian rupiah plunged, Steady Safe could not repay the debt. With markets in retreat across Asia, Peregrine's ambitions went up in smoke and after desperately trying to arrange a bail-out, it was forced to close its doors. Steady Safe's stock price had by then fallen to almost zero. Bizarrely, this triggered a buying frenzy as people rushed to acquire paper share certificates that they could frame as a keepsake. Somehow, Steady Safe avoided going bankrupt and its taxis are still a common sight on the clogged streets of Jakarta. The company remains listed on the Jakarta Stock Exchange. Rather like *dangdut*, it's all a bit confusing.

Steady Safe's share price never recovered after the Asian Financial Crisis in 1997. Neither did Peregrine.

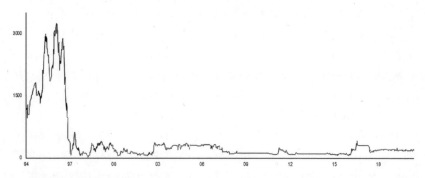

Note: Steady Safe's stock code is SAFE IJ
Source: Yahoo Finance

Legendary American investor Warren Buffett has always been ahead of his time. For example, in 1992, he said: "Only when the tide goes out do you discover who's been swimming naked." Mr Buffett made the comment after Hurricane Andrew, the most destructive storm to ever hit Florida, exposed the inadequacies of the insurance industry. He could have been talking about the aftermath of the Asian Financial Crisis.

All across the region, companies were caught with their pants down. Most, like Steady Safe, threw their hands in the air and told banks that the loans were now their problem. In Indonesia and Thailand, people rushed to bank counters and ATM machines to withdraw their savings. Those that succeeded bought gold or dollars, pushing the rupiah and baht even lower. The crisis was spiralling out of control and soon spread to South Korea. Stock markets tanked and in Hong Kong, property prices crashed.

Millions of people lost their jobs as companies collapsed. Some got angry. Indonesian students took their grievances to the streets and demanded the resignation of President Suharto. A few days later, I watched tanks rolling through Jakarta being pelted by rock-throwing students and saw troops firing on them. The whole city was on edge and there were rumours of a coup. Eventually, in May 1998, President Suharto stepped down after nearly 30 years of authoritarian rule. The Asian crisis had brought a government down.

Around the region, politicians and policymakers scrambled to respond, often with funding support from the International Monetary Fund (IMF). Banks in danger of collapse received huge injections of capital and massive amounts of debt were written off, allowing businesses that had survived to make a clean start. By 2000, Southeast Asia's stock markets slowly started to recover, but the hard lessons learned were never forgotten. Even today, many Thai and Indonesian firms are reluctant to take on debt, especially in US dollars.

If Peregrine was seen as a case study of everything going wrong, one man emerged as the symbol of resilience and recovery. Sirivat Voravetvuthikun graduated from the University of Texas at Austin in 1974 and took a job as a stock trader in Bangkok. He proved to be so adept at picking stocks that in the early 1990s, he had become known

in the industry as "The Phantom". The share price of companies took
off as soon as he went near them, and by the mid-1990s, he was a
multimillionaire. Life was a breeze.

His fortune, however, evaporated as soon as the crisis struck, and he
was left with a huge pile of debt. Unsure what to do, Sirivat turned to his
wife, Vilailuck, who came up with the idea of selling sandwiches made
with her favourite Japanese brand of bread, Yamazaki. He soon became
a familiar figure on the streets of Bangkok, selling his tasty snack from a
yellow foam box hanging from his neck to make just a few hundred baht
a day. He slowly built up his new business, Sirivat Sandwich, and today
he runs a chain of coffee shops and a catering operation. "The sandwich
man", as he is still known all over Bangkok, became a symbol of Thai
optimism and tenacity.

Similar stories of businesses looking for new opportunities emerged.
In Thailand, hospitals such as Bumrungrad and Bangkok Dusit Medical
Services saw their local market for high-end healthcare evaporate. Instead,
they focused on a new type of clientele. They offered tourists who flocked
to Thailand every year an annual health check, with additional surgery
if required, at a fraction of the prices charged in Hong Kong, Tokyo or
New York. Medical tourism has turned into a real success story. In the
Philippines, companies took advantage of the population's proficiency in
the English language to set up consumer call centres in Cebu, an island
which previously relied heavily on tourism.

But while capital was still being pumped into banks across ASEAN
and bank managers renegotiated debt payment schedules with fragile
businesses, the rest of the world had moved on. E-commerce and mobile
technologies were the new craze. The region was late to nurture home-
grown tech companies, which, with a few exceptions, are conspicuous by
their absence from stock markets in Southeast Asia. The star performer
in what is a pretty small field is Singapore's Sea Ltd.

The company was founded by entrepreneur Forrest Li in 2009 during
the depths of the Global Financial Crisis, which made the Asian crisis
look like a minor wobble. Sea's first product was a communication tool
for video games and it has since expanded into e-commerce (Shopee)
and digital payments (SeaMoney). It is now the largest internet platform

in Southeast Asia and China's Tencent has a stake in the company. Other successful internet companies have emerged, for example Gojek, a motorcycle delivery operation in Indonesia, but they are not listed.

This lack of large tech companies means that Southeast Asia's stock markets are largely populated with "traditional" companies which have been around since the 1980s, mostly food producers, beverage bottlers, tobacco makers, telecom operators, banks and local conglomerates.[4] Most are stable businesses which do not change much from one year to the next (at least until the coronavirus came along). There are also commodity businesses where profits can swing wildly – think palm oil plantations, coal miners or oil refiners – but they tend to be in the minority and, generally, these stock markets "think local".

New towns, new markets

As the years passed, the 1997 crisis slowly disappeared in the rear-view mirror. With their economies recovering, governments dusted off old plans to build roads, railways, hospitals and schools, and put them back on the drawing board. This desire to improve the region's infrastructure would have major consequences for stock markets.

By the mid-1990s, I had swapped my backpack for a suit and tie. As a stock analyst in Jakarta, I gained a whole new perspective on the region by flying from city to city to talk to companies that most western investors had never heard of. I toured cement factories in the Philippines, spoke to media outlets in Kuala Lumpur, and visited banks and shopping malls in Bangkok. My absolute favourite was a trip to visit *kretek* cigarette factories near Surabaya, where the fragrance of tobacco, sweat and sweet cloves filled giant halls as thousands of women rolled the cigarettes while listening to *dangdut*.

Wildly popular all over Indonesia, these cigarettes are often sold by the stick in small *warung* shops and represent a massive local consumer industry. The story goes that around 1850 in the Javanese town of Kudus, someone had the bright idea of adding dried clove buds to hand-rolled cigarettes and found that this relieved his chest pains.[5] The health benefits are questionable, but the *kretek* industry never looked back. The big brands are Sampoerna, Gudang Garam and Bentoel, and

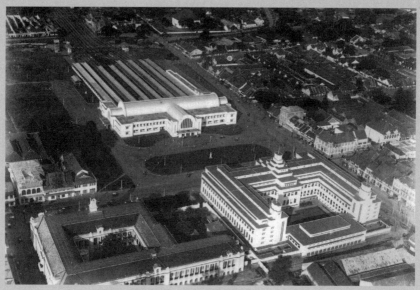

Remnants of the world's first listed company, the Dutch East India Company (VOC), are still visible in Jakarta. This is a 1935 photograph of the U-shaped building that was owned by the Netherlands Trading Society (NTS), also known as De Factorij, an early forerunner of ABN AMRO, a major Dutch bank. NTS was formed from the surviving businesses of the VOC after the giant went bankrupt in the late 18th century. The building stands opposite the Kota railway station in the north of the city and is today home to Museum Bank Mandiri, the corporate museum of Bank Mandiri. The word "Factorij" is still prominent on the front of the building. Source: Leiden University Libraries Digital Collections, KILTV 179130 <https://digitalcollections. universiteitleiden.nl/view/item/841827?solr_ nav%5Bid%5D=2925ff9666e43d5907d5&solr_ nav%5Bpage%5D=0&solr_nav%5Boffset%5D=11>.

Handel en Industrie.

DE BEURS.

Koersnoteeringen van de

Makelaars K. Goelst & Co. te Batavia.

Amsterdam, den 1sten Nevember.

	Gist.	Heden.
Certificaten N. H. M.	173 %	173 %
Javasche Bank	238 »	238 »
Ned. Ind. Hand.	216 »	217 »
Koloniale Bank	127 »	128 »
N. I. Escompto Mij	136 »	137 »
Handelsv. Amsterdam	187 »	187 »
Internationale	195 »	196 »
Pref. Paleleh	110 »	109 »
Gew. Paleleh	41 »	41 »
Redjang Lebong	238 »	238 »
Pref. Ketahoen	43 »	43 »
Gew. Ketahoen	31 »	32 »
Simau	352 »	352 »
Totok	44 »	44 »
Gloemboek	69 »	70 »
Ned. Scheepvaart Unie	146 »	147 »
Rott. Lloyd	139 »	139 »
Kon. Paketv. Mij	155 »	156 »
Java Ch. Japan	108 »	116 »
Sem. Ch. Tram	215 »	215 »
Sem. Joana Tram	177 »	177 »
Bat. Electr. Tram	86 »	86 »
Ned. Ind. Spoor	303 »	305 »
Tarakan Petr. Mij	10 »	110 »
Oost Borneo	83 »	83 »
Kon. Petr. Mij	503 »	513 »
Geconsolideerde	214 »	223 »
Linde Teves	217 »	217 »
Poerworedjo	92 »	92 »
Prolongatie-rente	4 %	4 %

From about 1912 onwards, stockbrokers, in this case K Goelst & Co in Batavia (now Jakarta), started to quote shares prices in local newspapers. Source: "Handel en Industrie" De Express, 1 November 1912 <http://resolver. kb.nl/resolve?urn=MMKB19:002789075:mpeg21:p00001>. Consulted on Delpher 9 May 2021.

their advertisements are seen everywhere – on large billboards, TV and stickers on the back of trucks blasting out *dangdut*. The shares are listed on the Jakarta Stock Exchange.

Back in those days, visiting factories in the hinterland was no easy feat. First, you had to escape the famously gridlocked Jakarta traffic, and then the challenge was to navigate the spider's web of single-lane roads that criss-crossed Java. Eventually, plans for a Trans Java highway to connect all the major cities along the northern coast of the island were signed off. After some serious delays, the new road opened in 2019. Suddenly, trips that took hours or even days were possible in a fraction of the time. This push for better roads, bridges and airports was not unique to Java, and the same was happening in Malaysia, Thailand, Vietnam and the Philippines.

The improved infrastructure started to open up all sorts of new opportunities. Factories, previously built near harbours to avoid trucks being caught in traffic jams, were now able to move further inland. This meant that those looking for work did not have to move to Jakarta, Manila or Bangkok, but could find employment in nearby factories. And women joined the search for jobs, too. They often had fewer children than their mothers and grandmothers, and as households grew smaller, they had more time to work. Growth was moving beyond the big cities and this changed, and is still changing, how and where people shopped and what they spent their money on.

New towns and higher incomes have also unleashed powerful consumer forces, which often follow a similar pattern.

First up is the move from a motorcycle to a car, preferably one that can transport the whole extended family, nieces and nephews included, to the mall for weekend entertainment. Almost every Filipino, Thai or Indonesian has been in a Toyota Avanza, possibly the most popular family car in the region. They are made by Toyota's partners such as Indonesia's Astra International, Southeast Asia's largest car and motorcycle group, which is partly owned by Jardine Matheson, the *hong* that originated in Hong Kong.

After the car, it's time to get on the property ladder for the first time or buy a bigger house. And that's good news for real estate companies.

Thailand's Land and Houses was hit hard by the 1997 crisis but found a willing investor in GIC, the Government of Singapore Investment Corporation,[6] the country's sovereign wealth fund. This allowed the company to restart its property business just when demand was picking up. It is now one of Thailand's prime developers of houses and condominiums in and around Bangkok and it also has large projects in Chiang Mai, Ayutthaya and Phuket.[7] In the Philippines, it's a similar story for Ayala Land. The company is part of the Ayala conglomerate, which has businesses ranging from banks (Bank of the Philippine Islands or BPI) to telecoms (Globe Telecom) and utilities (Manila Water).

All these new property owners need lots of stuff, so a visit to Homepro in Thailand and Ace Hardware in Indonesia to buy paint, lamps, cupboards or kitchen equipment is in order. This is great business for the operators of malls and shopping centres in these new, fast-growing towns and cities. Major players include Indonesia's Matahari and Ramayana (both Sanskrit names of old Indian epics), the Philippines' SM Supermalls, as well as smaller convenience stores such as Puregold in the Philippines or Alfamart in Indonesia.

A study by business consultancy McKinsey[8] concluded that as many as 90 million people in Southeast Asia are expected to move to these new fast-growing towns by 2030. By then, Cebu is expected to be the region's fourth-largest market for detergent, Khon Kaen in Thailand the sixth-biggest market for facial moisturiser, and Bekasi in Indonesia, a city just east of Jakarta, the sixth-largest market for diapers[9].

The improved infrastructure also helped to boost tourism. For example, after Phuket International Airport was upgraded and a new international terminal added, annual passenger capacity doubled. This helped Phuket to make the transition from backpacker paradise to upmarket tourist destination in a decade, and the island is now a hotbed of five-star hotels. Tourism makes a huge contribution to Thailand's economy, generally accounting for 12% of the GDP before the pandemic struck.

One of the country's more unlikely entrepreneurs to benefit from the tourism windfall is Bill Heinecke. As the name suggests, he's not Thai. The American started his own office cleaning business in Bangkok with a bucket and a mop when he was still in high school. He is now the chairman of Minor International, the listed company that runs a chain of luxury hotels, food companies and a lifestyle business. Minor was hammered by coronavirus, but with Mr Heinecke at the helm, it survived both the Asian Financial Crisis and the Global Financial Crisis, so expect it to bounce back quickly, along with the rest of the tourism industry in Thailand.

But there is also a flip side to having better transport systems, which makes it easier for newcomers to enter these markets. The difficulty of distributing goods and products around sprawling archipelagos such as the Philippines and Indonesia throws up all sorts of physical barriers – single-lane roads, traffic jams, congested ports. These barriers are slowly being broken down. That could be bad news for the industries and sectors where local companies have become accustomed to having the market to themselves because outsiders have struggled to find a way to compete. Like so much else in Southeast Asia, that is beginning to change.

Take Indonesia's cement market, for example. This was a cosy local industry until Conch Cement Indonesia, a subsidiary of China's Anhui Conch, entered the fray. With the financial muscle of the Chinese company behind it, the newcomer soon became the third-largest cement producer following the acquisition of a local player.[10] The domestic companies had to roll up their sleeves to deal with the increased competition, but this has come at the expense of their profit margins.[11] Similarly, the local retail market was shaken up when Lotte, a sophisticated rival from Korea, opened new hypermarkets across Jakarta. Again, profit margins suffered.

And then everyone in Southeast Asia went online.

An online love affair

Maybe it's the combination of having extremely sociable people and the fearsome traffic jams in cities such as Jakarta, Bangkok and Manila that force people to spend hours in cars away from family and friends. Whatever the cause, Indonesians, Thais and Filipinos are obsessed with communicating with each other online and have a love affair with Twitter. Indonesia is also one of the most Facebook-friendly nations on Earth.[12] In 2019, over 6% of the total global Facebook users were Indonesians, no small feat given that only a quarter of the population between the ages of 15 and 49 had access to the internet at the time.

And they are not just chit-chatting or watching *dangdut* videos. They are also amazingly effective at pushing for social justice and embarrassing misbehaving government officials. In Thailand, social media erupted after Facebook users began counting the number of expensive watches worn in public by a government minister – they included 11 Rolexes – raising questions about how a former general on a public servant's salary could afford such expensive accessories.

All this constant tweeting and messaging has been great news for anyone selling their wares online. The millions of consumers in towns and villages who were previously well off the beaten track were suddenly within reach. Somewhat surprising, the region's banks were among the first to see the huge opportunities that were opening up. After the Asian crisis, they had undergone root and branch surgery to repair their balance sheets and were now in far better shape. They wanted to expand but faced a familiar problem: many people in the Philippines and Indonesia didn't (and still don't) have access to even the most basic of banking services such as a bank account, credit card or mortgage. In large parts of Southeast Asia, less than 50% of the population has a bank account.[13] But they all have mobile phones.

Digital banking had arrived, and it grew fast. As did the competition. Surveys suggest that half of those who don't have access to digital banking want to get it soon. Alternative payment platforms such as e-wallets, a type of electronic card connected to a bank account, sprang up all over the place.[14] Ride-hailing apps such as Singapore's Grab went into the digital payment business, with its offshoot GrabPay now available in Malaysia and the Philippines. Meanwhile, money remittance firms like Ayannah have rolled out new apps in the Philippines, and Singapore's Shopee, part of Sea Ltd, is a big player, too. China's digital giants have also discovered these markets, with Tencent and Alibaba competing with home-grown Tokopedia in Indonesia. In short, it's a pretty crowded space.

But despite all the competition, the banks have done very well for themselves. A deft digital touch and an ability to sign up new customers in the faster-growing towns and cities has turned some of the region's banks into the most profitable in the world.[15] The rush to get online has also been good news for telecom operators such as Telkom in Indonesia, AIS in Thailand and Axiom in Malaysia. The rapid growth in social media and e-commerce activity also led to an inevitable explosion in mobile data, allowing telecom tower operators such as Towers Bersama to sit back, relax and count the profits. And now, the first tech companies are now planning to IPO in the Jakarta stock market.

But the digital revolution is not over. Not only are more and more people who used to keep their cash in a box at home putting their money into bank accounts for the first time, they are also starting to buy mutual funds and stocks. As a result, local investors have become a force to be reckoned with on their own stock markets. In Thailand, they have overtaken the large international funds that traditionally dominated the market and now account for roughly half of daily trading volumes. There are early signs that something similar might be happening in Indonesia. And in Singapore and Malaysia, local pension funds already dominate their respective markets.[16]

The common perception is that these retail traders punt stocks by the hour, but this is not always the case. Many invest for the long term and, unlike foreign investors, they don't run for the hills when there is a wobble in the market, creating big swings in currencies. Malaysia has become one of the most stable stock markets in the region for the very simple reason that a large domestic pension fund is happy to pick up stocks when foreigners sell.[17]

The Nguyens as neighbours

Vietnam was one of the few countries in Southeast Asia to avoid the pain of the 1997 meltdown. The economy was still at an early stage of development, and most companies were state-owned, and so had no US dollar debt. There was no stock market to crash and there was no recession. The country's home-grown crisis came much later, starting in 2007. The problem was eerily familiar; foreign investors had woken up to the country's growth potential as the economy started to open up. Money poured in, far too much in fact, and far too quickly.

These huge capital inflows led to rapid growth in credit. This, combined with higher public sector spending and a surge in energy and food prices, created high levels of inflation and large trade deficits. After overheating in 2007, the economic situation deteriorated in the first half of 2008. Banks were bursting with bad debt, the currency tanked, and the fledgling stock market, opened only in 2000, lost 70% of its value. It was like 1997–1998 all over again, but this time in Vietnam. As had happened in Indonesia and Thailand, foreign investors fled, and the government had to write off loans and pump money into the banking system.

Memories are, however, famously short in the world of investment. The stock market, no-go territory for several years, quickly went from almost total anonymity to achieving celebrity status as Asia's most promising frontier market, ahead of Bangladesh and Sri Lanka. Vietnam was back, big time. It's easy to see why as the country has so much going for it. Aside from its proximity to China, Vietnam is liberalising its economy in order to attract foreign industry, it has a number of deep-water ports and a large pool of young, hardworking and well-educated workers. Like China, it has become a workshop for the world and has welcomed some very big corporate names to its shores.

The biggest name of all is Samsung. The company employs more than 100,000 people in Vietnam and has helped to make the country the second-biggest exporter of smartphones in the world, after China. Samsung alone accounts for about a fifth of Vietnam's total exports.[18] Its factories are more like cities than production centres, offering a full range of shops, restaurants and other amenities. At one of these, a Korean vet is available to treat the pets of the expatriate staff.

The benefits are mutual. Samsung has diversified its supply chain away from China and Vietnam is an attractive alternative as the workforce is younger and cheaper. And it's not just Samsung that has changed the industrial landscape. Many other big overseas companies have followed in the footsteps of the Korean giant, including LG Electronics, Intel, Apple and Foxconn.

This is transforming the economy. People now enjoy higher incomes, have fewer children and live in smaller households. More women have joined the workforce. And just like in Indonesia and Thailand a decade earlier, smaller towns started to grow as road access improved and job opportunities spread. Restaurants, hotels and shops opened, and consumers moved from motorcycles to cars, bought new houses, and started to bank online and take holidays overseas.

Excitement about Vietnam's stock market started in earnest in 2015, when restrictions on foreigners buying real estate were scrapped. Overnight, the country with beautiful beaches, amazing food and a thriving economy turned into Asia's property investment hotspot. The stock market soared. Companies rushed to list their shares and get access to funds, and the government started to sell off stakes in moribund state-owned enterprises. The market was soon trading more stocks every day than some of its ASEAN neighbours. The largest listed firms are banks, real estate players and a large diary company, all local businesses.

There are still some restrictions in place. For example, the level of foreign investment in some companies in certain sectors are not permitted to exceed 49%, which can result in shares trading at a premium when the ownership limits are reached, but the government has made it clear that it will try to address some of these anomalies. If it does, expect this market to become a full-fledged member of the region's stock market family and be promoted from frontier to full emerging market status.

Bangladesh

Bangladesh's DSE Broad Index.

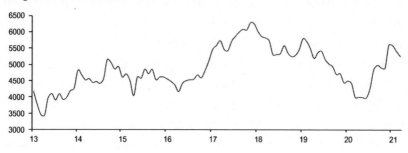

Source: Factset

There's never a dull moment in Dhaka.* The capital of Bangladesh is a maze of chaotic streets and has the worst traffic I have ever seen (which is saying something). Women dressed in brightly coloured sarees meander through the gridlock selling street food such as *fuchka*, crisp bread filled with chickpeas, yogurt, tamarind syrup and chili. Delicious! The bedlam is occasionally interrupted by tranquil open spaces, featuring imposing palaces and temples. The pinkish Dhakeshwari Temple houses the city's deity, Dhaka, who gave her name to the city. Although a bit overwhelming at first, those willing to explore will find a city full of charm and friendly people.

Bangladesh's economy is growing fast, led by the world's second largest textile industry with support from a steady stream of remittances from Bangladeshis working in the Middle East. The country will need to reduce its reliance on garments as cheap alternatives emerge in Africa, and the good news it is already attracting a new breed of investors. Korea's Samsung Electronics and Japan's Honda have opened factories that are starting to churn out mobile phones and motorbikes. It seems that the country is taking a page from the Vietnam playbook.

There are two stock exchanges. The Dhaka Stock Exchange (DSE) is the largest as well as the oldest, having begun trading in 1954, before the country became independent in the 1970s. The second is the Chittagong Stock Exchange, which began operations in 1995. The largest stocks are a mobile phone operator (Grameenphone), electric appliance maker Walton, British American Tobacco Bangladesh and Square Pharma, a local producer of pharmaceuticals (another domestic industry that is growing rapidly).

Although Bangladesh is still not on the radar screen of many investors, the DSE is taking big steps forward. By 2021, its combined market cap stood at US$46 billion and there were seven stocks worth more than US$1 billion, up from four in 2015. Daily trading amounts to US$125 million – not a lot for large investors but good enough for most others.

---

*   By 2030, Dhaka will be one of Asia's largest cities, taking fourth place after Delhi, Tokyo and Shanghai. See United Nations, Department of Economic and Social Affairs, Population Division, *World Urbanization Prospects 2018: Highlights* (2019).

A paradox: how Southeast Asian stock markets work

The shock waves that rolled over these markets in 1999–1998 and again in 2008–2009 have given them a distinct shape and flavour. Yes, they have been overtaken by China and missed out on the emergence of tech giants, but they still enjoy many of the benefits of the digital revolution. They also offer investors access to all sorts of companies not often seen elsewhere, from kretek cigarette makers and Thai hospitals to some of the most profitable small banks on the planet.

Many of the larger companies have succeeded by having a straightforward business model that has allowed them to penetrate the small towns and villages which dot the landscape, and where most consumers live and work. With the exception of a few oil and commodity stocks – in Thailand, PTT Global Chemical, a refiner, and PTTEP, an oil exploration firm, are the two biggest listed companies – it is local stories that drive these stock markets.

This is further amplified by the fact that Southeast Asian markets are also the most concentrated across the region. The top five companies in Indonesia account for over 60% of the total market. To put this into perspective, in China, the top-five concentration is 38% and in India, the least concentrated market in Asia, it's just over 30%. In short, a handful of large, locally-oriented stocks set the pace.

This dominance of local over global themes comes with two other advantages: steady earnings and diversification. Most of the companies sell consumer goods and services – noodles, cigarettes, motorcycles, telecom services – which tend to generate a remarkably stable flow of earnings. Southeast Asia's stock markets also make it easy for investors to diversify their portfolios. These smaller markets have their own pulse, one that is not dictated by the movements of the global giants such as the US and China.[19] In the years when the US and China markets are down, it is not unusual for stocks in Indonesia or Thailand to shine. This is usually not the case in the Hong Kong, Korea or Taiwan markets, which often get pounded if stocks in mainland China fall sharply.

The big disadvantage of investing in these markets is the exposure to local currencies. With the exception of Singapore, these countries do not have a large pool of domestic savings that can be tapped to make the investments the region so badly needs. Despite the recent improvement in infrastructure, there's still a long way to go. As a result, they have to borrow from foreign investors through the bond markets. This lack of domestic savings has many side effects. For example, foreign investors can be a fickle bunch. They tend to flee when markets fall and this in turn weakens the currency, creating a vicious circle. This is unlikely to change until the pool of local savings is large enough to meet these countries' domestic investment needs.

Like *dangdut*, Southeast Asia is a study in contrasts: new versus old, urban versus rural and stability versus volatility. And that means it can be a maddening, confusing place. Prime ministers and presidents sometimes try to balance these opposing forces by making contradictory statements which have investors running for the hills, only for them to return soon afterwards when they discover the latest policy announcement has achieved the opposite of what was intended.

Take, for example, Indonesia's President Joko Widodo, commonly referred to as Jokowi. A brilliant, instinctive politician, he lived in a riverside shack and made a living as a humble furniture seller before becoming the mayor of Jakarta and, in 2014, the president of the country. He was voted in on a wave of hope for change. Jokowi has simultaneously promised big bang reforms to reinvigorate foreign investment, while at the same time promoting self-sufficiency, calling for imports to be curbed and even urging Indonesians to "hate foreign products".[20] It is perhaps not a complete surprise that the first English language biography of the president is titled *Man of Contradictions*.[21]

Herein lies the very thing, a paradox really, that makes these markets attractive. While the companies tend to be stable, the same thing cannot be said about the currencies or the stock markets. Profit growth is among the steadiest in the region, but large swings in currencies make these markets among the most volatile in the region.[22] At the same time, they offer access to an unusual potpourri of stocks not seen elsewhere and opportunities to diversify portfolios. For stock pickers, these markets are at times significantly mispriced. Like the region itself, they often tease and tantalise.

That's why treating them as a sideshow to the big markets further north in Asia can be a big mistake.

Endnotes

1 Andrew Weintraub, *Dance drills, faith spills: Islam, body politics, and popular music in post-Suharto Indonesia*, published online by Cambridge University Press, 2008.

2 The average return on equity in Thailand, for example, fell from 13% in 1992 to 5% by 1996. Return on capital employed (pre-tax) dropped from 9% to 5% in the same period and in Indonesia, it declined from 12% to 10%. For more details, see Pomerleano 1999.

3 "Peregrine: hawk turned prey", *The Economist*, 22 November 1997.

4 Here are some examples. Food producers: Charoen Pokphand in Thailand , Indofood in Indonesia, Universal Robina in the Phillippines. Beverage bottlers: Thaibev, San Miguel in the Philippines. Tobacco makers: Sampoerna and Gudang Garam in Indonesia, British American Tobacco (BAT) in Malaysia. Telecom: Telkom Indonesia, AIS in Thailand, Axiata in Malaysia, PLDT and Globe in the Philippines. Banks: Bank Central Asia (BCA) in Indonesia, Siam Commercial Bank in Thailand, Bank of the Philippines. Local conglomerates: Astra International in Indonesia, Ayala Corp in the Philippines, Sime Darby and YTL Corp in Malaysia.

5 Hanusz 2000, p 10–12.

6 GIC now owns 8% of this company.

7 Land and Houses Annual Report 2019.

8 Woetzel 2014.

9 Woetzel 2014, p 7.

10 That was Holcim Indonesia. By late 2019, Semen Indonesia and Indocement controlled 70% of local installed capacity across both integrated and grinding plants. Conch Cement Indonesia is the next biggest. See Perilli 2019.

11 For example, in Indonesia, Semen Indonesia's EBITDA margin fell from 35% and 33% in 2010 and 2011 to 21% and 22% in 2018 and 2019. For department store Matahari, they dropped from 30% and 31% in 2011 and 2012 to 26% and 21% in 218 and 2019.

12 Wahyudi 2018.

13 In Thailand, three out of four Thais access banking through mobile devices and in Indonesia, mobile penetration is 70%. See "ASEAN needs smart regulation to boost financial inclusion", *Nikkei Asian Review*, 6 January 2020.

14 The number of Indonesians making payment through their phones grew 2.5x between 2019 and 2014, and they now make up 32% of the banked population. Indonesia's BCA saw its mobile transactions rise from 300 million end-2017 to 1.7 billion end-2020. Source: BCA website.

15 Indonesia's BCA had interest margins of over 6% in 2019 and generated return on assets of 4% and return on equity of 18%. This is about double that of most banks in Asia. The massive clean-up of bad debt after the Asian crisis has helped, too.

16 In Malaysia, there are, for example, the Retirement Fund Inc (KWAP) or Employees Provident Fund (EPF), as well as unit trusts and mutual funds like Public Mutual or CIMB Principal Asset Management. In Singapore, there is the Central Provident Fund (CPF) and Employee Provident Fund (EPF). Both are defined contribution plans and have been trailblazers for other pensions systems across Southeast Asia.

17 The standard deviation in monthly returns in the FTSE Malaysia index over 2000–2020 stands at

3.7%, which is the lowest across the region. It is 5.0% for FTSE Asia ex Japan, Australia and New Zealand, 6.8% for the FTSE Indonesia and 6.1% for the FTSE Thailand.

18 In 2018, Samsung Vietnam's exports were just over US$60 billion, accounting for 25% of Vietnam's total export turnover. Source: *Hanoi Times*, 21 December 2018. In 2020, when the coronavirus hit global economies, total export turnover of Samsung Vietnam was about US$57 billion, 20% of Vietnam's total exports. Source: *Nhân Dân*, 25 April 2021.

19 This can be measured by looking at correlations between these markets. The five-year correlation (from 1 January 2016 to 1 January 2021) with the US S&P500 and the Shanghai index is the lowest for the Philippines at 0.61 and 0.28, followed by Indonesia at 0.64 and 0.30, then Malaysia at 0.64 and 0.36. The highest are Thailand at 0.76 and 0.32, and Singapore, where the correlation stands at 0.77 and 0.49.

20 Dian Septiari, "Jokowi's 'hatred' of foreign products raises eyebrows", *Jakarta Post*, 6 March 2021.

21 Bland 2020.

22 The standard deviation in annual profit growth for the top ten largest stocks in Indonesia stands at 22%, in the Philippines it is 23% and in Malaysia 28%. Earnings volatility is much higher in Thailand, a standard deviation of 67%, but that's partially because of the two large oil companies that dominate that stock market. Most of these markets exhibit much lower earnings volatility than China (24%), Hong Kong (28%), Korea (43%) and Taiwan (42%). Only India is lower at 20%. All data for annual growth measured from 2000 to 2020.

Chapter 9

Japan
株式市場

Swimming I

Mieko Nagaoka had never been much of a swimmer, but she decided to give it a try in her 80s after a doctor told her it would help her recover from a knee injury. Initially, she struggled to finish a single lap but little by little, she swam further and faster. When she was 100, she became the world's first centenarian to complete a 1,500-metre freestyle race. She may have been an hour off the world record, but she is the age group champion. Mieko wrote a book, titled *I'm 100 years old and the world's best active swimmer*.[1] At the age of 105, she held 18 world records and was still entering swimming competitions.

Japan is ageing. It has entered what demographers call a period of "super-aged" society, with senior citizens 65 and above accounting for more than 28% of the population.[2] Japan might be the first, but the rest of north Asia will soon join this club. First Taiwan, then South Korea, followed a few years later by China. What happens in Japan should give us clues about the implications for its neighbours. As we will see, demographics help drive stock markets.

There are a lot of Miekos out there. Long seen as being a burden on family and society, elderly people don't want to be seen as nuisance – *meiwaku* in Japanese, a word that can also describe a number of social ills, such as spam e-mail or speaking loudly on a mobile phone. Rather than sit at home and watch soap operas all day, many have adopted a super-charged senior lifestyle. They keep working, go for hikes and generally do everything they can to stay active. It is not uncommon to hail a taxi in Tokyo that is driven by someone in their 80s. A staggering 50% of Japanese aged 70 and above are either working or engaged in volunteer activities, doing community service or have hobbies.[3]

The truth is that ageing scares us. Newspapers are full of headlines predicting the apocalypse – "Japan's population is in rapid decline"[4] and "Worse than Japan: how China's looming demographic crisis will doom its economic dream".[5] Yes, it is true that ageing populations strain pension systems and increase healthcare costs as people live longer, but, for businesses and investors, this also creates new opportunities.

Take robots, which help to keep people happy and healthy in Japan. Panasonic and Nara-based Atoun have developed a smart walker, a kind of robot-suit that looks like a small backpack that enables its mainly older users to get out and about. Sohgo Security Services created a portable, thumb-size electronic device that tracks dementia patients who wander from their homes or care facilities, an increasing problem across Japan. And at nursing homes in Tokyo, robots keep the elderly entertained. Paro, a mechanised furry seal, cries softly when someone pets it; Pepper, a humanoid, leads groups of senior citizens in exercise routines; and DFree is a wearable sensor which uses ultrasound to detect changes in bladder conditions. It's big in the incontinent community.

Care robots are not just for the elderly and have a number of different uses. My first interaction with one was in an elevator in a Japanese hotel back in 2015. It appeared we were both going to the fifth floor, so I decided to have a chat: "Are you going to the fifth floor?" I asked. I guess the answer was too obvious and the robot didn't reply. Dumb foreigner. On arrival, it waited so I could leave the elevator first, and then navigated its way around a pillar on its way to a destination further down the corridor. Room service had arrived. When the guest opened the door, a lid opened, revealing a tasty hot meal. Mission accomplished, the robot returned to the elevator. Impressed, I later ordered room service. Imagine my disappointment when a very human lady appeared at the door with a steaming bowl of ramen noodles.

Of course, the rise of robots has implications for far more than Japan's old peoples' homes and its hotel industry. Robots improve productivity and reduce labour costs, and are now used around the world to perform a wide range of production tasks in agriculture, food preparation, warehousing and manufacturing. Japan is the robot king, especially when it comes to high-end automatons. More on that later.

What Japan has taught us is that many of the fears about an impending grey apocalypse are wide off the mark. The elderly are very well aware that they are likely to live much longer than their parents and will need a large amount of cash to see them through an extended period of retirement.[6] As mentioned earlier, pension pots will not be sufficient for many, which is why so many people in Korea, Taiwan and China are working for longer.[7]

With a bit of simple arithmetic, it is possible to calculate how much the whole of the Asian population will need to put aside before 2050 in order to retire in comfort – it's a staggering US$157 trillion.[8] To put that figure in context, it is 157x Apple's market cap.

All this cash will need to be invested somewhere, so expect elderly Asians to be big buyers of stocks, bonds, gold, property, and, of course, care robots. That's very good news for banks, insurers, stock brokers, wealth managers and the makers of sensors that tell us when to go for a wee. A lot of it will end up in bank deposits, at least to start with. But when banks are awash in cash, deposit rates fall, as do mortgages rates and bond yields – as we know, they are all connected. When interest rates turn negative, customers have to pay to put their money into banks, which in turn make no returns from lending money to businesses.[9] Then the stock market beckons.

Japan knows all about this as it has been there before.

Swimming II (naked this time)

In the late 1980s, Tokyo was on steroids. Even on a regular Tuesday, hundreds of men with baggy suits and their *wan-ren-bodi-kon-gyaru* ("one length hair, body conscious girls") with enough bling to start a small jewellery shop, lined up to get into clubs to party until dawn. One in particular, Juliana's Tokyo, encapsulated this era and people travelled from afar just to be able to say they had been there.

The rest of the country was fizzing, too. Osaka housewives sipped cups of coffee sprinkled with gold dust and Nagoya businessmen quaffed extraordinarily expensive bottles of Bordeaux over lunch. Those were crazy times. Tokyo's Imperial Palace was reported to be worth more than all the property in France. Japanese tourists and businessmen flew to New York, Paris and London in droves to snap up the latest Louis Vuitton handbag or Armani suits and, while they were at it, pick up some prime real estate as well.

Japan's boom was also highly visible in the western world through companies like Sony and Toshiba and their ubiquitous Walkmans, VHS recorders and Betamax tapes. Aside from electronics, Japan was also home to the world's largest auto plants and Nissan, Honda and Toyota sold cars all over the US and Europe. When Mitsubishi Estate struck a deal to take control of New York's Rockefeller Center in late 1989, the latest in a string of acquisitions that included other US trophy assets such as Firestone Tire & Rubber and Columbia Pictures, it was evident that Japan was about to take over the reigns as world's greatest economic power.

Its stock market was valued as such; ordinary Japanese companies traded at price to earnings (PE) multiples of between 50x and 70x, while the rest of the world traded at around 15x. As the 1980s drew to a close, eight of the top ten global companies by market cap were Japanese. The country's stock market was almost as big as all other global stock markets combined.[10] But even before the ink had dried on that celebrated Rockefeller Centre deal in late 1989, the Japanese stock market peaked. Tokyo's Nikkei 225 index – Asia's longest running stock index – finished the year at 38,915, a six-fold increase from 1980, when it stood at 6,315.

What had fuelled the rally – ultra low interest rates, a wave of money sloshing around banks and markets, and big spending projects by the government[11] – went into reverse as Japan's central bank started to mop up all this money by raising interest rates. Initially, people were not fazed. They assumed it was just a blip, a temporary setback before the market zoomed higher again. As the bulls said, no one wanted to call an end to the party, least of all the government.

That turned out to be a big mistake. It soon became clear that a "Minsky moment" – a major collapse of asset values marking the end of a growth cycle – had arrived. The stock and property markets went in reverse, starting a slow-motion collapse. The Nikkei eventually bottomed in February 2009 at 7,416, a drop of 80% over 20 years and not far from the levels when the party started in 1980, some 30 years earlier. At the end of 2020, the Nikkei 225 was still languishing about 30% below this 1989 peak.[12]

It turned out that a lot of companies had also made speculative bets in the stock market that turned sour. Newspapers were filled with stories of businesses going bankrupt or banks seeing their investments go up in smoke. Some had borrowed from the violent and heavily-tattooed *yakuza*, Japan's mafia,[13] whose procedures for collecting overdue debts involved meat cleavers and amputated fingers. In 1993, Koyama Toyosaburô, vice president of Hanwa Bank, was shot dead, and it was widely assumed that his killer was a gangster.[14] Others had entangled themselves in complex financial products that looked great as long as stock prices went up but turned into horror movies when the market turned. This was so common that journalists invented a new word for it: *zaitech* or "financial engineering trickery".

A few years later, larger banks were forced to merge as the banking system digested an enormous amount of bad loans. As we mentioned earlier, Warren Buffett, the "oracle of Omaha", once said that you only find out who is swimming naked when the tide goes out.[15] In Japan, it seemed like almost everybody had been skinny dipping. The economy had entered what came to be known as "the lost decade", a period when economic growth halted for more than ten years.

Farewell samurai, hello private enterprise

Japan has a long history of being a fiercely independent group of islands. The Japanese repulsed the Mongols in the Middle Ages and fought off Europeans in the 1600s and 1700s. For a long time, they only traded with the Dutch East India Company (VOC) – the firm behind the very first stock exchange in Amsterdam in 1602 – and then only on the small man-made island of Dejima in Nagasaki harbour.[16] This isolation did not stop them from creating their own financial markets. In 1730, shogun Tokugawa Yoshimune authorised trade in rice futures at the Dojima Exchange in Osaka, the world's first organised futures market.[17] The rule of the shoguns came to an end during the Meiji Restoration in 1868, when Japan opened its doors to the outside world again.

Dojima rice exchange. Water was used to drive off people who stayed after official closing hours. Painting by Hiroshige (1797–1858). Source: Honolulu Museum of Art, Japanese woodprint, gift of James A. Michener, 1991 (23082), ID 5421.

Under Emperor Meiji, the samurai warrior class was phased out and the government sold the small industries the shogunate had developed to the highest bidder. These "Meiji men" built large conglomerates that they passed on to their sons. And so a large network of family-controlled businesses emerged with close ties to the government.[18] These *zaibatsu* or "financial cliques" became the hubs around which business life in Japan revolved, led by Sumitomo, Mitsubishi, Mitsui and Yasuda. A few decades later, they would become the template for Korea's *chaebol*.

In 1878, the government approved the opening of new stock exchanges in several leading cities, including Tokyo and Osaka. The Tokyo Stock Exchange was built in Kabuto-cho, a district which became synonymous with finance, similar to Wall Street in New York or Dalal Street in Mumbai. Those were the days when boys in kimonos carried buy and sell instructions from customers to stockbrokers. Investors had their first real taste of a bear market between 1920 and 1924, when Japan's economy slowed after World War I and, of course, far worse was to follow in World War II.

After the war, the stock markets in different cities merged into a new exchange which eventually morphed into the Tokyo Stock Exchange in 1949. The index that monitors the pulse of this market is the Nikkei 225, which was Asia's first stock index. It has been calculated by the *Nihon Keizai Shimbun* (*The Nikkei*) newspaper since 1950. The Topix, another widely used index in Japan, came into use in 1969.[19]

With Japan's economy in tatters, the US occupying forces, led by General Douglas A MacArthur, put in place a series of economic reforms.[20] The family-owned *zaibatsu* were seen as unhealthy monopolies with too much power, and some were broken up. The US soon changed course when the reindustrialisation of Japan became a priority during the Cold War, a time when Washington needed a strong ally in Asia. The *zaibatsu* were back in favour, although this time they were grouped around a particular bank rather than a family and encouraged to co-operate with each other.

They were called *keiretsu*, meaning "series" or "sequence". The leading *keiretsu*, which still dominate the country's corporate landscape, are Fuyo, Mitsui, Mitsubishi, Sumitomo, Sanwa and the DKB Group. In the Fuyo *keiretsu* we find Sapporo Brewery, Nissan and Canon, while Sony, Fujifilm, Suntory Whiskey and Toshiba are in another. During an economic slump, employees are transferred from one company to another to avoid them losing their jobs.

The plan worked. Japan became one of the great success stories of the post-war era. By the late 1970s, it was a manufacturing powerhouse and the world's second-largest economy (now overtaken by China), setting the stage for the stock market frenzy that would peak in 1989.[21] The *keiretsu* are household names and sell their products all over the world. This is why nearly half of all profits generated on the Tokyo Stock Exchange come from outside Japan, and why it's so sensitive to movements in the yen and conditions in markets such as the US and China.

As with the *chaebol* in Korea, cross-holdings keep out other companies. It's like a drawbridge that protects managers from shareholder criticism or revolt. These managers shuffle employees from one part of the *keiretsu* to another and maintain long-term relations with suppliers and customers, even if this does not obviously benefit the bottom line. Boards and executive suites are dominated by long-time insiders, who act less as representatives of shareholders and more as heads of a family. It allows them to do what is best for them or the rest of the *keiretsu*, not necessarily what is best for the shareholder.

This is one of the reasons why Japanese companies tend to be much less profitable and pay lower dividends than many other companies in Asia or the US. It is also why they are often found at the bottom of all sorts of corporate governance rankings in Asia.[22] And it explains why Japanese stocks, in the past decade or so, have traded at lower valuations than their peers in the US. This tradition of entangling companies in a net of cross-holdings is, however, slowly changing. More about that later.

The triumphs and tribulations of Toshiba, Toyota and Nissan

Some of Japan's big companies have fascinating back stories, often accompanied by a strong whiff of scandal. Take, for example Toshiba, part of the Mitsui *keiretsu*. The company traces its history back to 1875 in the early Meiji days, when it built its first factory in Tokyo to make equipment for the big innovation of the day: the telephone. It was called Tanaka Engineering Works and eventually amalgamated with others to form Toshiba in 1939.[23] After World War II, Toshiba made a name for itself by manufacturing many innovative products, from the world's first colour TV and video phones to laptops and DVDs. By 2015, it was involved in industries as diverse as semiconductors, home appliances, nuclear power and medical equipment, and was one of the largest stocks on the Tokyo Stock Exchange.

Then, in May 2015, disaster struck. A whistle-blower revealed that the company was cooking the books: charges and other costs were being delayed in order to inflate profit numbers. Until then, Toshiba had been perceived as a totem of good corporate governance, so these allegations really shook the country. An investigation put the blame on Toshiba's corporate culture. Senior executives set unrealistically high profit targets, while also signalling to division heads that failure was not an option. The only way to achieve these targets (and safeguard jobs) was through large amounts of creative accounting. Toshiba's CEO resigned but several other scandals[24] have since plagued the company and, in 2021, three private equity firms started to circle the Japanese conglomerate with the aim of a hostile takeover. This, too, led to the departure of another CEO, Nobuaki Kurumatani, given his ties with one of the bidders.[25] By then, the stock price was still below the level it was in May 2015.

Toyota Motors has had no such problems. Now one of the world's most valuable auto companies, it started life in a completely different industry. Sakichi Toyoda, an inventor known as Japan's Thomas Edison, was the man behind the introduction of the automatic loom to Japan's textile industry. His son, Kiichiro Toyoda, worked in his father's textile company but was soon making plans for expansion. In 1933, he established an automobile division and, two years later, started to sell cars.

The first model, the Toyota AA, was an homage to (or a blatant copy of) a Chevrolet sedan. In 1936, the company changed its name to Toyota because the number of strokes to write Toyota in Japanese (eight) was thought to bring luck and prosperity.[26] The company has long been cautious about making all-electric vehicles, favouring gasoline/electric hybrids, where it leads the market, but it is developing its own battery technology, which should allow it to make a big splash in the electric vehicle market in due course. It also owns a stake in Southeast Asian ride-hailing firm Grab as traditional automakers race to team up with disruptive tech companies.[27]

Other auto companies have had a bumpier ride. The raciest story to hit the industry for years involved Carlos Ghosn, the Brazilian-Lebanese-

French executive who was head of Renault-Nissan-Mitsubishi, the world's leading automotive alliance. Allegations surfaced in 2018 that Mr Ghosn had under-reported his rather substantial compensation. He argued that the charges were false, part of a corporate coup to stop him from orchestrating a merger between Renault and Nissan, one of the crown jewels of Japan's auto industry. Mr Ghosn was released on bail but as proceedings dragged on, he became convinced that he could never get a fair trial in Japan.[28]

His escape reads like a Hollywood-style thriller – a series of rendezvous in shady cafés in Istanbul and Beirut, secret meetings in hotel rooms, and an ex-special forces officer specialising in extracting executives from sticky situations. Having made his way covertly from Tokyo to Osaka, Mr Ghosn was concealed in a large, box-like piece of luggage that evaded scrutiny by customs officers and was then loaded on to a private jet. He succeeded in returning to his childhood home, Lebanon, which has no extradition treaty with Japan. Despite the drama, the Renault-Nissan-Mitsubishi alliance has survived.

Abenomics and the three arrows

While some of Japan's leading companies are phenomenal successes, largely because of their huge international footprints, the same can't be said for the domestic economy. Growth got stuck in a rut after the market crash of 1989 and the lost decade dragged on well into the new century. Then the Global Financial Crisis came along and gave both the economy and the stock market another good kicking. There was a strong feeling among the public, politicians and policymakers that something needed to be done.

In 2012, Shinzo Abe was elected prime minster after campaigning aggressively for radical change. His plans, dubbed Abenomics, were presented as "three arrows" based on an old samurai story. The first two were relatively straightforward in terms of policy: a large increase in government spending and a programme of quantitative easing (QE), with the Bank of Japan making large injections of money into the economy in the form of bond purchases.[29] But after this monetary and fiscal stimulus was unleashed came the hard part – the third arrow, the promise of massive structural reforms to reshape a stagnant economy hobbled by low productivity, a rigid labour market and an ageing population.

Part of the strategy was to make Japanese companies more profitable. This had been tried before with little success. Company executives had been threatened with laws to force them to pay more dividends and dismantle stock cross-holdings, but to no avail. The Abe government's plan was to create a new stock market index, the JPX-Nikkei400, comprising Japan's 400 best-run and most profitable companies.[30] To give it real impetus, the huge state-run government pension fund said it would invest in the companies that were part of the index.

The innovation was an instant success. Companies lined up to be part of this exclusive group. Every summer, Nikkei announces which have made the cut and those that will be dropped from the index. The names of the losers are published prominently on the front page of major newspapers. That's why it's become known as the "shame index" (Toshiba got the boot in 2015).[31] It's all very *meiwaku* for the companies which don't make the grade.

There are broad-based benefits, especially in the sensitive area of corporate governance. Many companies have appointed more independent directors and set up compensation committees to provide advice on how much executives should be paid. Maybe, slowly, the old way of doing business in Japan is changing.[32] The jury this is still out on this, but if true, Japanese companies might become more profitable and the stock market may trade at a lower valuation discount compared to the US.[33]

The IMF concluded that[34] "Abenomics has improved economic conditions and engendered structural reforms", though the approach "has not yet achieved a durable exit from deflation". Growth has hardly been robust and things worsened when the coronavirus wreaked havoc on Japan. Stocks fell in early 2020 but, as elsewhere, this was quicky followed by a boom as bond yields collapsed in the aftermath of the pandemic.

Japan's new prime minister is Yoshihide Suga, a long-time lieutenant of Mr Abe. He is also a reformer and wants to maintain the "three arrows" approach. His priorities include consolidating the smaller regional banks – there are far too many of them – and cutting mobile phone costs, effectively shaking up the cosy world of Japanese telecoms. Docomo, one of the largest mobile phone operators, promptly announced a new and competitive 5G services plan for lower-income users. Even before the new policy was announced, e-commerce giant Rakuten had attracted a lot of attention by entering the market with a low-cost plan to challenge the established companies.

Change is (perhaps) possible in Japan. It's just not easy.

Small is big

The Japanese stock market generally lacks the big tech companies that dominate the US stock market, and there is no equivalent to the tech-heavy NASDAQ. While four companies in Japan have market caps of more than US$100 billion, the US has about 81. A tech exception is SoftBank, now a poster child for the "new Japan". When the company listed in 1994, it was a small cap, but it has been so successful that it's now one of the country's largest companies. SoftBank's founder (and now chairman), Masayoshi Son, was educated in the US and the firm's Vision Fund, the world's largest technology-focused venture capital fund, owns a large chunk of China's Alibaba. Other new tech names that have made a splash are e-commerce companies Rakuten, Mercari and Zozo Town, the latter headed by flamboyant entrepreneur Yusaku Maezawa, who hopes to be the first commercial passenger to fly to the moon in 2023.[35]

But the giant presence of SoftBank and the rise of e-commerce websites cannot obscure a simple truth. Much of Japan's success is built on a tradition of manufacturing excellence. There's even a word for it – *kaizen* – which translates as "continuous improvement". The concept covers everything from quality control and just-in-time delivery to the use of advanced, efficient equipment, and the elimination of waste. It reflects a love of detail. As a result, aside from the country's high-profile industrial behemoths, Japan also has a large number of smaller, specialist companies that represent a potential treasure trove for sharp-eyed stock investors.

Keyence is a leader in factory automation, Daikin Industries has few peers in air-conditioning, Nidec makes electric motors and Makita cordless leaf blowers and hedge trimmers. Meanwhile, Nitto Denko may not be a household name but draws on nearly a century of manufacturing prowess and makes thousands of products that are used in a variety of global industries. Better known are some of the video gaming companies, such as Nintendo in Kyoto, Capcom in Osaka, and Sega-Sammy and Konami in Tokyo.

Fanuc is another good example. Spun off from Fujitsu (the large electronics conglomerate) in 1972, its factories and offices are located in a village at the foot of Mount Fuji.[36] It initially focused on automation, maintenance and repair services overseas, helping Japanese automakers and machinery manufacturers make inroads into foreign markets. The company started to export industrial robots as early as 1977, and over the years it gained control of a large chunk of the global market in highly-specialised computer-controlled machine tools.[37]

As a result, it is now a world leader in robotics and automation. Its charismatic founder, Dr Seiuemon Inaba, who passed away in 2020 at the age of 95, was known in Japan as the king of industrial robots. A real stickler for procedures, processes and cost controls, he ensured that every single yen was accounted for.[38] The company loathes debt and has been criticised for having too much cash on its balance sheet (as have so many other Japanese companies).

Fanuc made headlines in March 2011 after the devastating earthquake and tsunami crippled the Fukushima nuclear power plant. Despite huge disruption to supply chains, the company informed its customers there would not be any delay in deliveries, a big relief to automakers and smartphone producers across the world. But just as soon as Fanuc had made these assurances, it received news that much-needed semiconductors could not be delivered. Mr Inaba instructed his engineers to change the design of the products so they could be made without semiconductors. They worked day and night to ensure that the deliveries were made on time. It established Fanuc's reputation as a company everybody wanted to deal with.

Japan is a stock picker's paradise and some smaller companies have done very well.

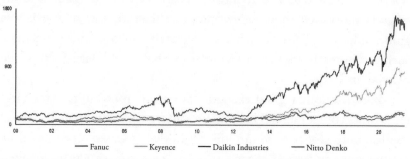

Note: Stock prices are set at 100 on 1 January 2000. The stock codes are 6954 JP (Fanuc), 6861 JP (Keyence), 6367 JP (Daikin Ind) and 6988 JP (Nitto Denko). Source: Yahoo Finance.

Japan is full of "Fanuc-style" firms. Their share prices tend to go their own way – driven by whatever happens in the market for gardening tools, robotics, video gaming or air conditioners – rather than trends in the broader market. This also means that these smaller stocks can go up while the rest of the market falls (and *vice versa*).[39] Indeed, as the Japanese stock market went into its long decline after the 1989 peak, some of these smaller stocks skyrocketed. While the Nikkei 225 fell 80% over two decades, Keyence went up 50x, Nidec 35x, and Pigeon, a producer of high-quality baby goods, 33x.[40]

This teaches us an important lesson – stock markets might be depressed for a long time, but there are always companies that will defy the odds. The trick to spotting them is to have a keen eye for new trends.

How the Japan stock market works

Juliana's Tokyo, the jewel in the crown of late 1980s excess, is back in business. It reopened in 2018 in Osaka and patrons, now a little longer in the tooth, were soon reliving past glories on the raised dance floor, a reproduction of the Tokyo prototype. But are the good old days really returning? After all, some 30 years on, Japan's stock market is still 30% below 1989 levels. There are reasons to be optimistic – for example, corporate governance seems to be improving – but understanding what drives this idiosyncratic market has never been more important. There are three ways to look at the Japanese market.

First, it is highly sensitive to the global business cycle, which makes it a "cyclical" market. Japanese stocks are highly concentrated in the auto and hardware sectors, which react to what happens in the big markets in the US, China and Europe.[41] As Japanese firms have a habit of avoiding massive lay-offs – remember the shuffling of employees by the *keiretsu* – the impact on profits is amplified when there are quick changes in demand. This makes the stock index more volatile and even more sensitive to the cyclical nature of the global economy. Auto and hardware stocks tend to react a bit slower than, say, commodities such as oil, steel or copper, which are driven almost entirely by economic data. As a result, Japan is sometimes labelled a "late cyclical" market. A friend of mine once compared it to the back wheel of an airplane – it goes up last and is the first to come down.

The second approach is to look at changing fashions. The dowdy old *keiretsu* business jacket and tie is starting to be discarded in favour of a smarter and more modern corporate style. If the old *keiretsu* structure really is being dismantled, the drawbridges lowered, Japanese companies might start to churn out hefty dividends. If this is so, investors will applaud. In addition, many of these companies have also started to be far more selective about the products they make to ensure that they are competitive at the global level.

Lastly, remember Mieko Nagaoka, the centenarian swimming champion. The ageing population is creating opportunities for highly specialised smaller companies that reflect the country's broader genius for detail and production processes, part of the secret sauce that makes them the best in the world.

The lessons learned in the past few decades are clear. When market euphoria spills over to nightclub dance floors, don't put all your cash into Japanese stocks. And when the stock market deflates slowly, as it did in Japan, it is best to identify smaller companies that are developing new technology or creating new market trends. That is why Japan is often seen as being a classic example of a stock picker's market.

Endnotes

1   Published in Japanese by Kobunsha, 2014.

2   Based on data for 2019.

3   Cabinet Office, Government of Japan (2019), "Annual Report on the Aging Society: 2019 (Summary)".

4   Ingber 2018.

5   Yi 2019 (*South China Morning Post*, 4 January 2019).

6   In Chapter 7 on Korea and Taiwan, we mentioned that Koreans now work well into their 70s. Note also the changes that have taken place in just one generation. In 1960, Japan still had the lowest life expectancy at birth of any OECD country at 67 years. Mortality conditions in other countries of Asia were worse than in Japan. In China, life expectancy was only 44 years in 1960.

7   Hong Kong launched a pension system in 2000 and although Korea had a pension law in place since 1986, it was not until 2007 that the National Pension Service was set up. This means that most Koreans over 40 are under-funded when it comes to retirement.

8   Lee *at al* 2011, p 16. It was US$26 trillion in 2010.

9   This process also impacts inflation expectations. Japan continues to have the lowest rate of inflation in the G7, despite the Bank of Japan's aggressive efforts since 2013. The primary factor seems to be the persistent downward pressure on inflation expectations and on wage demands.

10   At its peak, Japan accounted for 45% of all global stock market capitalisation.

11   A lot of this was, again, the result of very loose financing conditions required to deal with a re-set in the exchange rate following the 1984 Plaza Accord. After the bubble, the government needed to support companies and banks with a combination of bailouts, allowing them to nurse their balance sheets back to health. As a result, the government found itself hugely in debt and its citizens had lots of assets, so income taxes and goods and services taxes have been steadily on the rise.

12   On 30 December 2020, the last day of trading of the year, the Nikkei 225 stood at 27,444. That is 29.5% below the 38,915 peak in December 1989.

13   Sugawara 1995.

14   Hill 2003.

15   Buffett used the line in 2008 in reference to the follies of large financial institutions exposed by falling home prices.

16   In 1641, the shogun permitted the Dutch to move to the island of Dejima, in the bay of Nagasaki. The shogun had faced resistance from the Japanese who had converted to Christianity. The Dutch had supported him in a conflict with these converts and were allowed to stay. All other Europeans were banned from Japan.

17   Moss and Kintgen 2009.

18   Addicot 2017.

19   The Nikkei 225 is a price-weighted equity index, just like the Dow Jones index in the US. It consists of 225 stocks and was first quoted in September 1950. The Topix is a free-float adjusted market capitalisation-weighted index (just like the S&P500 index in the US) with a base date of 4 January 1968 when it was set at 100 points. It was first quoted on 1 July 1969.

20   This was between 1945 and 1952.

21   What helped as well was very loose financing conditions after the Plaza Accord 1984.

22   Japanese companies often carry too much cash and make acquisitions that don't seem very profitable. See Jones 2015.

23   That name was only adopted in 1983. Before that, it was called Tokyo Shibaura Denki.

24   After the first reports of irregularities, it was revealed that Tosiba's accounting shenenigans had been going on since 2008, putting a US$1.22 billion hole in their profits. A few months later, on 21 July 2015, Toshiba's CEO Hisao Tanaka resigned.

25   Kurumatani served as head of CVC's Japan operations before being appointed Toshiba's CEO. CVC was one of the private equity firms that offered to take Toshiba private. It led to allegations of conflict of interest. Kuramatani resigned in April 2021.

26   "Kiichiro Toyoda, Founder of the Toyota Motor Corporation, Dies." 24 March 2021, History.com <https://www.history.com/this-day-in-history/toyota-founder-dies>.

27   Reuters, 13 June 2018.

28   This is not an unreasonable assumption as nearly all criminal cases that go to trial in Japan end in a guilty verdict; Japan has a 99% conviction rate. See Toshikuni 2019.

29   Abe's plan was for the Bank of Japan to undertake massive Quantitative Easing (QE), large injections of money into the economy in the form of bond purchases. Rates were already at zero in 2013 and they ended up in negative territory in 2016 when they reached -0.1%.

30   Every year, it selects the 400 most profitable large and liquid firms.

31   A unique feature of JPX400's selection criteria is that its algorithm is explicit, transparent, and, with the exception of a small number of "qualitative adjustments", based on publicly available financial performance data. Although the JPX does not publish the underlying rankings, they are highly replicable. These features sharply distinguish the JPX400 from the Nikkei225, whose selection criteria are opaque and determined by Japan's top financial publication, owned by Nikkei Inc. See also Chattopadhyay 2018.

32   The notion that a stock index incentivises managers to change behaviour is possibly also applicable to East Asian economies, such as China, Korea, Singapore or Taiwan, that share cultural roots with Japan as well as patterns of low capital efficiency and weak de facto shareholder rights. Chattopadhyay 2018.

33   A Japanese fund manager summed it up like this: "Corporate Japan now works for you more than it ever has before. You can benefit from rising stock prices as companies are on a journey of increasing returns on the capital you have invested in them and you can benefit from higher returns already achieved in companies in which you own a piece for the long term."

34   IMF, Asia and Pacific Department, 31 July 2017.

35   In 2018, SpaceX CEO Elon Musk announced that by 2023, his company will send Maezawa to the moon as its first private customer.

36   Oshino in the Yamanashi Prefecture.

37   These are so-called computer numerical control (CNC) devices.

38   Fanuc's operating profit margin stood at 17%, a very respectable level for manufacturers.

39   Japanese small-cap stocks generally have low correlations with global markets.

40   All multiples measured from January 1989 to December 2020.

41   Schuenemann et al 2020.

Chapter 10

Travel in Style

Hawkers, curries and cobwebs

Singapore's Maxwell Food Centre does not win many awards for its architecture or aesthetics. It is an unassuming, low-rise building right in the middle of Chinatown. But it takes the top prize for what's on offer inside: enticing aromas, around-the-clock buzz and, the main attraction, delicious street food. The mouth-watering dishes on offer include spicy chilli crab, grilled chicken satay, oyster cake, fragrant fish porridge and oodles of noodles, all freshly prepared at brightly-lit stalls that line a kind of inner courtyard full of hard plastic tables. It's the proverbial Asian melting pot – the flavourful infusion of Chinese, Malay and Indian food, available for just a few Sing dollars, and all to be washed down by gallons of ice-cold beer.

It is tempting to see Asia's stock markets as one big, buzzing hawker centre – Hainanese chicken rice on the left, Indian curry on the right, satay in the middle – but that would be a mistake because they are far more than individual stalls. Rather, the region's stock markets are like a large spider's web, where movements in one can be picked up in another through vibrations along invisible silk fibres. These connections are called investment "styles" and only become visible when we look across all the markets. There are many to choose from, so to get a sense of what they are all about, let's start with the easiest to grasp – "size".

When size is in style

For the moment, let's assume Asia's stock markets have just experienced a rout. For now, it doesn't matter why the market collapsed, all we need to know is that investors ran for the hills. As stock prices came crashing down, they sold their Asian stocks and converted the proceeds into US dollars, always a safe haven in times of turmoil. This left Asian currencies weak and the US dollar strong. The market is in crisis and has entered the first stage of a new cycle after a crash – the "revulsion" stage – a period when most of the bulls have become bears.

Now, let's also assume that after a while, there are signs of the pendulum swinging back in the opposite direction. This transition begins with the "displacement" stage, when a small number of investors, attracted by low valuations, start to buy back into the market. At first, they are swimming against the tide. While most investors are selling or are already long gone, they do exactly the opposite: sell US dollars to buy, for example, Indian rupee, Indonesian rupiah or Korean won to buy shares. As more money comes back into the markets, these Asian currencies get stronger, the US dollar weakens and stocks start to rise again.

At first, most investors pick up the largest stocks in the region: Samsung in Korea, TSMC in Taiwan, Hindustan Unilever in India, Telkom in Indonesia, or China's Tencent that is listed in Hong Kong. Highly liquid, they are the easiest stocks to buy during and just after a sharp market correction. As a rule of thumb, large cap stocks pull ahead in the early stage of a recovery in Asian stock markets. It is as if there is an invisible connection between them signalling that large caps are back in vogue.

The recovery continues and shifts to the "expansion" stage as more and more investors jump back in. Regional currencies continue to strengthen, prices start to rise faster and investors begin to buy the stocks of smaller companies, simply because the big names that pulled ahead earlier now look expensive. There are cheaper alternatives available in mid-caps and small-caps and, suddenly, this is the size that is in favour with investors. It's good news for markets with many smaller listed companies: Japan, for example, but China has plenty, too, as do the markets in Southeast Asia. The more daring investors might decide to look at adventurous "frontier" markets, like Vietnam, Bangladesh and Sri Lanka.

The switch from an obsession with large caps to a frantic search for small caps goes hand in hand with movements in the US dollar. Put another way, investors tend to become interested in smaller stocks when the US dollar weakens, boosting local currencies and the value of their shareholdings. This phenomenon affects all Asia's stock markets, like an invisible thread connecting the region.

Bond yields

This is a very important style. As discussed in an earlier chapter, movements in interest rates – bond yields – often set the tone in markets. Remember that stock markets are like a tug of war between bond yields and profits. For most companies, rising profits are good news, but higher bond yields are not, especially in the absence of any meaningful change in their profits. There are, however, exceptions. Banks, for example, benefit from higher bond yields as they can lend money at a higher rate. Their profits go up as bond yields rise. This is why stock markets that are chock-full with banks, such as Singapore and Thailand, tend to do better in these circumstances, as in the first half of 2021, for example.

Some companies are more sensitive to bond yields than others. Their share prices fall more as bond yields increase and rise faster when they fall. Remember that bond yields discount profits made in the future. Some companies that are not making any money at the moment are expected to generate big profits in the future. Start-ups or firms involved in new technologies yet to go mainstream fall into this category.

Take the electric vehicle industry, for example. It is generally assumed that this will be a massive market in a decade or so but, for now, there are relatively few electric vehicles on the road as the technology is still evolving. Quite a few electric vehicle makers lost money in 2020. The value of these stocks is determined by the prospects of big profits in the distant future. The discount rate helps us to put a price tag on those future profits. And, like sushi sitting on supermarket shelves, the further we look into the future, the bigger the discount.

Discount rates are set by bond yields. So, if bond yields rise, the discount we give to future profits is much bigger. That means that the value we assign to future profits is lower, more so for firms that have all their value married to profits to be made at a much later date. When bond yields rise, their stock prices will come down faster than the rest of the market. This is exactly what happened when bond yields rose in late 2020 and early 2021. Chinese electric vehicle stocks fell sharply, but companies with highly visible earnings, such as consumer brands, did much better.

Commodities, exports and governance

This time, let's assume China's economy is gaining strength and mainland construction companies are busy building new high-rise apartment blocks and laying tracks for the latest high-speed rail connection. Across the nation, factories are humming at full speed and industrial and consumer companies need commodities – oil, steel, copper, aluminium, zinc and palm oil – and their prices are rising fast.

However, higher commodity prices don't necessarily mean higher share prices. Different stock markets react differently. Take rising oil prices, for example. This is good news for Thai refiners and Thailand's stock market pushes higher. China's small group of oil refiners benefit, too. But it is the reverse for India, a big importer of oil. Indian stocks tend to be put under pressure when oil prices move sharply higher.[1] In this example, commodity prices are the invisible connection that impact similar types of stocks (refiners) in different parts of Asia and can simultaneously cast a long shadow over a whole market (India).

There are many other styles that connect markets. Sometimes exporters are in vogue, while on other occasions firms that serve domestic markets are in demand. Not surprisingly, movements in currencies play a major role in this narrative. If exporters are "in style", Taiwan and Korea – the two large (tech) export markets in Asia – tend to do better than, say, Indonesia, a mostly domestic market.

"Governance" can also act as the invisible thread that runs through markets. This is especially the case after a big market scandal when people want to focus on strong companies with good reputations. Korea and Japan generally score lower in corporate governance rankings because of the multitude of cross-holdings in their *chaebol* and *keiretsu*. The structure of Indian and Taiwanese companies is much more straightforward, so they tend to perform better when "governance" is a force in the market.

The rise of Asia's retail army

Maybe they were bored, stuck at home during the COVID-19 pandemic. Perhaps it was the proliferation of online trading apps. Whatever the reason, mirroring event in the US, Asian retail investors have dived into stock markets in numbers never seen before. In Korea, they traded more than the large pension funds and investment institutions combined in 2020.* Even in Indonesia, where retail investors were previously pretty much non-existent, there was a surge in the number of new trading accounts being opened. Even my 25-year-old nephews in Jakarta, Anur and Vandi, joined in the fun, piggybacking on the big rally in Asian stocks.

These individual retail investors are a tech savvy bunch, meeting online in messaging groups and chat forums to discuss the latest moves in the market. Quite a few also invest with money borrowed from banks, brokers, and friends of family,** an approach that can add considerable misery to your investment portfolio as well as your marriage.

Some professional institutional investors have expressed concerns about these armies of amateurs increasing volatility and over-inflating share prices. But there are also benefits. Many of these new Asian investors are much more willing to invest in smaller stocks often overlooked by the likes of large pension funds. And while it is true that some have a "casino" approach, many others may invest for the long term. But whatever their motives, it's people like Anur and Vandi who are part of a trend that is starting to change the way Asian stock markets behave.

* By end 2020, Korean retail investors accounted for nearly 80% of all trading in the market. The total amount traded that year was more than all trading done in the ten years prior, added together. That was the highest in Asia. In 2020 in Taiwan, retail trading accounted for 60% of all activity in the market, in India it stood at 58%, in Thailand it was 40% and in Malaysia it was 35%. Not all markets disclose information on retail investors' activity.
** Borrowing from your bank or broker to play in the stock market is margin trading. Margin trading typically accounted for about 12% of total market cap in Korea from 2010 to 2019, but rose to 25% in 2020.

Let it all soak in

Travel is exciting. Stumbling into a shop on a tiny lane in Bali, sampling street food at a hawker stall run by a grinning chef in Singapore, renting bikes and getting lost in the paddy fields of Yangshuo, or steaming in an *onsen* in central Japan – these are the experiences that make travel special and meaningful. But travel also calls for contemplation, and at some point it is nice to sit down, put your feet up, imbibe a refreshing ale and let it all soak in. And so it is with a journey through Asia's stock markets.

Thinking in terms of styles can help investors to see the big picture. Something that is hard to spot when only looking at a single market becomes a visible thread connecting all the markets in the region. If large caps are in vogue not just in China but also in Korea, Singapore and India, it tells us something about the state of mind investors are in. The process can be hugely rewarding. An investor who can spot the next change in style will be the first to enjoy the rise in stock prices before the crowd arrives on the scene. It's like being first in the queue at the popular Hainanese chicken rice stall in Maxwell Food Centre.

Endnotes

1   This is a simplified version of reality. For example, when oil prices are rising from low levels, Indian stocks might not react, but if prices move to a level deemed to be really negative, stocks can fall very quickly. Finance geeks call this a non-linear reaction.

Chapter 11

Goodness! Responsible Investing

How Luckin Coffee didn't live up to its name

For a business named Luckin, its luck sure ran out quickly. This ambitious upstart, which opened its first stores in October 2017, was meant to push Starbucks in China aside and take over as the country's leading chain of coffee shops. The approach was simple. First, get people hooked on the app where all sorts of vouchers and discounts were available, and worry about profits later. Memberships and visible foot traffic to the stores were more important than actual sales. Prices were also much cheaper than those charged at Starbucks, offering aspirational Chinese consumers an affordable alternative to bland instant coffee or cheap canned offerings. Luckin Coffee had everything that a unicorn start-up needed: an all-star founding team, a famed CEO, a ton of money and a relatively untapped market.

What could possibly go wrong? As it happens, just about everything.

At first, all seemed to be going to plan. By late 2018, just a year after the launch, Luckin Coffee was running 2,000 stores across China. Investors wanted in and valued the company at US$2 billion. By May 2019, it had listed on the NASDAQ in the US and Luckin's value had jumped to US$4 billion. The number of stores doubled to more than 4,000, and at the peak, the company's market cap ballooned to US$12 billion. Watch out Starbucks, Luckin Coffee's on your tail.

Turned out, it was all froth. Things started to go wrong when Muddy Waters, the prominent US short-seller, accused the company of fabricating sales.[1] At first, the company denied any wrongdoing but admitted after an internal investigation that the sales numbers had been inflated by the equivalent of hundreds of millions of dollars. The stock was delisted from the NASDAQ and, on 17 December 2020, the *Financial Times* reported that the US Securities and Exchange Commission had hit Luckin Coffee with a US$180 million penalty for "defrauding investors by materially misstating revenue and expenses, inflating its growth rates and understating its losses".[2] The chain is still operating in China.

The Luckin saga illustrates the risks that come with single-stock investments. You can lose a lot of money. It also shows the importance of thinking about corporate governance, how a company is run and who runs it (remember Toshiba). After all, buying stocks is, in essence, an investment in the integrity and ingenuity of the people who are in charge of the business. Turns out Luckin had lots of ingenuity, especially with numbers, but zero integrity.

Luckin was not so lucky.

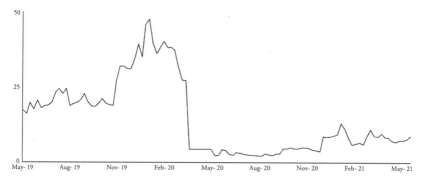

Note: The stock code is LKNCY US. This is an ADR traded in the US.
Source: Yahoo Finance

The oligarchs' playground and policy risk in China

Luckin-style deception has always been an issue for investors, especially in Asia. For one, it is not always clear who the real owners of a business are. Quite often, a family controls the shares of a typical Asian firm by means of stock pyramids[3] and cross-shareholdings. Their ownership is hidden by layers of companies, and it is not always clear what they want out of a business, so their interests are unlikely to be closely aligned with those of investors.

Korea's *chaebol* and Japan's business groups are good examples of complex ownership structures which, when drawn on a piece of paper, look like a bowl of noodles. This creates strong defences against corporate raiders and hostile takeovers, especially in countries where weak legal systems and poor law enforcement mean that few tools are available to mount a proper legal defence.[4]

But it's not just families that we have to watch. Across Asia, relations between businesses, politicians, governments and regulators have always been fuzzy. I met companies in Indonesia in the 1990s that listed on the stock market to avoid being forced to sell to the ruling family of the day, the Suharto clan. Being listed provided them with some comfort, as any takeover had to be done in broad daylight, for all to see. For a far more recent and higher profile example of how governments and larger companies can be at loggerheads, look no further than China. As discussed in Chapter 4, Alibaba and a number of other leading internet companies have run into trouble with the regulator because their commercial power and reach has started to concern Beijing.

Mixing politics and business is, of course, not exclusive to China. In 2015, a member of an Indian parliamentary committee on health made the remarkable claim that there were no health risks associated with tobacco use. The media wasted no time in pointing out the obvious – the man in question, Shyama Charan Gupta, was one of the largest players in the Indian tobacco business.[5] And in Indonesia, the former presidential candidate and chairman of Golkar, one of the largest political parties, was Aburizal Bakrie of the Bakrie Group, which has interests that stretch across the property, agri-business, construction, media and mining industries.

In Asia, be aware that politics is often the playground of oligarchs. And in China, in particular, never underestimate the potential scale of policy risks, both positive and negative. While Jack Ma and the internet sector feel the wrath of the regulators, companies linked to the semiconductor industry benefit from policy support as China's strives to boost home-grown technologies.

The ABC of ESG

In the past few years, corporate governance and investing for the good of society and the planet in general has become a hot topic. It's a global trend that arrived in Asia in many different guises – responsible, social, ethical, green, or sustainable investing – which the financial industry now groups under one banner: environmental, social and governance (ESG).

What started out as a rather vague wish list has hardened into very clear guidelines with very real outcomes. For example, some asset managers no longer invest in companies linked to fossil fuels and banks are under increasing pressure to stop lending to these firms. Broadly speaking, the idea is that, in addition to profits, investors should also look at the impact companies have on the environment and society as well as how they are run. And it has been a hit. By 2020, ESG-aligned investments around the world totalled more than US$40 trillion, the equivalent of 40x Apple's market cap.

Like most new ideas, it is actually anything but. Jewish documents dating back 3,500 years lectured about the responsibility that came with investing. And in 1613, a group of Dutch East India Company stockholders claimed that the corporation was badly run, an early attempt at a shareholder revolt.[6] Much later, in the 18th century, Quakers and Methodists in the US laid out clear guidelines to followers about the type of companies in which they should invest.

These factors were relevant long before ESG became common currency in modern financial markets. In 1971, a group of Methodists in the US established the PaxWorld Fund that avoided investment in businesses involved in armaments, alcohol and gambling.[7] In the 1980s, pressure was building on investors to avoid investing in South Africa, which at the time pursued harsh racial segregation policies (apartheid). Environmental disasters also played a role in raising investor awareness. A gas leak at a pesticide plant in the Indian city of Bhopal killed thousands of people in 1984, and five years later, Exxon Valdez spilled millions of gallons of crude oil into Alaska's Prince William Sound, the worst oil spill in US history until the Deepwater Horizon disaster in 2010.

Then the world started to wake up to the dangers of climate change and in 2008 to 2009, the Global Financial Crisis reminded investors that corporate governance standards were still pretty lax, even in the most advanced economies and markets. As a result, climate change and a series of corporate scandals put more "E" and "G" into ESG. More recently, the outbreak of COVID-19 showed the importance of "S". The pandemic brought out the best and the worst of the corporate world – while some carmakers switched to making ventilators, a lot of attention was also paid to how companies treated their employees during the crisis.

Asia has its own take on responsible investing. In the past few years, Islamic banking and finance has boomed in Indonesia and Malaysia, leading to the launch of religious stock market indices. They include the Jakarta Islamic Index (JII),[8] four Sharia compliant indices in Malaysia and in India, Dharma indices[9] cater to Hindu, Buddhist, Sikh and Jain investors. Alcohol and meat processing firms are often excluded, along with some defence and pharmaceutical companies. In Dharma indices, financial stocks are included but this is often not the case in Islamic indices.[10]

But the biggest force pushing the ESG agenda is generational. Millennials, born in the 1980s and 1990s, tend to be far more aware of environmental and social issues than their parents. Having grown up in a digital age, they are also more likely to use a range of different electronic investment tools. This powerful combination of demographics and technology bodes well for the future of ESG investments. The millennials will inherit trillions of dollars from the baby boomers – the largest ever transfer of intergenerational wealth[11] – so it is no surprise that investment managers come calling as the number of ESG funds in Asia increases. The range of investment options is now deeper and broader. For example, ESG exchange traded funds (ETFs) are now available – Yuanta, a financial firm, launched Taiwan's first ESG-focused ETF in August 2019.[12]

But, as ever, the ancient principle of *caveat emptor* – buyer beware – still applies. It is wise to exercise caution about products that claim to be ESG investments. The concept remains broad and largely ill-defined, and some funds include holdings in companies that struggle to pass the

ESG sniff test. At the same time, consultants and equity analysts are grappling with the issue of how to measure ESG factors when it comes to company profits and valuations. It's not easy[13] as crucial data points are not always available, and levels of disclosure vary.

According to a report by Ping An, a leading finance and insurance company in China, an increasing number of mainland Chinese companies now release annual ESG reports. In 2019, 85% of companies in the blue chip China Securities Index (CSI) 300 did so, up from 54% in 2013. However, among those companies that disclose ESG reports, only 12% had audited reports. The report – "ESG in China", released in June 2020 – also noted that, on average, the scope and quality of ESG disclosures among CSI300 companies ranked the lowest among firms that are part of major stock market indices in Asia.

Aside from a lack of data, the broader problem is the subjective nature of ESG investment. What I find to be good or bad about a company reflects my personal values, which might well differ from those of others. It's best to do some research into what a fund considers to be sustainable, to see if it matches your own preferences. On the plus side, perhaps the biggest benefit is that there is little downside from socially responsible investing. There is evidence that firms which adopt better ESG practices are less likely to experience large drops in their share prices.[14] This is probably because socially responsible firms tend to be better run and are less likely to be caught up in controversies and legal problems.

Many of us want to make a positive contribution to the world that we live in. One way to do so is through our investments in companies that take environmental, social and governance issues to heart. ESG may be a relatively new force in Asian financial markets, but all the indications are that it is only going to get stronger. As ESG evolves, so will the tools we use to measure its impact on stock prices. And look on the bright side – the principles behind ESG should help investors avoid being burnt by companies such as Luckin Coffee.

Endnotes

1   Muddy Waters, the prominent US short-seller, has a good track record in this area.

2   "Luckin Coffee to pay $180m in accounting fraud settlement", *Financial Times*, 17 December 2020 <https://www.ft.com/content/4db3b074-829f-4f1c-a256-11c7e28a31d1>.

3   This is how a simple pyramid works: company A is 51% owned by company B. This company B is 51% owned by company C. If you own 51% of company C, you have effective control over company A.

4   Claessens and Fan 2002.

5   Ghosh 2015.

6   Petram 2011, p 32.

7   Louche *et al* 2012.

8   The first Islamic stock index was launched in Indonesia on 3 July 2000.

9   Louche *et al* 2012.

10 A survey suggested the negative screens most used by religious organisations are the following: nuclear weapons (70%), military armaments (68%), tobacco (62%), pornography (60%) and abortion (51%). See Louche [et al] 2012.

11 Srivinas and Goradia 2019.

12 Cruz 2020.

13 Berg *et al* 2020 looked at data from six prominent rating agencies – MSCI ESG KLD Stats, Sustainalytics, Vigeo Eiris (Moody's), RobecoSAM (S&P Global), Asset4 (Refinitiv) and MSCI— and found all sorts of differences.

14 Hoepner *et al* 2016.

Chapter 12

The Future of Asia

Spirits, *feng shui* and stock market forecasters

In Java, spirits are everywhere. At my mother-in-law's house in south Jakarta, they were said to live near the cemetery. In our own house in central Jakarta, they occupy a small alley that runs behind the kitchen and the garden. Spirits like to hide in all kinds of places – bushes, temples, houses or mountaintops. The woods are full of them and some have a particular liking for banyan trees, where they can disappear in the tangle of roots and branches.

There are similar ancient beliefs elsewhere in Asia. India has its *vastu shastra*, which is generally more concerned with architectural matters and act as a guide to constructing a happy home. The Philippines has its *manghuhulas*, or fortune-tellers, as does Hong Kong's Temple Street. For bigger issues, a visit to the city's incense-filled Wong Tai Sin Temple is the place to go for advice, and before making an important decision. This often involves shaking fortune sticks (and parting with a few dollars).

The big bucks, however, are made by Hong Kong's traditional *feng shui* masters. *Feng shui* is the Chinese traditional practice of aligning objects in their environment so as to create harmony, and *feng shui* experts are also consulted about the most propitious date to get married or move into a new house. In Hong Kong, *feng shui* is everywhere.

The two bronze lions, Stephen and Stitt, which sit in front of HSBC's headquarters in Hong Kong, are considered guardians of wealth and prosperity.

When the two lions returned after a cleaning in late 2020, a *feng shui* master was called in. He performed his rituals and predicted that good fortune would return to HSBC "in mid-December – 49 days after the two lions had their eyes painted red".[1] And so it was. HSBC's share price had fallen to a 25-year low and a few months after the lions were returned to their original location in front of the bank with their eyes duly dotted with red paint, the stock rallied more than 30%.

The HSBC lions now located at the bank's headquarters in Hong Kong were, in the 1920s, located outside the bank's building in Shanghai, as pictured above. It was then, as it is now, a tradition to pat the lion's paw for good luck, as can be seen in the picture. Source: Wikimedia Commons <https://commons.wikimedia.org/w/index.php?curid=74861300>.

Unfortunately, when it comes to investing in stocks, most of us do not have access to such unworldly gifts of foresight. At cocktail parties, dinners and barbecues, people always have a view on the market and want to know how my predictions have turned out. But they confuse the art of prediction, the stuff of the spirit world, with the more mundane existence of stock market strategists, who inhabit a very different universe, where little is certain and nothing is pre-determined.

We live in a world of hard data and spreadsheets, and need to constantly reassess our views and opinions as markets move and new information becomes available, and, of course, be prepared to eat humble pie when we are wrong. One very useful tool when it comes to forecasting is to take the opposite approach and look back to see what we can learn from the past.

The rear-view mirror

Let's start by looking at how Asian stock markets have performed since the start of the millennium. Assume we invested $100 in each market in January 2000. Fast forward 21 years and these investments would have grown to $936 on the Hang Seng China Enterprises Index (HSCEI), $795 in Shenzhen, $746 in the Indian market, $626 in Indonesia and $746 in Thailand.[2] Not bad at all.

A similar investment in the US S&P500 would be worth $284 but the $100 invested in Japan would have grown to only $104. Remember, after peaking in 1989, Japanese markets continued to fall until 2009. Meanwhile, our investment in Singapore would be worth $142. This tells us that there are no easy conclusions to be drawn – over a period of 21 years, the performance of each stock market has been quite different. This also tells us nothing about the future. It is quite possible that the reverse will happen in the next two decades and that Japan and Singapore will do spectacularly well.

We can, however, draw important lessons from this data. For example, some Southeast Asian markets were among the best performers because they were still recovering from the Asian Financial Crisis in 2000. Stocks were cheap and their economies were in tatters. But local businesses were just starting to pick themselves up, like Bangkok's indomitable sandwich man. That was a good moment to buy into these markets, straight after a market crash.

Next, let's look at the best performing stocks in Asia in the last 20 years. This, too, is a mixed bag,[3] but two types of companies stand out. The first are those that emerged as global leaders in a fast-growing industry. A good example is China's Sunny Optical, which leads the world in making specialised lenses used in cameras, smartphones, cars, security surveillance and robots. Another is Japan's Keyence, a leader in robotics. There are also several Indian names in this group, the successful IT and pharma companies referred to in Chapter 6.

In the second group are domestic market leaders, companies that have unmatched distribution capabilities and phenomenally strong local brands. Think of Tencent, Alibaba and Moutai in China, or Nippon Paint in Japan. While not in the top ten, other strong performers in this category are Hindustan Unilever in India and Astra International in Indonesia.

History tells us that buying when the chips are down and focusing on either (emerging) global or local industry leaders was the best way to make money in Asia in the past two decades. We can add this knowledge to our investment toolkit. Let's now swivel the mirror around and ask what Asian stock markets might look like in the future. This involves using different tools for different time frames.

If we look at the very near future – say a few hours, days or weeks – it's news that dominates stock prices. This can include earnings reports, a merger or a takeover, the launch of a product, a corporate scandal or the announcement of new regulations. Swings in bond yields are important, too, and looking at technical indicators like the relative strength index (RSI) also helps. The RSI is based on average gains and losses, with a value between zero and 100; a move towards 70 indicates excessive buying at high-price conditions and a reading lower than 30 points to oversold conditions, that is, selling below its true value.

The medium term outlook covers the next few quarters, stretching out to a year or more. To answer questions like how fast companies are growing, how the market values a stock and the likely direction of bond yields requires an assessment of earnings growth, valuations and policy statements made by the US Federal Reserve. But if we look at stock prices a long way out, say over a decade, things get much murkier. There is so much we don't know about 2030 – which companies will still be around, advances in medicine, the impact of climate change, what earnings will be like, and how high or low interest rates will be – that it looks like an impossible task.

But there are also things that we do know. For example, we know that the population will have aged ten years and we can be pretty sure that advances in technology will continue at a rapid clip. This has huge implications for the consumer sector, healthcare and the tech supply chain. As China's economy grows, the geopolitical outlook may be very different, too. These tectonic shifts can provide us with at least an inkling of what 2030 might look like.

Let's start with demographics.

Why demographics matter

Demographics have a lot in common with the weather – everybody seems to have an opinion on the subject. The planet either has too many people for its own good, ageing will spur social collapse or there are too few babies. In some corners of Asia, such as Korea and Japan, there are fears about what rapid declines in population levels will mean for the future of these countries.

However, unlike the weather, demographics provide us with a lot of certainty. We can measure pretty accurately how fast different societies are ageing and forecast with great confidence that India is going to overtake China as the most populous nation by 2025. But there's more. While languages, cultures, religions and cuisines may differ widely, there are also common demographic threads linking the region. Every day, at dinner tables throughout Asia, middle class families tuck into comfort food, share details about their day and toast each other's successes. And as their incomes rise, families tend to have fewer children, which spurs a near-universal reshuffling of where and how people shop and spend their money.

As growing financial resources are dedicated to a tighter, smaller, nuclear household, new goals come into focus, irrespective of whether you are Indian, Korean or Thai. For example, it means more money for travel. The Chinese enjoy visiting Korea, Indonesian Muslims make the pilgrimage to Mecca (the haj), Hong Kongers fly to Thailand for annual health check-ups and Indians want to visit casinos in Singapore. These families also spend more on their wellbeing – from medical care and yoga to insurance and ayurvedic medicines – as well as on educating their children.

Then there are the trends that are unique to certain parts of Asia. One of the most prominent is the rise of China's empty-nesters, households where the only child has left home to make his or her way in the world. These empty-nesters will shape the consumer landscape in China.[4] By 2030, this group of 40 to 65-year-olds with an annual income of over USD50,000 will outnumber their counterparts in the US. In 2020, they were only about a third of the size of their US peer group, so the empty-nesters are a very fast-growing bunch of super consumers. They are in the market for overseas travel, upscale restaurants, good wine, household renovations and gym memberships.

There is another demographic trend that we can forecast with a reasonable degree of certainty: even more Asians will flock to cities from the countryside, especially in China and Indonesia. This "urbanisation rate", as demographers call it, is currently 51%[5] in Asia and is expected to rise to 58% by 2030. This is not surprising because cities offer jobs, education and opportunities, while the simple, impecunious life on the farm has lost its allure years ago.

What is a surprise is that Asians will no longer simply flock to mega cities such as Shanghai, Tokyo, Jakarta or Mumbai. Many will head to smaller and less well-known places such as Makassar in Indonesia, Cebu in the Philippines, Chon Buri in Thailand and Surat in India. As the big cities reach saturation point, these will become the new growth hotspots where new arrivals live, work and shop. The majority of Asia's urban population will not live in giant metropolises but in mid-sized cities,[6] whose numbers swelled from 99 in 1990 to 269 in 2020 and are forecast to rise to 330 in 2030.[7]

Aside from smaller families and urbanisation, there is another powerful demographic force shaping Asia. Ageing represents possibly the biggest social transformation of the 21st century. Here, Japan leads the way, while Taiwan and Korea are fast following in its footsteps, with China not far behind. Experiences in Japan show us that that the elderly like to stay active, go swimming, make use of robots, work longer and save for retirement, which has been a boon to wealth managers, insurance companies, stock markets and, as seen in Chapter 9 on Japan, sellers of incontinence devices.

China and US

Beyond demographics, a second trend that will shape Asia and its stock markets over the next decade is the relationship between China and the US. A good place to start is China's entry into the WTO in 2001. According to John J Mearsheimer, a professor of political science who specialises in great power politics, it was a seminal moment in modern history:[8]

> The US, over the course of the 1990s and the first decade-and-a-half of the 2000s, went to great places to make China more and more economically powerful. We, in fact, have created a potential peer competitor. This is remarkably foolish.

In his view, the US and China are now locked in a struggle for power and influence in the region. The theatres of conflict are not battlefields but the crucial technologies that drive the modern world. The stakes are high – whoever wins this struggle is likely to become the dominant superpower in the 21st century. And the weapons of choice are computer chips, the semiconductors which run everything from personal computers, smartphones and electric vehicles to televisions, washing machines and refrigerators, not to mention military applications.

Asia is central to this narrative. Korea's Samsung Electronics is the largest manufacturer of semiconductors, followed by Intel in the US. Samsung is what is called an integrated chip maker: it designs chips and then produces them itself. This is in contrast to Taiwan's TSMC, which is the world's largest pure foundry: it makes chips designed by other companies. US companies such as Qualcomm and Broadcom are among the biggest "fabless semiconductor companies" which design chips and outsource their production to companies like TSMC. Taiwan's Mediatek is another chip designer which has a big following with China's smartphone producers.

While China is a producer of basic computer chips, the reality is that the country's electronics industry is still heavily reliant on US, Taiwanese, Korean and Japanese suppliers for many important components, particularly high-end semiconductors. China's leaders have made closing this technology gap a major policy priority.

One very high profile area of competition is 5G,[9] the fifth generation of wireless technology. 5G's super-fast connectivity has many uses. It can enable download of a high-definition movie in a few seconds or stream several movies at the same time, and also enable thousands of robots and sensors in a factory to interact with each other simultaneously. Ericsson, Samsung, Nokia and China's Huawei and ZTE are all major players in 5G equipment and they all need chips made by Samsung or TSMC.

Huawei dominates the global 5G wireless infrastructure and is at the centre of the tech power struggle between the US and China. The US claims Huawei is a national security threat and has imposed sanctions on the company, reducing its access to crucial components, particularly computer chips. The dispute has spread and US allies like Australia and the UK have blocked Huawei from their 5G networks.

As this geopolitical struggle unfolds, it makes sense for countries to support strategically important technologies. This explains China's drive to make rapid advances in chip technology. China's key producer is Semiconductor Manufacturing International Corporation (SMIC), based in Shanghai, but its access to US technology, like Huawei, has also been restricted. Unless Beijing's domestic initiatives to move up the tech ladder bear fruit – billions of dollars have been invested in semiconductor development – China will remain years behind Taiwanese, Korean and US producers.

Self-reliance is a theme that is also visible in other parts of the region. India, for example, wants to ensure that it has the capability to grow its pharma industries and aims to make the pharmaceutical ingredients needed to produce pills, powders and drugs domestically. The government has made money available to make this happen, which should be good news for some of its leading listed pharma makers.

It's not just technology that is important, but also access to food and energy. Cultivating secure, stable and advanced seed varieties is a crucial element of China's efforts to beef up the nation's food security. And while China has huge resources in terms of metals and minerals, it still needs plenty of oil and gas from abroad to power its factories and warm its houses. That's why it's investing heavily to ensure that China is a world leader in renewable energy, particularly wind, solar and hydro.

Green energy also helps to reduce the suffocating air pollution that has blighted major cities like Beijing for years. The government officially declared war on pollution in 2014 and since then, air quality has improved and the renewable share of the country's energy mix has risen. Again, it is never wise to underestimate the power of policy support in China.

India, another big importer of oil, also faces massive pollution problems. Of the top 20 most polluted cities on the planet, 14 are now in India.[10] No wonder renewable energy is a policy priority. The rapid decline in the prices of solar panels and wind turbines means that renewable energy is now cheaper than coal-fired power, traditionally the least expensive source of power generation in India.

Talking of policy support, look no further than the electric vehicle industry. By far the largest market for the sale of electric cars, China was home to nearly half of the world's production in 2020. While the leading models are international brands, Chinese companies dominate the component supply chain. When I first visited Shenzhen in southern China in 1990 and marked my first day in the country by getting bashed on the nose, bicycles were still abundant. The city now boasts the most electric vehicles of any city in the world, including the largest e-bus and e-taxi fleets.[11]

The battle for technological supremacy will be fought for many years to come. Investors should follow the contours of this narrative closely as it is likely to create many winners and losers in the region's equity markets.

What to do in a gold rush
"Gold!" cried San Francisco newspaper publisher Samuel Brannan, when he walked the city's streets holding aloft a flashy flake of gold.

It was March 1848 and the California Gold Rush was underway, with some 300,000 people arriving in the hope of making a fortune.

Miners of all nationalities set up camp and many also headed straight for the most ubiquitous forms of entertainment: drinking and gambling. In the mining towns, tables made of planks with sheets of canvas for shade became rowdy gambling saloons. Miners paid to watch performances on a stage made of packing crates. One popular show was called "The Bandit Chief", which one member of the audience described as "filled with the usual amount of fighting and terrible speeches".[12]

As for making large amounts of money, only a handful of miners struck gold and Brannan was one of them. But he did it without getting his hands dirty. Brannan became the first Gold Rush millionaire to get rich by not mining gold, but by selling picks, shovels and pans.[13] His hardware store made enormous profits. Levi Strauss and Jacob Davis followed a similar path. They stitched together strong, practical pairs of work pants for the miners who worked in tough conditions. Inventing the first "jeans" made Levi Strauss famous but he and his partner also had a lucrative side business selling shovels, buckets and wheelbarrows.

The moral of the story is simple: don't pan for gold – it's dangerous, dirty, back-breaking work that rarely changes your life. Instead, sell the stuff that the gold miners need: margins are fat and there's no shortage of customers. Or invest further down the supply chain in entertainment and saloons.

And so it is with picking stocks and sectors. When a big, new investment story is in full cry – think clean energy or electric vehicles – everyone is trying to get a piece of the action. Crowded markets can get very expensive, very quickly. Competition is intense and there are many casualties. Think about the picks and shovels. Fast forward to today and the modern equivalents are parts for solar panels or wind turbines, and battery components for electric vehicles. They may not be fancy but they are often a much safer bet for investors.

How a trade works

At the grocery store, prices are clearly marked on a shelf. Not so in stock markets. There, prices move continuously and the price quoted on a screen is simply the last one someone paid for it. There's no guarantee that you'll get that price if you place an order to buy or sell shares. That is because stock exchanges match buyers and sellers. Buyers "ask" for a price, while sellers "bid". When bid and ask are the same, a trade takes place.

This is usually a simple, orderly process unless there are rapid movements in share prices. Then, circuit breakers are put in place to let the market cool off. For example, the Shanghai and Shenzhen stock exchanges suspend trading for 15 minutes when the CSI300 Index rises or falls by 5% or more from its previous close for the first time in a day. If the index rises or falls by 7% or more from the previous close, trading will be halted for the day.

To understand how a trade works, its best to walk through the process of buying a stock.

Day 1: 20 July

Let's assume you purchase 100 shares in a listed company. The share price is HK$20, so the total purchase price is HK$2,000. The date is 20 July and we call this the Trade Day or "T-Day". Once the trading day ends, your bank (or broker) takes HK$2,000 (plus charges) from your account. However, the stocks are not in your account yet.

Day 2: 21 July

This is known and as "Trade Day + 1" or "T+1". The money has already been debited from your bank account but you haven't received the shares yet. In the background, however, things are moving. The stock exchange collects the purchase amount and charges from the bank.

Day 3: 22 July

This is "T+2". The shares are taken from the account of the person who sold them and put into your account. If, in the meantime, the share price has risen from HK$20 to HK$30, the value shown in your account will be HK$3,000 (100 shares x HK$30). On the same day, the HK$2,000 taken from your bank account on T-Day is added to the seller's bank account.

A trade takes three full days to complete. This time-consuming process will probably become obsolete in the next few years due to Blockchain, a new technology that is already used to trade Bitcoin, a digital currency. Blockchain reduces trading time to a few seconds, which has implications for traditional stock markets. For example, the same stock could be traded multiple times in the same day, dramatically improving market liquidity.*

---

* Various initiatives are underway across Asia. For example, in Hong Kong, the exchange is working with the Australian Stock Exchange to develop a blockchain platform focused on over-the-counter trading. In India, the NSE, along with ICICI Bank, IDFC Bank, Kotak Mahindra Bank, RBL

Bank and HDFC Securities have used blockchain start-up Elemental's blockchain to test know-your-customer procedures and real time information updates using blockchain. In Japan, the Japan Exchange Group (JPX) worked with IBM in 2016 to explore blockchain's use in trade and settlement for low liquidity markets. It is also working with Nomura Research Institute to explore the reach of blockchain technology in security market processes. In Korea, the exchange launched a Korea Startup Market (KSM), where equity shares of start-up companies can be traded in the open market, using blockchain-based technology. For more details, see "The Potential for Blockchain Technology in Public Equity Markets in Asia", OECD Capital markets series, OECD, 2018.]

Back to the future and good luck

So, after our long journey through Asia's stock markets, what have we learnt? We know a little about how Asia might look like in 2030. It will be greyer, technology will be far more advanced, more people will live in smaller cities, and they will generally be richer and spend more money on themselves. We also know from past experiences that investing in leaders in new industries, difficult-to-beat domestic brands and companies with unmatched distribution capabilities is a profitable strategy. History also teaches us to invest in Asian stock markets when they are out of favour, straight after a stock market rout. And, like making money in the gold rush, it is best not to always focus on the shiny stuff, but to go for the shovels, jeans or start a saloon.

All this information should be part of the toolkit for investing in Asian stock markets. But looking ahead, we also need to be both humble and nimble. The future is bound to be full of surprises, and without the services of Javanese *dukun* or Hong Kong *feng shui* masters, the best advice is to be open to new ideas and react quickly to events.

Finally, be optimistic. Equity markets are generally associated with optimism, while bond investors tend to be bearish and cautious. And, from my long experience of living and working in Asia, optimists always have more fun.

Good luck.

Endnotes

1   Wang, *The Standard*, 23 October 2020.

2   These are total returns, price increases and dividend payments, measured in US dollars.

3   This focuses on the best performers in what is now the top 100 largest stocks across Asia. They include the following top ten performers: Bajaj Finance in India, Sunny Optical, TAL Education, Alibaba Health Information, Technology Shenzhou International, Tencent, Moutai, Techtronics, Netease in Hong Kong and China, and Celltrion in Korea. This is a selection outside Japan. In Japan, we find top performers such as M3, Nippon Paint and Keyence.

4   Global Demographics, a consultancy, estimates that this group of 40 to 64-year-olds will contribute 55% of total urban consumption in China by 2028.

5   United Nations, Department of Economic and Social Affairs, Population Division, *World Urbanization Prospects 2018: Highlights.*

6   In 2018, 55% of Asia's population will live in cities with fewer than 1 million inhabitants. This growth in medium-sized cities is a global phenomenon. Note also that in 1990, there were ten cities with more than ten million inhabitants, hosting 153 million people, which represents less than 7% of the global urban population. Note that the number of megacities has tripled to 33, and most of them are in Asia, including five that have recently joined the group: Bangalore, Bangkok, Jakarta, Lahore and Madras. By 2020, Tokyo's population is projected to begin to decline and Delhi is projected to become the most populous city in the world in 2028. By 2030, Asia's largest cities will be Delhi, Tokyo, Shanghai and Dhaka. See United Nations, Department of Economic and Social Affairs, Population Division, *World Urbanization Prospects 2018: Highlights.*

7   United Nations, Department of Economic and Social Affairs, Population Division, *World Urbanization Prospects 2018: Highlights.*

8   "US foolishly fed the rise of China: Famed international relations expert John Mearsheimer", *India Today*, 20 June 2020. See also his website for many more articles on the topic of US-China rivalry.

9   1G brought us the brick phone in the 1980s, 2G came in the late 1990s in the form of SMS text messaging and 3G arrived in the early 2000s with voice, video and data services. After 2010, 4G allowed for continuous video streaming and all sorts of other applications; 5G is super-fast connectivity, fast enough to download a high-definition movie in a few seconds; and 6G – still on the engineers' drawing boards – will be even faster.

10   IQAir 2019.

11   Li *et al* 2020.

12   "Gaming and Entertainment in Gold Rush Towns", PBS website <https://www.pbs.org/wgbh/americanexperience/features/goldrush-gaming-and-entertainment/>.

13   Bringhurst 1997.

Asian Stock Market Indices

Bangladesh: DSE Broad Index (DSEX)

USD100 invested on January 2013 in this index would be 135 by June 2021

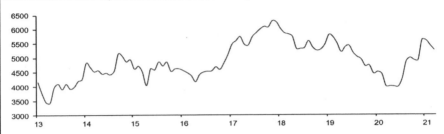

Description: DSE Broad Index reflects the performance of all stocks listed on Dhaka stock exchange. It is one of the markets that has only come to investor's attention in the past few years. Bangladesh is, like Vietnam, a so-called frontier market.

Sector composition

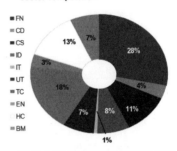

- FN
- CD
- CS
- ID
- IT
- UT
- TC
- EN
- HC
- BM

Top 5 stocks in this index

Company name	Ticker	Size	ADTV (*)
Grameenphone Ltd	GRAM BD	6	1
British American Tobacco	BATBC BD	3	3
Robi Axiata Ltd	ROBI BD	3	3
Square Pharma	SQUARE BD	2	2
United Power Generation	UPGO BD	2	0

Note: Size in USDbn. ADTV is average daily trading value in USDm, last 3 months

Note: FN=Financials, CD=Consumer Discretionary, CS=Consumer Staples, ID=Industrials, IT=Technology, RE=Real Estate, UT=Utilities, TC=Telecommunications, EN=Energy, HC=Health Care, BM=Basic Materials

Largest ETFs that follow this index

Fund	Ticker	Size
There are no ETFs for this market		

Note: Size in USDmn   Source: ETF.com

Index earnings growth

Based on top 10 companies

Period	2014-19	2017-2019
DS 30 index	14%	41%

Source: author's calculations

Stock market chart from Factset. All data as per Jun 2021

China: Shanghai Composite Index (SSE index)

USD100 invested on January 2000 in this index would be 508 by June 2021

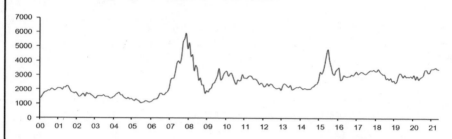

Description: This is one of Asia's biggest stock market. The index was launched in 1991 and is made up of all (A and B) stocks on the Shanghai Stock Exchange (that have been listed for over a year). There are many subindices, such as the SSE 50 index for the 50 largest companies.

Sector composition

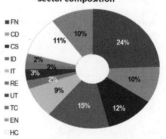

- FN
- CD
- CS
- ID
- IT
- RE
- UT
- TC
- EN
- HC

Top 5 stocks in this index

Company name	Ticker	Size	ADTV (*)
Kweichow Moutai	600519 CH	370	1444
Ind & Com.Bk.Of China	601398 CH	218	232
China Merchants Bank	600036 CH	173	550
Agri. Bank Of China	601288 CH	161	121
Ping An Insurance	601318 CH	118	967

Note: Size in USDbn. ADTV is average daily trading value in USDm, last 3 months

Note: FN=Financials, CD=Consumer Discretionary, CS=Consumer Staples, ID=Industrials, IT=Technology, RE=Real Estate, UT=Utilities, TC=Telecommunications, EN=Energy, HC=Health Care, BM=Basic Materials

Largest ETFs that follow this index

Fund	Ticker	Size
Fullgoal SSE ETF	510210 CH	71
Guotai SSE Composite ETF	510760 CH	57

Note: Size in USDmn Source: ETF.com

Index earnings growth

Based on top 10 companies		
Period	2014-19	2017-2019
SSE	1%	6%

Source: author's calculations

China: Stock market chart from Factset. All data as per Jun 2021

China: Shenzhen Composite Index (SZ Comp)

USD100 invested on January 2000 in this index would be 956 June 2021

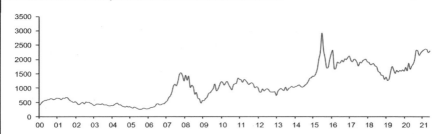

Description: This index is made up of all listed stocks on the Shenzhen Stock Exchange. Technology and healthcare are prominent in this market. In 2009, the Chinext was introduced as a new market on the Shenzhen stock exchange.

Sector composition

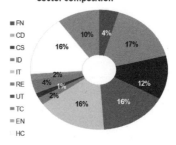

Note: FN=Financials, CD=Consumer Discretionary, CS=Consumer Staples, ID=Industrials, IT=Technology, RE=Real Estate, UT=Utilities, TC=Telecommunications, EN=Energy, HC=Health Care, BM=Basic Materials

Top 5 stocks in this index

Company name	Ticker	Size	ADTV (*)
Wuliangye Yibin	000858 CH	164	1008
Contemporary Amperex Te	300750 CH	132	957
Midea Group	000333 CH	82	514
Shn.Mindray Bmed. Eltn	300760 CH	80	307
Yihai Kerry Arawana Hldg	300999 CH	62	367

Note: Size in USDbn. ADTV is average daily trading value in USDm, last 3 months

Largest ETFs that follow this index

Fund	Ticker	Size
SZSE COMPONENT INDEX ETF	159903 CH	47
China Universal SZSE 300 ETF	159912 CH	15

Note: Size in USDmn   Source: ETF.com

Index earnings growth

Based on top 10 companies		
Period	2014-19	2017-2019
SZSE	2%	(6%)

Source: author's calculations

Stock market chart from Factset. All data as per Jun 2021

Hong Kong: Hang Seng China Enterprises Index (HSCEI)

USD100 invested on January 2000 in this index would be 1150 by June 2021

Description: This index follows the largest Chinese companies that are listed in Hong Kong. Over the years the Chinese "H-shares" have become the largest stocks in this index. It has in total 50 stocks.

Sector composition

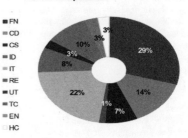

Top 5 stocks in this index

Company name	Ticker	Size	ADTV (*)
Tencent	700 HK	754	2124
Alibaba	9988 HK	619	822
China Construction Bar	939 HK	191	268
Ping An Insurance	2318 HK	78	411
Xiaomi	1810 HK	67	721

Note: Size in USDbn. ADTV is average daily trading value in USDm, last 3 months

Note: FN=Financials, CD=Consumer Discretionary, CS=Consumer Staples, ID=Industrials, IT=Technology, RE=Real Estate, UT=Utilities, TC=Telecommunications, EN=Energy, HC=Health Care, BM=Basic Materials

Largest ETFs that follow this index

Fund	Ticker	Size
HSCEI ETF	2828 HK	2891
E Fund HSCEI ETF	510900 HK	1567

Note: Size in USDmn Source: ETF.com

Stock market chart from Factset. All data as per Jun 2021

Index earnings growth

Based on top 10 companies		
Period	2014-19	2017-2019
HSCEI	10%	17%

Source: author's calculations

Hong Kong: Hang Seng Index (HSI)

USD100 invested on January 2000 in this index would be 353 by June 2021

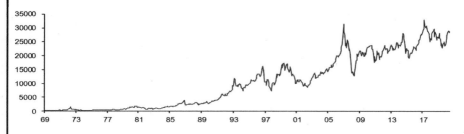

Description: This index started in 1969 and follows the largest Hong Kong listed companies. It has in total 55 stocks. The weight of any stock is limited to 10%. Traditionally, this index was dominated by banks and property, but now its dominated by Chinese stocks

Top 5 stocks in this index

Company name	Ticker	Size	ADTV (*)
Tencent	700 HK	741	2111
Alibaba	9988 HK	614	816
China Con.Bank	939 HK	193	267
Aia Group	1299 HK	158	270
Hsbc Holdings	5 HK	129	171

Note: Size in USDbn. ADTV is average daily trading value in USDm, last 3 months

Sector composition

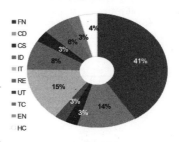

Note: FN=Financials, CD=Consumer Discretionary, CS=Consumer Staples, ID=Industrials, IT=Technology, RE=Real Estate, UT=Utilities, TC=Telecommunications, EN=Energy, HC=Health Care, BM=Basic Materials

Largest ETFs that follow this index

Fund	Ticker	Size
Hang Seng Inv. Index Funds	2833 HK	7000
China AMC Hang Seng ETF	159920 CH	1871

Note: Size in USDmn Source: ETF.com

Index earnings growth

Based on top 10 companies		
Period	2014-19	2017-2019
HSI	6%	10%

Source: author's calculations

Hong Kong: Stock market chart from Factset. All data as per Jun 2021

India: BSE SENSEX (SENSEX)

USD100 invested on January 2000 in this index would be 864 by June 2021

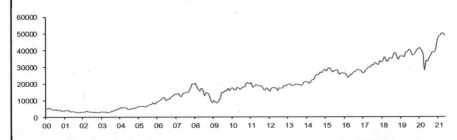

Description: This index is a free-float market-weighted stock market index of 30 stocks listed in Mumbai (the BSE). This stock market is the most diversified in the whole of Asia and belong to the least sensitive to movements in Chinese or US stocks.

Sector composition

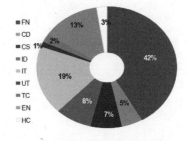

■ FN
■ CD
■ CS
■ ID
■ IT
■ UT
■ TC
■ EN
□ HC

Top 5 stocks in this index

Company name	Ticker	Size	ADTV (*)
Reliance Industries	RIL IN	189	246
HDFC Bank	HDFCB IN	114	192
Infosys	INFO IN	81	141
HDFC	HDFC IN	64	129
ICICI Bank	ICICIBC IN	62	190

Note: Size in USDbn. ADTV is average daily trading value in USDm, last 3 months

Note: FN=Financials, CD=Consumer Discretionary, CS=Consumer Staples, ID=Industrials, IT=Technology, RE=Real Estate, UT=Utilities, TC=Telecommunications, EN=Energy, HC=Health Care, BM=Basic Materials

Largest ETFs that follow this index

Fund	Ticker	Size
iShares MSCI India ETF	INDIA SP	5241
UTI Sensex ETF	UTISENX IN	1787

Note: Size in USDmn Source: ETF.com

Stock market chart from Factset. All data as per Jun 2021

Index earnings growth

Based on top 10 companies		
Period	2014-19	2017-2019
Sensex	5%	8%

Source: author's calculations

Indonesia: Jakarta Stock Exchange Composite index (JCI)

USD100 invested on January 2000 in this index would be 616 June 2021

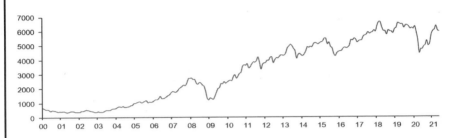

Description: IDX composite is an index that measures the stock price performance of all listed companies on the Indonesia Stock Exchange in Jakarta. This market is one of the most domestic-oriented markets and, thus, least sensitive to movements in China or the US stock markets.

Sector composition

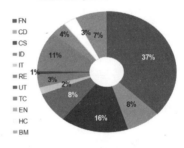

Top 5 stocks in this index

Company name	Ticker	Size	ADTV (*)
Bank Central Asia	BBCA IJ	56	45
Bank Rakyat Indonesia	BBRI IJ	37	40
Telekom Indonesia	TLKM IJ	24	23
Bank Mandiri	BMRI IJ	20	21
Unilever Indonesia	UNVR IJ	15	7

Note: Size in USDbn. ADTV is average daily trading value in USDm, last 3 months

Note: FN=Financials, CD=Consumer Discretionary, CS=Consumer Staples, ID=Industrials, IT=Technology, RE=Real Estate, UT=Utilities, TC=Telecommunications, EN=Energy, HC=Health Care, BM=Basic Materials

Largest ETFs that follow this index

Fund	Ticker	Size
iShares MSCI Indonesia ETF	EIDO US	347
HSBC MSCI Indonesia UCITS ETF	HIDR LN	52

Note: Size in USDmn   Source: ETF.com

Index earnings growth

Based on top 10 companies		
Period	2014-19	2017-2019
IDX Comp	7%	9%

Source: author's calculations

Stock market chart from Factset. All data as per Jun 2021

Japan: Tokyo Stock Price Index (TOPIX)

USD100 invested on January 2000 in this index would be 154 by June 2021

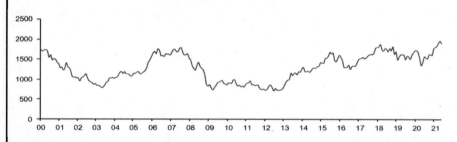

Description: TOPIX is a free-float adjusted market capitalization-weighted index. Industrials are the largest sector in this market. The other index in Japan is the Nikkei 225, the oldest index in Asia.

Sector composition

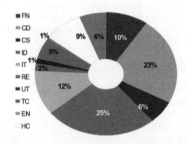

Top 5 stocks in this index

Company name	Ticker	Size	ADTV (*)
Toyota Motor	7203 JP	281	487
Softbank Group	9984 JP	129	1142
Sony Group	6758 JP	125	469
Keyence	6861 JP	120	305
Mitsubishi Ufj Finl.Gp.	8306 JP	78	394

Note: Size in USDbn. ADTV is average daily trading value in USDm, last 3 months

Note: FN=Financials, CD=Consumer Discretionary, CS=Consumer Staples, ID=Industrials, IT=Technology, RE=Real Estate, UT=Utilities, TC=Telecommunications, EN=Energy, HC=Health Care, BM=Basic Materials

Largest ETFs that follow this index

Fund	Ticker	Size
Amundi Japan TOPIX UCITS ETF	TPXU LN	1284
Daiwa ETF - TOPIX	1457 JP	65750

Note: Size in USDmn   Source: ETF.com

Index earnings growth

Based on top 10 companies		
Period	2014-19	2017-2019
Topix	6%	11%

Source: author's calculations

Stock market chart from Factset. All data as per Jun 2021

Korea: KOSPI

USD100 invested on January 2000 in this index would be 660 June 2021

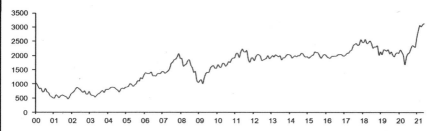

Description: The Korea Composite Stock Price Index (KOSPI) is made up of all companies traded on the Korea Stock Exchange. Technology makes up about 39% of the total market value. Together with Taiwan's index this market is most sensitive to Chinese and US stock markets.

Sector composition

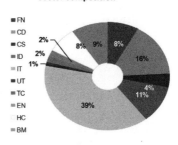

- FN
- CD
- CS
- ID
- IT
- UT
- TC
- EN
- HC
- BM

Top 5 stocks in this index

Company name	Ticker	Size	ADTV (*)
Samsung Electronics	005930 KS	435	1308
SK Hynix	000660 KS	85	506
Naver	035420 KS	55	244
LG Chem	051910 KS	53	306
Kakao	035720 KS	51	326

Note: Size in USDbn. ADTV is average daily trading value in USDm, last 3 months

Note: FN=Financials, CD=Consumer Discretionary, CS=Consumer Staples, ID=Industrials, IT=Technology, RE=Real Estate, UT=Utilities, TC=Telecommunications, EN=Energy, HC=Health Care, BM=Basic Materials

Largest ETFs that follow this index

Fund	Ticker	Size
Hanwha ARIRANG 200 ETF	152100 KS	724
Hanwha ARIRANG KOSPI TR ETF	328370 KS	156

Note: Size in USDmn Source: ETF.com

Stock market chart from Factset. All data as per Jun 2021

Index earnings growth

Based on top 10 companies		
Period	2014-19	2017-2019
KOSPI	1%	(5%)

Source: author's calculations

FTSE Bursa Malaysia (KLCI)

USD100 invested on January 2000 in this index would be 558 by June 2021

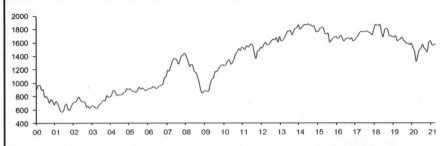

Description: The FTSE Bursa Malaysia KLCI, is a capitalisation-weighted stock market index, composed of the 30 largest companies. This stock markets is one of the least volatile in the region and tends to do better when other markets fall.

Sector composition

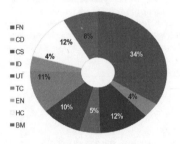

Top 5 stocks in this index

Company name	Ticker	Size	ADTV (*)
Malayan Banking	MAY MK	23	14
Public Bank	PBK MK	20	19
Tenaga Nasional	TNB MK	14	9
Cimb Group Holdings	CIMB MK	11	11
Top Glove Corporation	TOPG MK	10	37

Note: Size in USDbn. ADTV is average daily trading value in USDm, last 3 months

Note: FN=Financials, CD=Consumer Discretionary, CS=Consumer Staples, ID=Industrials, IT=Technology, RE=Real Estate, UT=Utilities, TC=Telecommunications, EN=Energy, HC=Health Care, BM=Basic Materials

Largest ETFs that follow this index

Fund	Ticker	Size
iShares MSCI Malaysia ETF	EWM US	270
Xtrackers MSCI Malaysia UCITS ETF	XCS3 GR	42

Note: Size in USDmn   Source: ETF.com

Index earnings growth

Based on top 10 companies		
Period	2014-19	2017-2019
KLCI index	(2%)	(1%)

Source: author's calculations

Stock market chart from Factset. All data as per Jun 2021

Philippines: Philippine Stock Exchange Index (PSEI)

USD100 invested on January 2000 in this index would be 344 June 2021

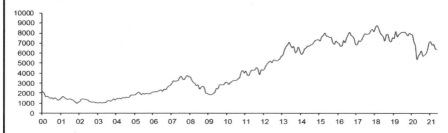

Description: The PSEI Composite Index, commonly known previously as the PHISIX and presently as the PSEi, is a stock market index of the Philippine Stock Exchange consisting of 30 companies.

Sector composition

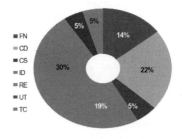

Note: FN=Financials, CD=Consumer Discretionary, CS=Consumer Staples, ID=Industrials, IT=Technology, RE=Real Estate, UT=Utilities, TC=Telecommunications, EN=Energy, HC=Health Care, BM=Basic Materials

Top 5 stocks in this index

Company name	Ticker	Size	ADTV (*)
Sm Investments	SM PM	25	6
Sm Prime Holdings	SMPH PM	23	5
Ayala Land	ALI PM	11	10
Jg Summit Hdg.	JGS PM	9	2
International Container Te	ICT PM	6	5

Note: Size in USDbn. ADTV is average daily trading value in USDm, last 3 months

Largest ETFs that follow this index

Fund	Ticker	Size
First Metro Philippine Equity ETF	FMETF PM	39
iShares MSCI Philippines ETF	EPHE US	128

Note: Size in USDmn   Source: ETF.com

Index earnings growth

Based on top 10 companies		
Period	2014-19	2017-2019
PSEi	10%	13%

Source: author's calculations

Stock market chart from Factset. All data as per Jun 2021

Singapore: Straits Times Index (STI)

USD100 invested on January 2000 in this index would be 315 by June 2021

Description: The Straits Times Index (STI) is made up of the top 30 companies listed on SGX. Many are banks, making this sector sensitive to trends in Asian banking. It started trading in 1988 (although it is a continuation of an index that was launched in 1966 and re-vamped in 1988).

Sector composition

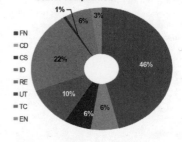

Note: FN=Financials, CD=Consumer Discretionary, CS=Consumer Staples, ID=Industrials, IT=Technology, RE=Real Estate, UT=Utilities, TC=Telecommunications, EN=Energy, HC=Health Care, BM=Basic Materials

Top 5 stocks in this index

Company name	Ticker	Size	ADTV (*)
Dbs Group Holdings	DBS SP	58	110
Jardine Matheson Hdg.	JM SP	46	23
Oversea-Chinese Bkg.	OCBC SP	42	60
United Overseas Bank	UOB SP	33	59
Singapore Telecom	ST SP	30	56

Note: Size in USDbn. ADTV is average daily trading value in USDm, last 3 months

Largest ETFs that follow this index

Fund	Ticker	Size
SPDR Straits Times Index ETF	STTF SP	1294
iShares MSCI Singapore ETF	EWS US	727

Note: Size in USDmn   Source: ETF.com

Stock market chart from Factset. All data as per Jun 2021

Index earnings growth

Based on top 10 companies		
Period	2014-19	2017-2019
STI	3%	4%

Source: author's calculations

Taiwan: TAIEX

USD100 invested on January 2000 in this index would be 390 by June 2021

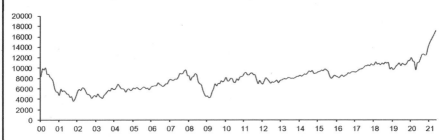

Description: The Taiwan Stock Exchange Weighted Stock Index (TAIEX) is the most tech-dominated market in Asia. The sector makes up 57% of the total market. Across Asia, this market is most sensitve to Chinese and US stock market movements.

Sector composition

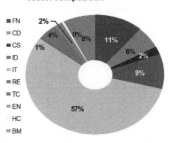

- FN
- CD
- CS
- ID
- IT
- RE
- TC
- EN
- HC
- BM

Top 5 stocks in this index

Company name	Ticker	Size	ADTV (*)
TSMC	2330 TT	561	958
Hon Hai	2317 TT	57	280
Mediatek	2454 TT	56	370
Formosa Petrochem	6505 TT	35	18
Chunghwa Telecom	2412 TT	32	39

Note: Size in USDbn. ADTV is average daily trading value in USDm, last 3 months

Note: FN=Financials, CD=Consumer Discretionary, CS=Consumer Staples, ID=Industrials, IT=Technology, RE=Real Estate, UT=Utilities, TC=Telecommunications, EN=Energy, HC=Health Care, BM=Basic Materials

Largest ETFs that follow this index

Fund	Ticker	Size
iShares MSCI Taiwan ETF	EWT US	7328
Yuanta/P-shares Taiwan Top 50 ETF	0050 TT	4922

Note: Size in USDmn   Source: ETF.com

Index earnings growth

Based on top 10 companies		
Period	2014-19	2017-2019
TAIEX	6%	1%

Source: author's calculations

Stock market chart from Factset. All data as per Jun 2021

Thailand: Bangkok SET Index (SET index)

USD100 invested on January 2000 in this index would be 558 by June 2021

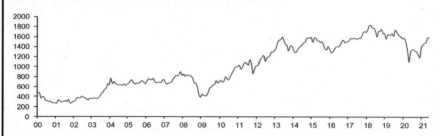

Description: The Bangkok SET Index is a capitalization-weighted index of stocks traded on the Stock Exchange of Thailand. Its base date is 30 April 1975, when it was set at 100. Its largest stock is an oil company, making this market one of the most senitive to oil price movements.

Sector composition

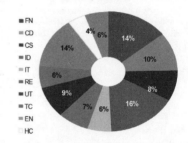

Note: FN=Financials, CD=Consumer Discretionary, CS=Consumer Staples, ID=Industrials, IT=Technology, RE=Real Estate, UT=Utilities, TC=Telecommunications, EN=Energy, HC=Health Care, BM=Basic Materials

Top 5 stocks in this index

Company name	Ticker	Size	ADTV (*)
Ptt	PTT TB	38	81
Airports Of Thailand	AOT TB	30	50
Delta Electronics	DELTA TB	23	59
Cp All	CPALL TB	17	66
Siam Cement	SCC TB	17	44

Note: Size in USDbn. ADTV is average daily trading value in USDm, last 3 months

Largest ETFs that follow this index

Fund	Ticker	Size
iShares MSCI Thailand ETF	THD US	435
ThaiDEX SET50 ETF	TDEX TB	115

Note: Size in USDmn   Source: ETF.com

Stock market chart from Factset. All data as per Jun 2021

Index earnings growth

Based on top 10 companies		
Period	2014-19	2017-2019
SET Index	1%	(2%)

Source: author's calculations

Vietnam: Ho Chi Minh City Stock Index (VN Index)

USD100 invested on January 2000 in this index would be 1238 by June 2021

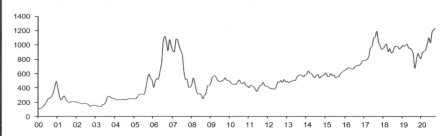

Description: The Vietnam Stock Index or VN-Index is a capitalization-weighted index of all the companies listed on the Ho Chi Minh City Stock Exchange. It is a frontier market, meaning it is not part of the "main" group of Asian stock markets. Vietnam had a stock market bubble in 2007.

Sector composition

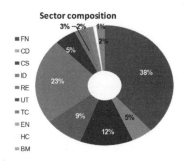

Top 5 stocks in this index

Company name	Ticker	Size	ADTV (*)
Vingroup Jsc	VIC VN	17	13
Bank For Foreign Trade Jsc	VCB VN	17	13
Vinhomes Jsc	VHM VN	15	23
Vietnam Js Commercial Ba	CTG VN	9	40
Bank For Investment And [	BID VN	9	14

Note: Size in USDbn. ADTV is average daily trading value in USDm, last 3 months

Note: FN=Financials, CD=Consumer Discretionary, CS=Consumer Staples, ID=Industrials, IT=Technology, RE=Real Estate, UT=Utilities, TC=Telecommunications, EN=Energy, HC=Health Care, BM=Basic Materials

Largest ETFs that follow this index

Fund	Ticker	Size
Fubon FTSE Vietnam ETF	00885 TT	356
KIM KINDEX VietnamVN30 ETF (Synth)	245710 KS	169

Note: Size in USDmn   Source: ETF.com

Index earnings growth

Based on top 10 companies		
Period	2014-19	2017-2019
VN index	8%	15%

Source: author's calculations

Stock market chart from Factset. All data as per Jun 2021

List of Referred Stocks (in alphabetic order)

Stock name	Stock code	Country	Size (Mcap in USD million) (*)	Daily trading activity in USD million (*)
Advanced Info Systems (AIS)	ADVANC TB	Thailand	16,569	35
Airtec	1590 TT	China	6,722	26
Alibaba	BABA US	China	573,320	3570
Amore Pacific	090430 KS	South Korea	14,743	50
Anta	2020 HK	China	56,663	163
Ascendas REIT	AREIT SP	Singapore	9,389	28
Ascott	ART SP	Singapore	2,442	3
Asia Paints	APNT IN	India	39,771	68
Astra International	ASII IJ	Indonesia	14,614	18
Aurobindo	ARBP IN	India	7,936	36
Axiom	AXIATA MK	Malaysia	8,733	4
Ayala Group	AC PM	Philippines	10,546	3
Ayala Land	ALI PM	Philippines	11,349	10
Baidu	BIDU US	China	65,956	2165
Bangkok Dusit Medical Services	BDMS TB	Thailand	11,686	25
Bank of China (HK)	3988 HK	China	130,956	127
Bank of Philippine Islands	BPI PM	Philippines	8,093	3
BAT	ROTH MK	Malaysia	1,009	2
Bawang	1338 HK	China	44	1
Bentoel	RMBA IJ	Indonesia	720	1
Bharti	BHARTI IN	India	40,607	86
Bilibili	BILI US	China	42,979	486
BTS	352820 KS	South Korea	9,301	88
Bumrungrad	BH TB	Thailand	3,419	7
Canon	7751 JP	Japan	31,770	92
Capcom	9697 JP	Japan	8,143	37

Stock name	Stock code	Country	Size (Mcap in USD million) (*)	Daily trading activity in USD million (*)
Capita land	CAPL SP	Singapore	14,814	31
Cathay Pacific	293 HK	Hong Kong	5,797	8
CDL Hospitality trust	CDREIT SP	Singapore	1,184	1
Cheung Kong	1113 HK	Hong Kong	24,430	57
China Life	2628 HK	China	123,085	83
China Mobile	941 HK	Hong Kong	126,615	185
China Unicom	762 HK	Hong Kong	16,556	31
Chroma ATE	2360 TT	Taiwan	3,028	8
Ciola	CIPLA IN	India	10,659	84
Citic Securities	600030 CH	China	46,688	351
Colgate	CLGT IN	India	6,349	14
COSL	2883 HK	China	8,762	19
Daelim	000210 KS	South Korea	1,526	23
Dah Sing Financial group	440 HK	Hong Kong	994	1
Daikin	6367 JP	Japan	54,446	143
DBS	DBS SP	Singapore	58,038	95
Delta	DELTA TB	Thailand	21,951	60
Dr Treddy's	DRRD IN	India	12,266	80
ENN Energy	2688 HK	China	21,082	36
Fanuc	6954 JP	Japan	49,808	172
Foxconn	2354 TT	Taiwan	3,326	26
Fraser & Neave	FNN SP	Singapore	1,586	0
Fujifilm	4901 JP	Japan	36,826	100
Galaxy	27 HK	Hong Kong	34,679	94
Giant	9921 TT	Taiwan	4,295	15
Globe Telcom	GLO PM	Philippines	5,251	2
Golden Agri	GGR SP	Singapore	2,151	5
Goldwind	002202 CH	China	7,600	110
Grameenphone	GRAM BD	Bangladesh	5,480	1
Gree	000651 CH	China	51,998	350
GS Retail	007070 KS	South Korea	2,613	14

Stock name	Stock code	Country	Size (Mcap in USD million) (*)	Daily trading activity in USD million (*)
Gudang Garam	GGRM IJ	Indonesia	4,680	3
Haidilao	6862 HK	China	26,731	71
HDFC Bank	HDFCB IN	India	112,076	185
Hengli Hydraulic	601100 CH	China	15,346	112
Hero Corp	HMCL IN	India	8,188	38
Hindustan Unilever Ltd	HUVR IN	India	76,597	63
Hiwin	2049 TT	Taiwan	4,577	26
Homepro	HMPRO TB	Thailand	6,124	10
Hon Hai	2317 TT	Taiwan	56,674	248
Honda	7267 JP	Japan	59,926	132
Hongfa	600885 CH	China	6,336	53
HSBC	5 HK	Hong Kong	124,599	129
Hyndai Department Stores	069960 KS	South Korea	1,852	16
Hynix	000660 KS	South Korea	83,663	429
Hyundai Heavy Industries	009540 KS	South Korea	8,640	62
Hyundai Motor	005380 KS	South Korea	45,288	210
ICBC	1398 HK	China	272,857	152
ICICI Bank	ICICIBC IN	India	60,894	177
Idea	IDEA IN	India	3,799	27
Infosys	INFO IN	India	85,597	144
Jardine Cycle and Carriage	JCNC SP	Singapore	6,463	8
JD.com	JD US	China	110,236	836
Jereh	002353 CH	China	5,891	57
Kakao	035720 KS	South Korea	57,369	346
Keppel Corp.	KEP SP	Singapore	7,182	14
Keyence	6861 JP	Japan	125,491	267
Konami	9766 JP	Japan	9,435	30
Kuaishou	1024 HK	China	110,265	192
Kweichau Moutai	600519 CH	China	430,048	1123

Stock name	Stock code	Country	Size (Mcap in USD million) (*)	Daily trading activity in USD million (*)
Land and Houses	LH TB	Thailand	3,204	14
Largan	3008 tt	Taiwan	14,656	58
Larsen &Toubro	LT IN	India	28,922	63
Las Vegas Sands	LVS US	Unites States	41,238	299
Li Ning	2331 HK	China	24,642	123
Link REIT	823 HK	Hong Kong	20,410	49
Lotte Department Stores	023530 KS	South Korea	3,061	14
Luckin Coffee	LKNCY US	China	2,369	14
Lupin	LPC IN	India	7,338	45
Mandarin Hotels	MAND SP	Hong Kong	2,564	1
Manila Water	MWC PM	Philippines	717	1
Mapletree	MINT SP	Singapore	5,415	15
Matahari	MPPA IJ	Indonesia	607	6
Mediatek	2454 TT	Taiwan	56,899	352
Meituan	3690 HK	China	238,074	1054
Mercari	4385 JP	Japan	7,879	47
Merry	2439 TT	Taiwan	806	7
MGM	MGM US	Unites States	20,732	314
Mitsubishi Real Estate	3481 JP	Japan	1,700	5
Nari Tech	600406 CH	China	20,763	73
Naver	035420 KS	South Korea	56,852	227
Nestle India	NEST IN	India	23,239	21
Netease	NTES US	China	74,432	205
Nidec	6594 JP	Japan	67,875	211
Nintendo	7974 JP	Japan	77,803	512
Nio	NIO US	China	74,127	2962
Nippon Paint	4612 JP	Japan	36,875	36
Nissan	7201 JP	Japan	21,579	79
Nitto Denko	6988 JP	Japan	11,519	52
Olam	OLAM SP	Singapore	4,327	2
Panasonic	6752 JP	Japan	28,219	81

Stock name	Stock code	Country	Size (Mcap in USD million) (*)	Daily trading activity in USD million (*)
Pegatron	4938 TT	Taiwan	7,033	37
PetroChina	601857 CH	China	141,848	89
Pigeon	7956 JP	Japan	3,646	27
Pinduoduo	PDD US	China	154,368	979
Ping An	2318 HK	China	189,886	345
Posco	005490 KS	South Korea	26,667	164
President Chain Stores	2912 TT	Taiwan	9,854	13
PTT Global Chemical	PTTGC TB	Thailand	8,536	41
PTTEP	PTTEP TB	Thailand	15,234	35
Puregold	PGOLD PM	Philippines	2,383	3
Rakuten	4755 JP	Japan	18,795	158
Ramayana	RALS IJ	Indonesia	353	2
Reliance Industries	RIL IN	India	200,879	250
RLX	RLX US	China	14,765	99
Sampoerna	HMSP IJ	Indonesia	9,621	4
Samsung Electronics	005930 KS	South Korea	431,920	1224
Samsung Electronics	005930 KS	South Korea	431,920	1224
Sany Heavy	600031 CH	China	37,221	636
Sea Ltd	SE US	Singapore	142,955	879
Sega-sammy	6460 JP	Japan	3,648	22
Shanghai Mechanical & Electric Corp	600835 CH	China	2,322	22
Shinsegae	004170 KS	South Korea	2,650	30
Singapore Exchanges	SGX SP	Singapore	8,842	19
Sinopec	600028 CH	China	83,453	97
SJM Holdings	880 HK	Hong Kong	6,360	15
SMIC	688981 CH	China	34,578	169
Softbank	9984 JP	Japan	125,826	1026
Sohgu Security Services	2331 JP	Japan	4,837	9
Sony	6758 JP	Japan	126,140	426
Square Pharma	SQUARE BD	Bangladesh	2,223	1
Steady Safe	SAFE IJ	Indonesia	8	1

Stock name	Stock code	Country	Size (Mcap in USD million) (*)	Daily trading activity in USD million (*)
Sun Hung Kai	16 HK	Hong Kong	45,134	49
Sun Pharma	SUNP IN	India	22,014	70
Sunny Optical	2382 HK	China	28,219	148
Suntec	SUN SP	Singapore	3,233	20
Suntory	2587 JP	Japan	11,996	21
Taj Hotels	IH IN	India	2,212	7
Tata Consultancy	TCS IN	India	164,491	124
Tata Power	TPWR IN	India	5,320	88
Techtronics	669 HK	Hong Kong	32,075	69
Telkom Indonesia	TLKM IJ	Indonesia	23,887	20
Tencent	700 HK	China	741,678	1784
Titan	TTAN IN	India	20,853	44
Tongwei	600438 CH	China	25,122	446
Toshiba	6502 JP	Japan	19,432	159
Toyota Motors	7203 JP	Japan	298,535	521
Tsingtao Brewery	168 HK	China	19,258	44
TSMC	2330 TT	Taiwan	571,311	799
UMC	UMC US	Taiwan	24,012	57
Walton	WALTONHI BD	Bangladesh	4,760	1
Wilmar	WIL SP	Singapore	22,425	29
Wipro	WPRO IN	India	41,662	88
Wuliangye	000858 CH	China	181,334	793
Wynn Resorts	WYNN US	Unites States	14,419	279
Xiaomi	1810 HK	China	90,921	576
Xinyi Glass	868 HK	Hong Kong	16,105	29
Xuji	000400 CH	China	1,982	38
Yue Yuen	551 HK	Hong Kong	3,984	5
Yum China	9987 HK	China	28,772	8
Zozo Town	3092 JP	Japan	10,499	28

(*) Data as per June 2021. All in USD million. Trading activity is average daily trading in USD million measured over April–June 2021.

Bibliography

Acemoglu, Daron, and James A. Robinson. *Why Nations Fail: The Origins of Power, Prosperity, and Poverty*. Illustrated Edition. New York: Currency, 2013.

Addicot, David A.C. "The Rise and Fall of the Zaibatsu: Japan's Industrial and Economic Modernization." *Global Tides* 11, no. 1 (2017): Article 5.

Agarwal, Sumit, Shashwat Alok, Pulak Ghosh, Soumya Ghosh, Tomasz Piskorski, and Amit Seru. "Banking the Unbanked: What Do 255 Million New Bank Accounts Reveal about Financial Access." Columbia Business School Research Paper No. 17–12, Georgetown McDonough School of Business Research Paper No. 2906523, HKUST Finance Symposium 2017, Indian School of Business WP 2906523, 26 October 2017. ttp://dx.doi.org/10.2139/ssrn.2906523.

Amenc, Noel, and Veronique Le Sourd. "The Performance of Socially Responsible Investment and Sustainable Development in France: An Update after the Financial Crisis." EDHEC Business School, September 2010. file:///Users/herald/Downloads/edhec_position_paper_-_the_performance_of_sri_0.pdf.

Anderson, T. D. "Revolution without Ideology: Demographic Transition in East Asia." *Philippine Geographical Journal* 24, no. 1 (March 1980): 33–44.

Anett, John, and Guanghua Wan. "Determinants of Urbanization." Asian Development Bank, July 2013. https://papers.ssrn.com/sol3/papers.cfm?abstract_id=2295736.

"ASEAN Needs Smart Regulation to Boost Financial Inclusion." Nikkei Asian Review. Accessed 22 September 2020. https://asia.nikkei.com/Opinion/ASEAN-needs-smart-regulation-to-boost-financial-inclusion.

Associated Press. "20 years on, scars from Asian financial meltdown linger." *Bangkok Post*, 29 June 2017. https://www.bangkokpost.com/business/1277891/20-years-on-scars-from-asian-financial-meltdown-linger.

"Automobile Industry in India." Indian Brand Equity Foundation. 21 October 2020. https://www.ibef.org/industry/india-automobiles.aspx.

Baird, Vanessa. *The No-Nonsense Guide to World Population*. New Internationalist, 2011.

Banerji, Gunjan. "Why Is the Stock Market Rallying When the Economy Is So Bad?" *Wall Street Journal*, 8 May 2020. https://www.wsj.com/articles/why-is-the-stock-market-rallying-when-the-economy-is-so-bad-11588974327.

Bank of England – History. Accessed 12 January 2021. https://www.bankofengland.co.uk/about/history.

Barquin, Sonia, Guillaume de Gantès, HV Vinayak, and Duhita Shrikhande. "Digital Banking in Indonesia: Building Loyalty and Generating Growth." McKinsey & Company, February 2019. https://www.mckinsey.com/id/~/media/McKinsey/Industries/Financial%20Services/Our%20Insights/Digital%20banking%20in%20Indonesia%20Building%20loyalty%20and%20generating%20growth/Digital-banking-in-Indonesia-final.pdf.

Bauer, Michael D., and Glenn D Rudebusch. "Why Are Long-Term Interest Rates So Low?" FRBSF Economic Letter. Federal Reserve Bank of San Fransisco, 5 December 2016. https://www.frbsf.org/economic-research/publications/economic-letter/2016/december/why-are-long-term-interest-rates-so-low/.

Benartzi, Shlomo, and Richard H. Thaler. "Heuristics and Biases in Retirement Savings Behavior." *Journal of Economic Perspectives* (2007) 21(3): 81–104. https://doi.org/10.1257/jep.21.3.81.

Berg, Florian, Julian Kölbel, and Roberto Rigobon. "Aggregate Confusion: The Divergence of ESG Ratings." 17 May 2020. Available at SSRN: https://ssrn.com/abstract=3438533 or http://dx.doi.org/10.2139/ssrn.3438533

Berlin, Isaiah. *The Hedgehog & The Fox*. Revised edition. London: Weidenfeld & Nicolson, 2014.

Bland, Ben. *Man of Contradictions*. Australia, Victoria: Penguin, 2020.

"Bombay Stock Exchange – History." Gulaq, 6 January 2020. Accessed 11 October 2020. https://medium.com/@gulaqfintech/bombay-stock-exchange-history-217e984d2.

Bonabeau, Eric. "Don't Trust Your Gut." *Harvard Business Review*, May 2003. https://hbr.org/2003/05/dont-trust-your-gut.

Bowen, H.V. "'The Pests of Human Society': Stockbrokers, Jobbers and Speculators in Mid-Eighteenth-Century Britain." *History* 78, no. 252 (1993): 38–53.

Bratton, William. *China's Rise, Asia's Decline: Asia's Difficult Outlook under China's Shadow*. Singapore: Marshall Cavendish Editions, 2021.

Brau, James C., Bill Francis, and Ninon Kohers. "The Choice of IPO versus Takeover: Empirical Evidence." *The Journal of Business* 76, no. 4 (2003): 583–612. https://doi.org/10.1086/377032.

Bray, Francesca. *The Rice Economies: Technology and Development in Asian Societies*. Berkeley: University of California Press, 1994.

Bringhurst, Newell G. "Samuel Brannan and His Forgotten Final Years." *Southern California Quarterly* 79, no. 2 (1997): 139–60. https://doi.org/10.2307/41171850.

Bruijn, J.R. "Schepen van de VOC En Een Vergelijking Met de Vaart Op Azië Door Andere Compagnieën." *BMGN – Low Countries Historical Review* 1, no. 99 (1984): 1–20. https://doi.org/10.18352/bmgn-lchr.2450.

Burgess, Robert. "The Daily Prophet: Carville Was Right About the Bond Market." *Bloomberg Businessweek*, 30 January 2018. https://www.bloomberg.com/news/articles/2018-01-29/the-daily-prophet-carville-was-right-about-the-bond-market-jd0q9r1w.

Byun, Suk Joon, Sonya S. Lim, and Sang Hyun Yun. "Continuing Overreaction and Stock Return Predictability." *The Journal of Financial and Quantitative Analysis* 51, no. 6 (2016): 2015–46.

Cabinet Office, Government of Japan (2019). "Annual Report on the Ageing Society [Summary] FY 2019." June 2019. https://www8.cao.go.jp/kourei/english/annualreport/2019/pdf/2019.pdf.

Carvalho, Carlos, Andrea Ferrero, and Fernanda Nechio. "Demographic Transition and Low U.S. Interest Rates." *FRBSF Economic Letter*, Federal Reserve Bank of San Fransisco, no. 2017–27 (25 September 2017). https://www.frbsf.org/economic-research/publications/economic-letter/2017/september/demographic-transition.

CFA Institute. *ESG Integration in Asia Pacific: Markets, Practices, and Data.* CFA Institute and PRI, 2019. https://www.cfainstitute.org/-/media/documents/survey/esg-integration-apac.ashx.

Chan, Hing Lin. "Chinese Investment in Hong Kong: Issues and Problems." *Asian Survey* 35, no. 10 (1995): 941–54. https://doi.org/10.2307/2645568.

Chan, Tara Francis. "South Korea has limited a working week to 52 hours, in order to stop overwork." World Economic Forum, 3 July 2018. Accessed 19 September 2020. https://www.weforum.org/agenda/2018/07/south-korea-is-trying-to-stop-overwork-by-limiting-the-maximum-workweek-to-52-hours/.

Chapman, Colin. *How the Stock Markets Work: A Guide to the International Markets.* London: Century, 1994.

Chattopadhyay, Akash, Matthew D. Shaffeer, and Charles C.Y. Wang. "Governance through Shame and Aspiration: Index Creation and Corporate Behavior." Harvard Business School, 1 November 2018. http://dx.doi.org/10.2139/ssrn.3010188.

Chavez, Chris. "Jurgen Klopp Fires Back on Coronavirus Question from Reporter." *Sports Illustrated.* 4 March 2020. https://www.si.com/soccer/2020/03/04/jurgen-klopp-coronavirus-question-reporter-liverpool.

Chavis, Jason. "The History of China's Stock Market." Bizfluent, 26 September 2017. https://bizfluent.com/about-5070399-history-chinas-stock-market.html.

"China is the world's largest producer of hydroelectricity." Country profile – China, International Hydropower Association. Accessed 15 September 2020. https://www.hydropower.org/country-profiles/china.

China Labour Bulletin. "Migrant Workers and Their Children." 11 May 2020. https://clb.org.hk/content/migrant-workers-and-their-children.

China National Renewable Energy Centre. "The Energy System for Beautiful China 2050," n.d. http://boostre.cnrec.org.cn/wp-content/uploads/2018/04/Beautiful-China-2050-EN.pdf.

"China's New Consumer." Global Demographics. Accessed 18 September 2020. https://www.globaldemographics.com/china-new-consumer.

"Chow Tai Fook 2020/2021 Interim Results Presentation." Chow Tai Fook Jewellery Group, 19 December 2020. http://ir.ctfjewellerygroup.com/pre201124_en.pdf.

Chuang, Wen-I, Bong-Soo Lee, and Kai-Li Wang. "US and Domestic Market Gains and Asian Investors' Overconfident Trading Behavior." *Financial Management* 43, no. 1 (2014): 113–48.

Chung, Sungchul. "Excelsior: The Korean Innovation Story." *Issues in Science and Technology* XXIV, no. 1 (Fall 2007). https://issues.org/chung/.

Claessens, Stijn, and Po-Hung Fan. "Corporate Governance in Asia: A Survey." *International Review of Finance* 3 (1 February 2002): 71–103. https://doi.org/10.2139/ssrn.386481.

Conover, C. Mitchell, Gerald R. Jensen, and Robert R. Johnson. "Emerging Markets: When Are They Worth It?" *Financial Analysts Journal* 58, no. 2 (1 March 2002): 86–95. https://doi.org/10.2469/faj.v58.n2.2525.

Cornell, Bradford, and Aswath Damodaran. "The Big Market Delusion: Valuation and Investment Implications," 10 December 2019. http://dx.doi.org/10.2139/ssrn.3501688.

Cruz, Bayana S. "Investors, Asset Managers Using ETFs to Boost Responsible Investments." Theasset.com, 6 July 2020. https://theasset.com/article-esg/40923/investors-asset-managers-using-etfs-to-boost-responsible-investments.

Custodio, Yuri. "An Introduction to Esports: What Are Esports?" ESTNN, 23 November 2020. https://estnn.com/an-introduction-to-esports/.

Damodaran, Aswath. *Investment Valuation: Tools and Techniques for Determining the Value of Any Asset.* Third edition. Hoboken, NJ: John Wiley & Sons, 2012.

———. *Narrative and Numbers: The Value of Stories in Business.* New York: Columbia Business School Publishing, 2017.

———. *The Little Book of Valuation: How to Value a Company, Pick a Stock, and Profit.* Hoboken, NJ: John Wiley & Sons, 2011.

Davidi, Einat. "Penso de La Vega and the Question of Jewish Baroque." In *Religious Changes and Cultural Transformations in the Early Modern Western Sephardic Communities,* edited by Yosef Kaplan, 54:469–84. Brill, 2019. https://doi.org/10.1163/j.ctvrzgvqk.25.

Davies, Roger J., and Osamu Ikeno, eds. *The Japanese Mind: Understanding Contemporary Japanese Culture.* Boston: Tuttle Publishing, 2002.

Daw, James. "Responsible Investing: Weighing the Impact." *Corporate Knights* 10, no. 4 (2012): 20–21.

De Bondt, Werner F. M., and Richard H. Thaler. "Financial Decision-Making in Markets and Firms: A Behavioral Perspective." NBRE Working Paper No. 4777, June 1994. https://doi.org/10.3386/w4777.

Dennett, D. C. *From Bacteria to Bach and Back: The Evolution of Minds.* First edition. New York: W. W. Norton & Co, 2017.

———. *Intuition Pumps and Other Tools for Thinking.* First Edition. New York: W. W. Norton & Co, 2013.

Dian, Septiari. "Jokowi's 'hatred' of Foreign Products Raises Eyebrows." *The Jakarta Post,* 6 March 2021. https://www.thejakartapost.com/news/2021/03/06/jokowis-hatred-of-foreign-products-raises-eyebrows.html.

Dimson, Elroy, Paul Marsh, and Mike Staunton. *Triumph of the Optimists: 101 Years of Global Investment Returns.* Princeton, NJ: Princeton University Press, 2002.

Dorbolo, Jon. "Intuition Pumps and Augmentation of Learning," 164–67, 2012. https://doi.org/10.1007/978-1-4419-1428-6_827.

Dorling, Daniel, and Stuart Gietel-Basten. *Why Demography Matters.* Medford, MA: Polity Press, 2018.

Dunne, Timothy, Milja Kurki, and Steve Smith, eds. *International Relations Theories: Discipline and Diversity.* Third edition. Oxford: Oxford University Press, 2013.

Elton, Edwin J., Martin J. Gruber, and Andre de Souza. "Are Passive Funds Really Superior Investments? An Investor Perspective." *Financial Analysts Journal* 75, no. 3 (1 July 2019): 7–19. https://doi.org/10.1080/0015198X.2019.1618097.

Enoch, Charles, Barbara Baldwin, Oliver Frecout, and Arto Kovanen. "Indonesia: Anatomy of a Banking Crisis – Two Years of Living Dangerously 1997–1999." International Monetary Fund, May 2001. https://www.imf.org/external/pubs/ft/wp/2001/wp0152.pdf.

Fabozzi, Frank J., and H. Markowitz, eds. *Equity Valuation and Portfolio Management*. The Frank J. Fabozzi Series. Hoboken, NJ: John Wiley & Sons, 2011.

Fama, Eugene, Laurence Fisher, Michael C. Jensen, and Richard W. Roll. "The Adjustment of Stock Prices to New Information." *International Economic Review* 10 (15 February 1969): 28. Https://Ssrn.Com/Abstract=321524 or Http://Dx.Doi.Org/10.2139/Ssrn.321524.

Feddes, Fred. *1000 Jaar Amsterdam: Ruimtelijke Geschiedenis van Een Wonderbaarlijke Stad*. Bussum: Uitgeverij Thoth, 2012.

Feenstra, Robert, Gary Hamilton, and Eun Lim. "Chaebol and Catastrophe: A New View of the Korean Business Groups and Their Role in the Financial Crisis*." *Asian Economic Papers* 1 (1 May 2002): 1–45. https://doi.org/10.1162/15353510260187373.

Feng, Rebecca. "'Taiwan Fund Managers Rush to Roll out Sustainable ETFs.'" *Financial Times*, 4 May 2021. https://www.ft.com/content/42c40636-a003-4661-8645-318476d63cec.

Fisher, Stanley. "Why Are Interest Rates So Low? Causes and Implications." Board of Governors of the Federal Reserve System, 17 October 2016. https://www.federalreserve.gov/newsevents/speech/fischer20161017a.htm.

"For Asia, the path to prosperity starts with land reform." *The Economist*, 12 October 2017. https://www.economist.com/asia/2017/10/12/for-asia-the-path-to-prosperity-starts-with-land-reform.

Frederick, William H. "Rhoma Irama and the Dangdut Style: Aspects of Contemporary Indonesian Popular Culture." *Indonesia* 34 (1982): 103–30. https://doi.org/10.2307/3350952.

Fukuda, Shin-Ichi. "The Impacts of Japan's Negative Interest Rate Policy on Asian Financial Markets." Tokyo: Asian Development Bank Institute, 2017.

Gagnon, Etienne, Benjamin K. Johannsen, and Lopez-Salid David. "Understanding the New Normal: The Role of Demographics." Finance and Economics Discussion Series 2016-08. Washington DC: Board of Governors of the Federal Reserve System, 2016. http://dx.doi.org/10.17016/FEDS.2016.080.

"Game Changers: Women and the Future of Work in Asia and The Pacific." International Labour Organization, 2018. https://www.ilo.org/wcmsp5/groups/public/---asia/---ro-bangkok/---sro-bangkok/documents/publication/wcms_645601.pdf.

Geanakoplos, John, Michael Magill, and Martine Quinzii. "Demography and the Long-Run Predictability of the Stock Market." *Brookings Papers on Economic Activity* 2004, no. 1 (2004): 241–325. https://doi.org/10.1353/eca.2004.0010.

Ghosh, Abantika. "MP Shyama Charan Gupta Who Said Nothing Wrong with Beedis Flaunts His Beedi Empire." *Indian Express*, 2 April 2015. https://indianexpress.com/article/india/india-others/mp-shyama-charan-gupta-who-said-nothing-wrong-with-beedis-flaunts-his-beedi-empire/.

Giant Bicycles official website. Accessed 26 October 2020. https://www.giant-bicycles.com/global/about-us.

Gietel-Basten, Stuart. "Aging Need Not Be a Threat to China's Future." *China Daily*, 14 November 2020. http://global.chinadaily.com.cn/a/202011/14/WS5faf2e34a31024ad0ba94043.html.

Goetzmann, William, and Dasol Kim. "Negative Bubbles: What Happens After a Crash." National Bureau of Economic Research, Working Paper 23830 (September 2017). https://doi.org/10.3386/w23830.

Gordon, Robert J. *The Rise and Fall of American Growth: The U.S. Standard of Living since the Civil War*. The Princeton Economic History of the Western World. Princeton: Princeton University Press, 2016.

Greber, Jacob. "Trump's Trade War Is about to Test Market Complacency." Australian Financial Review, 4 December 2019. https://www.afr.com/world/north-america/trump-s-trade-war-is-about-to-test-market-complacency-20191204-p53gr5.

Greenwood, John. *Hong Kong's Link to the US Dollar*. Hong Kong: Hong Kong University Press, 2016.

Hanusz, Mark. *Kretek: The Culture and Heritage of Indonesia's Clove Cigarettes*. Jakarta: Equinox Publishing, 2000.

HDFC Bank official website. "Overview." Accessed 22 September 2020. https://www.hdfcbank.com/personal/about-us/overview.

Hill, Peter. "Heisei Yakuza: Burst Bubble and Bôtaihô." *Social Sciences Japan Journal* 6, no. 1 (2003): 1–18.

Hindustan Lever. "Annual Report 2019–20." https://www.hul.co.in/investor-relations/annual-reports/.

Hirsch, Jeffrey A. *The Little Book of Stock Market Cycles: How to Take Advantage of Time-Proven Market Patterns*. Little Book Big Profits Series. Hoboken, NJ: John Wiley & Sons, 2012.

History.com Editors. "Kiichiro Toyoda, Founder of the Toyota Motor Corporation, Dies." History, 13 November 2009 (updated 24 March 2021). https://www.history.com/this-day-in-history/toyota-founder-dies.

HKEX official website. Accessed 7 September 2020. https://www.hkex.com.hk/?sc_lang=en.

———. "Hong Kong Stock Market Historical Events." 29 December 2020. https://www.hkex.com.hk/-/media/hkex-market/news/news-release/2006/060116news/30.

———. "Shanghai Connect, Shenzhen Connect; Information Book for Investors." Hong Kong, August 2020. https://www.hkex.com.hk/-/media/HKEX-Market/Mutual-Market/Stock-Connect/Getting-Started/Information-Booklet-and-FAQ/Information-Book-for-Investors/Investor_Book_En.pdf.

———. "Stock Connect." Accessed 14 September 2020. https://www.hkex.com.hk/Mutual-Market/Stock-Connect?sc_lang=en.

Ho, Johnny, Felix Poh, Jia Zhou, and Daniel Zipser. "China consumer report 2020: The many faces of the Chinese consumer." McKinsey & Co, December 2019. https://www.mckinsey.com/~/media/McKinsey/Featured%20Insights/China/China%20consumer%20report%202020%20The%20many%20faces%20of%20the%20Chinese%20consumer/China-consumer-report-2020-vF.pdf.

Hoepner, Andreas G. F., Ioannis Oikonomou, Zacharias Sautner, Laura T. Starks, and Xiaoyan Zhou. "ESG Shareholder Engagement and Downside Risk." *SSRN Electronic Journal*, 2016. https://doi.org/10.2139/ssrn.2874252.

Horner, Rory. "The World Needs Pharmaceuticals from China and India to Beat Coronavirus." Medical Xpress, 25 May 2020. https://medicalxpress.com/news/2020-05-world-pharmaceuticals-china-india-coronavirus.html.

Hoshi, Takeo, and Anil K. Kashyap. "Will the U.S. and Europe Avoid a Lost Decade? Lessons from Japan's Postcrisis Experience." *IMF Economic Review* 63, no. 1 (2015): 110–63.

Houlder, Vanessa. "Richard Thaler's Advice: Be a Lazy Investor – Buy and Forget." 22 December 2017. https://www.ft.com/content/90d1289e-daa9-11e7-a039-c64b1c09b482.

Housel, Morgan. *The Psychology of Money: Timeless Lessons on Wealth, Greed, and Happiness*. Hampshire: Harriman House, 2020.

Hruska, Joel. "14nm, 7nm, 5nm: How low can CMOS go? It depends if you ask the engineers or the economists ..." Extreme Tech, 23 June 2014. Accessed 17 September 2020. https://www.extremetech.com/computing/184946-14nm-7nm-5nm-how-low-can-cmos-go-it-depends-if-you-ask-the-engineers-or-the-economists.

ICICI Bank official website. "About Us." Accessed 22 September 2020. https://www.icicibank.com/aboutus/about-us.page.

International Monetary Fund, Asia and Pacific Department. "Japan: 2017 Article IV Consultation – Press Release; Staff Report; and Statement by the Executive Director for Japan." IMF Staff Country Reports (31 July 2017). https://www.imf.org/en/Publications/CR/Issues/2017/07/31/Japan-2017-Article-IV-Consultation-Press-Release-Staff-Report-and-Statement-by-the-Executive-45149.

"In bleak times for banks, India's digital-payments system wins praise." *The Economist*, 9 May 2020. https://www.economist.com/finance-and-economics/2020/05/09/in-bleak-times-for-banks-indias-digital-payments-system-wins-praise.

Ingber, Sasha. "Japan's Population Is In Rapid Decline." NPR.org, 21 December 2018. https://www.npr.org/2018/12/21/679103541/japans-population-is-in-rapid-decline.

Jao, Y. C. "The Rise of Hong Kong as a Financial Center." *Asian Survey* 19, no. 7 (1979): 674–94. https://doi.org/10.2307/2643989.

Japan Exchange Group corporate site. "History." Accessed 20 October 2020. https://www.jpx.co.jp/english/corporate/about-jpx/history/01-02.html.

Jeong, May. "How Carlos Ghosn Escaped Japan, According to the Ex-Green Beret Who Snuck Him Out." *Vanity Fair*, July/August 2020 (23 July 2020). https://www.vanityfair.com/news/2020/07/how-carlos-ghosn-escaped-japan.

Jia, Jin, Qian Sun, and Wilson H. S. Tong. "Privatization through an Overseas Listing: Evidence from China's H-Share Firms." *Financial Management* 34, no. 3 (2005): 5–30.

Jin, Byoungho, and Junghwa Son. "Indian Consumers: Are They the Same across Regions?" *International Journal of Emerging Markets* 8 (18 January 2013). https://doi.org/10.1108/17468801311297255.

Jones, Randall S., and Myungkyoo Kim. "Enhancing Dynamism and Innovation in Japan's Business Sector." OECD Economics Department Working Papers, no. 1261 (2 September 2015). OECD iLibrary. https://doi.org/10.1787/5jrtpbtkbhs1-en.

Jorda, Oscar, Sanjay R. Singh, and Alan M. Taylor. "Longer-Run Economic Consequences of Pandemics." Federal Reserve Bank of San Francisco, Economic Research Working Papers, 30 June 2020. https://www.frbsf.org/economic-research/publications/working-papers/2020/09/.

Kahneman, Daniel. *Thinking, Fast and Slow*. First edition paperback. New York: Farrar, Straus and Giroux, 2013.

Kaplan, Robert D. "Why John J. Mearsheimer Is Right (About Some Things)." The Atlantic, January/February 2012. Accessed 8 September 2020. https://www.theatlantic.com/magazine/archive/2012/01/why-john-j-mearsheimer-is-right-about-some-things/308839/.

Kennedy, Paul M. *The Rise of the Anglo-German Antagonism, 1860–1914*. London-Boston-Sydney: George Allen & Unwin, 1980.

Kindleberger, Charles P., and Robert Z. Aliber. *Manias, Panics, and Crashes: A History of Financial Crises*. Fifth edition. Wiley Investment Classics. Hoboken, NJ: John Wiley & Sons, 2005.

Klement, Joachim. "What's Growth Got to Do With It? Equity Returns and Economic Growth." *The Journal of Investing* 24 (1 May 2015): 74–78. https://doi.org/10.3905/joi.2015.24.2.074.

Kobler, Daniel, and Sven Probst. "The Deloitte International Wealth Management Centre Ranking 2018: The Winding Road to Future Value Creation." Deloitte Centre for Financial Services, 2018. https://www2.deloitte.com/cn/en/pages/financial-services/articles/the-deloitte-wealth-management-centre-ranking-2018.html.

Komenkul, Kulabutr, and Santi Kiranand. "Aftermarket Performance of Health Care and Biopharmaceutical IPOs." *Inquiry* 54 (2017): 1–11. https://doi.org/10.2307/26369684.

Kung, James J., and Wing-Keung Wong. "Profitability of Technical Analysis in the Singapore Stock Market: Before and after the Asian Financial Crisis." *Journal of Economic Integration* 24, no. 1 (2009): 135–50.

Kurtz, Lloyd, and Dan diBartolomeo. "The Long-Term Performance of a Social Investment Universe." *The Journal of Investing* 20, no. 3 (31 August 2011): 95. https://doi.org/10.3905/joi.2011.20.3.095.

Kwan, Stanley S. K., and Nicole Kwan. *The Dragon and the Crown: Hong Kong Memoirs*. Hong Kong: Hong Kong University Press, 2011.

Kwatra, Nikita. "Can India Replace China as the World's Factory?" *Mint*, 5 October 2020. https://www.livemint.com/news/india/can-india-replace-china-as-the-world-s-factory-11601691617840.html.

Lach, Donald Frederick. *Asia in the Making of Europe. Asia in the Making of Europe.* Chicago: University of Chicago Press, 1994.

Lardy, Nicholas R. "Issues in China's WTO Accession." *Brookings* (blog), 2001. https://www.brookings.edu/testimonies/issues-in-chinas-wto-accession/.

Latoja, Ma. Concepcion G. "Remittances to Asia in 2018: Sources and Costs." Asia Regional Integration Center. Accessed 22 September 2020. https://aric.adb.org/blog/remittances-to-asia-in-2018-sources-and-costs.

Laurent, Clinton R. *Tomorrow's World: A Look at the Demographic and Socio-Economic Structure of the World in 2032.* Singapore: John Wiley & Sons, 2013.

Lee, Sang-Hyop, Andrew Mason, and Donghyun Park. "Why Does Population Aging Matter So Much for Asia? Population Aging, Economic Growth, and Economic Security in Asia." ADB Economics Working Paper Series, No. 284. October 2011. https://www.econstor.eu/bitstream/10419/109416/1/ewp-284.pdf.

Lee, Sang-Hyop, Cheol-Kon Park, and Andrew Mason. "Better Work Opportunities for Older Adults Would Benefit the South Korean Economy." E3G, 2020. JSTOR. https://doi.org/10.2307/resrep24947.

Lewis, Michael. *Boomerang: The Biggest Bust.* London: Penguin, 2011.

Li, Mengnan, Haiyi Ye, Xiawei Liao, Junping Ji, and Xiaoming Ma. "How Shenzhen, China pioneered the widespread adoption of electric vehicles in a major city: Implications for global implementation." *WIREs Energy and Environment* 9, no. 4 (July/August 2020): e373. https://doi.org/10.1002/wene.373.

Li, Shi. "The Economic Situation of Rural Migrant Workers in China." *China Perspectives* 2010, no. 4 (15 December 2010). https://doi.org/10.4000/chinaperspectives.5332.

Lim, Stanley, and Cheong Mun Hong. *Value Investing in Asia: The Definitive Guide to Investing in Asia.* Hoboken, NJ: John Wiley & Sons, 2017.

London Stock Exchange official website. "Homepage | London Stock Exchange." Accessed 7 September 2020. https://www.londonstockexchange.com/.

Louche, Celine, Daniel Arenas, and Kathinka C. van Cranenburgh. "From Preaching to Investing: Attitudes of Religious Organisations Towards Responsible Investment." *Journal of Business Ethics* 110, no. 3 (5 January 2012): 301–320. https://doi.org/10.1007/s10551-011-1155-8.

Maddison, Angus. *The World Economy: A Millennial Perspective.* Paris: OECD, 2001.

Mak, Geert. *Amsterdam a Brief Life of a City.* London: Harvill Press, 2001.

Malmendier, Ulrike, and Timothy Taylor. "On the Verges of Overconfidence." *The Journal of Economic Perspectives* 29, no. 4 (2015): 3–7.

Margolis, Joshua D., Hillary A. Elfenbein, and James P. Walsh. "Does It Pay to Be Good … And Does It Matter? A Meta-Analysis of the Relationship between Corporate Social and Financial Performance." 1 March 2009. http://dx.doi.org/10.2139/ssrn.1866371.

Maroney, Neal, Atsuyuki Naka, and Theresia Wansi. "Changing Risk, Return, and Leverage: The 1997 Asian Financial Crisis." *The Journal of Financial and Quantitative Analysis* 39, no. 1 (2004): 143–66.

Mason, Andrew, and Tomoko Kinugasa. "East Asian Economic Development: Two Demographic Dividends." *Journal of Asian Economics* 19, no. 5–6 (November–December 2008): 389–99. https://doi.org/10.1016/j.asieco.2008.09.006.

Mason, Andrew, Ronald Lee, Michael Abrigo, and Sang-Hyop Lee. "Support Ratios and Demographic Dividends: Estimates for the World." Technical Paper No. 2017/1. New York: United Nations Department of Economic and Social Affairs, Population Division, 2017. https://www.un.org/en/development/desa/population/publications/pdf/technical/TP2017-1.pdf.

Mccauley, Robert, John Cairns, and Corrinne Ho. "Exchange Rates and Global Volatility: Implications for Asia-Pacific Currencies." *BIS Quarterly Review*, 1 January 2007.

McCloskey, Deirdre N. "Measured, unmeasured, mismeasured, and unjustified pessimism: a review essay of Thomas Piketty's capital in the twenty-first century." *Erasmus Journal of Philosophy and Economics* 7, no. 2 (1 December 2014): 73–115. https://doi.org/10.23941/ejpe.v7i2.170.

McMorrow, Ryan, and Sun Yu. "The vanishing billionaire: how jack ma fell foul of Xi Jinping." *Financial Times*, 15 April 2021. https://www.ft.com/content/1fe0559f-de6d-490e-b312-abba0181da1f.

Mearsheimer, John J. *The Great Delusion: Liberal Dreams and International Realities*. The Henry l. Stimson Lectures Series. New Haven, CT: Yale University Press, 2018.

———. *The Tragedy of Great Power Politics*. Updated Edition. New York: W. W. Norton & Co, 2014.

Meng, Wang, and Kohlbacher Florian. "The Chinese 'Dama' as Consumer Cohort." *China Economic Review* (blog), 1 June 2015. https://chinaeconomicreview.com/op-ed-chinese-dama-consumer-cohort/.

Mladina, Peter, and Steve Germani. "The Enigma of Economic Growth and Stock Market Returns." Northern Trust, October 2016. https://cdn.northerntrust.com/pws/documents/commentary/investment-commentary/the-enigma-economic-growth-and-stock-market-returns.pdf.

Mobron, Jaap-Jan, and The History Team of Museum Bank Mandiri. *The Factorij: Bank, Museum, Monument*, 2011.

Mohanty, Ranjan Kumar, and N.R Bhanumurthy. "Assessing Public Expenditure Efficiency at Indian States." NIPFP Working Paper. New Delhi: National Institute of Public Finance and Policy, 19 March 2018. https://www.nipfp.org.in/media/medialibrary/2018/03/WP_2018_225.pdf.

Morris, Jan. *Hong Kong: Epilogue to an Empire*. Vintage Departures ed. New York: Vintage Departures, 1997.

Moss, David A., and Eugene Kintgen. "The Dojima Rice Market and the Origins of Futures Trading." *Harvard Business School Case 709-044*, January 2009.

MSCI AC Asia ex Japan Index (USD). "MSCI.Com." 31 May 2021. https://www.msci.com/documents/10199/43000c0b-7078-4d82-a59d-9a23792cc21e.

"Mutually Assured Existence | Special Report " *The Economist*, 15 May 2010. Accessed 21 September 2020. https://www.economist.com/special-report/2010/05/15/mutually-assured-existence?story_id=16078466%3B.

Naipaul, V. S. *India: a Million Mutinies Now*. First Vintage International edtion. New York: Vintage Books, 2011.

Nakagawa, Keiichirō, and Henry Rosovsky. "The Case of the Dying Kimono: The Influence of Changing Fashions on the Development of the Japanese Woolen Industry." *The Business History Review* 37, no. 1–2 (1963): 59–80. https://doi.org/10.2307/3112093.

Negara, Siwage Dharma. "Dutch Commerce and Chinese Merchants in Java: Colonial Relationships in Trade and Finance, 1800–1942." *Bulletin of Indonesian Economic Studies* 50, no. 3 (2 September 2014): 498–500. https://doi.org/10.1080/00074918.2014.980390.

Neuburger, Hugh, and Houston H. Stokes. "The Anglo-German Trade Rivalry, 1887–1913: A Counterfactual Outcome and Its Implications." *Social Science History* 3, no. 2 (Winter, 1979): 187–201. https://doi.org/10.2307/1171200.

Nison, Steve. *Japanese Candlestick Charting Techniques: A Contemporary Guide to the Ancient Investment Techniques of the Far East*. Second edition. New York: New York Institute of Finance, 2001.

OECD. "OECD Employment Outlook 2020." https://www.oecd-ilibrary.org/content/publication/1686c758-en.

———. "Pensions at a Glance 2017: OECD and G20 Indicators." Accessed 19 September 2020. https://www.oecd-ilibrary.org/social-issues-migration-health/pensions-at-a-glance-2017_pension_glance-2017-en.

———. *PISA 2018 Results (Volume I): What Students Know and Can Do*. PISA. OECD, 2019. https://doi.org/10.1787/5f07c754-en.

———. "'The Potential for Blockchain Technology in Public Equity Markets in Asia.'" OECD Capital Markets Series. OECD, 2018. https://www.oecd.org/daf/ca/The-Potential-for-Blockchain-in-Public-Equity-Markets-in-Asia.pdf.

Park, Young Jin. "The Rise of One-Person Households and Their Recent Characteristics in Korea." *Korea Journal of Population and Development* 23, no. 1 (1994): 117–29.

Partridge, Matthew. "Great frauds in history: the Bre-X gold-mining scandal." *Moneyweek*, 20 February 2019. https://moneyweek.com/502188/great-frauds-in-history-the-bre-x-gold-mining-scandal.

Patnam, Manasa, and Weijia Yao. "The Real Effects of Mobile Money: Evidence from a Large-Scale Fintech Expansion." International Monetary Fund Working Paper, 2020.

"Paytm Targets 1.5 Billion Merchant Payments During Festive Season." *Businessworld*, 24 September 2019. http://www.businessworld.in/article/Paytm-Targets-1-5-Billion-Merchant-Payments-During-Festive-Season/24-09-2019-176636/.

Perilli, David. "Update on Indonesia in 2019." Global Cement, 6 November 2019. <https://www.globalcement.com/news/item/10055-update-on-indonesia-in-2019>.

Persson, Karl Gunnar. *An Economic History of Europe: Knowledge, Institutions and Growth, 600 to the Present*. Second edition. New Approaches to Economic and Social History. Cambridge-New York: Cambridge University Press, 2015.

Petram, Lodewijk. *The World's First Stock Exchange*. New York: Columbia Business School Publishing, 2014.

———. "What was the return on VOC shares?" 1 October 2020. VOC dividends: mace and cloves, n.d. https://www.worldsfirststockexchange.com/2020/10/01/what-was-the-return-on-voc-shares/.

———. "The world's first stock exchange: how the Amsterdam market for Dutch East India Company shares became a modern securities market, 1602-1700." PhD thesis, University of Amsterdam, 2011. https://pure.uva.nl/ws/files/1427391/85961_thesis.pdf.

Pomerleano, Michael. *The East Asia Crisis and Corporate Finances: The Untold Micro Story*. The World Bank, 1999.

PwC Experience Centre. "The Rise of China's Silicon Dragon," May 2016. https://www.pwc.com/sg/en/publications/assets/rise-of-china-silicon-dragon.pdf.

"Rakesh Jhunjhunwala." Forbes Lists, Billionaires 2021 and India's Richest 2020. https://www.forbes.com/profile/rakesh-jhunjhunwala/?sh=61cde14a174b.

Rasmussen, Dan, John Klinger, Georgi Koreli, Nick Schmitz, and Igor Vasilachi. "Emerging Markets Crisis Investing." Verdad. Accessed 1 March 2021. https://static1.squarespace.com/static/5db0a1cf5426707c71b54450/t/601da88946f6aa3a2d177c28/1612556446187/Emerging+Markets+Crisis+Investing.pdf.

Ray, Saon, and Smita Miglani. "India's GVC integration: An analysis of upgrading efforts and facilitation of lead firms." Indian Council for Research on International Economic Relations, Working Paper 386, February 2020. http://icrier.org/pdf/Working_Paper_386.pdf.

Reuters Staff. "Toyota pumps $1 billion in Grab in auto industry's biggest ride-hailing bet." 13 June 2018. https://www.reuters.com/article/us-grab-toyota-investment-idUSKBN1J907E.

Roegholt, Richter, ed. *A Short History of Amsterdam*. Second edition. Amersfoort: Bekking & Blitz, 2006.

Rosling, Hans, Ola Rosling, and Anna Rosling Rönnlund. *Factfulness: Ten Reasons We're Wrong about the World and Why Things Are Better than You Think*. London: Sceptre, 2018.

Rude, Jana. "Half the World's New Single Person Households to Emerge in Asia Pacific." *Market Research Blog* (blog), 26 August 2020. https://blog.euromonitor.com/half-the-worlds-new-single-person-households-to-emerge-in-asia-pacific/.

Sahgal, Sujit. *A Wall Street View of Rural India*. S.l.: Olympia Publishers, 2020.

Sass, Steven A., and Jorge D. Ramos-Mercado. "Are Americans of All Ages and Income Levels Shortsighted About Their Finances?" *Centre for Retirement Research* 15, no. 9 (May 2015): 1–10.

"SBI Annual Report 2019–20." State Bank of India, 2020. https://www.sbi.co.in/documents/17826/35696/23062020_SBI+AR+2019-20+%28Time+16_3b11%29.pdf/a358b5ec-1d32-a093-d9ac-13071fda9ff6?t=1592911831224.

Schalk, Ruben, and Jan Bruin. "Leven, Werk En Financiën van Pieter Harmensz, de Eigenaar van Het Oudste Aandeel Ter Wereld." *Steevast* Schalk, R. (2011). Leven, werk en financiën van Pieter Harmensz, de eigenaar van het oudste aandeel ter wereld. *Steevast* 2011 (74–104). Enkhuizen, Met Jan de Bruin (Westfries Archief, Hoorn). (1 January 2011): 74–104.

Schlingemann, Frederik P., and Rene M. Stultz. "Have Exchange-Listed Firms Become Less Important for the Economy?" National Bureau of Economic Research, Working Paper 27942, October 2020. https://doi.org/10.3386/w27942.

Schmeltzing, Paul. "Eight centuries of global real interest rates, R-G, and the 'suprasecular' decline, 1311–2018." Bank of England. Staff Working Paper 845, January 2020. https://www.bankofengland. co.uk/-/media/boe/files/working-paper/2020/eight-centuries-of-global-real-interest-rates-r-g-and-the-suprasecular-decline-1311-2018. pdf?la=en&hash=5197703E8834998B56DD8121C0B64BFB09FF4881.

Schmidt, Hilary. "Singapore's Shrinking Stock Market." *International Banker*, 2 April 2019. https://internationalbanker.com/brokerage/singapores-shrinking-stock-market/.

Schuenemann, Jan-Hendrik, Natalia Ribberink, and Natallia Katenka. "Japanese and Chinese Stock Market Behaviour in Comparison – an Analysis of Dynamic Networks." *Asia Pacific Management Review* 25, no. 2 (1 June 2020): 99–110. https://doi.org/10.1016/j.apmrv.2019.10.002.

Seven Dollar Millionaire, ed. *Happy Ever After: Financial Freedom Isn't a Fairy Tale.* Chichester, UK: John Wiley & Sons, 2021.

Shabarisha, N. "Heuristic and Biases Related to Financial Investment and the Role of Behavioral Finance in Investment Decisions – A Study." *ZENITH International Journal of Business Economics & Management Research* 5, no. 12 (December 2015): 82–101.

Sahni, Urvashi. "Primary Education in India: Progress and Challenges." Brookings Institution India Centre, 20 January 2015. https://www.brookings.edu/research/primary-education-in-india-progress-and-challenges/.

Shin, Inseok. "Evolution of the KOSDAQ Stock Market: Evaluation and Policy Issues." Korea Development Research Institute. AT10 Research Conference, 7–8 March 2002. https://www.nomurafoundation.or.jp/en/wordpress/wp-content/uploads/2014/09/20020307-08_Inseok_Shin.pdf.

Shor, Russell. "New York Stock Exchange (NYSE)." FXCM Markets, 11 December 2014. Accessed 6 September 2020. https://www.fxcm.com/markets/insights/new-york-stock-exchange-nyse/.

Shorto, Russell, Otto Biersma, and Luud Dorresteyn. *Amsterdam: geschiedenis van de meest vrijzinnige stad ter wereld.* Amsterdam: Ambo, 2013.

SIFMA. "2020 Capital Markets Fact Book." September 2020. https://www.sifma.org/wp-content/uploads/2020/09/US-Fact-Book-2020-SIFMA.pdf.

Singapore Exchange (SGX) official website. Accessed 7 September 2020. https://www.sgx.com/.

Singh, Pratima. "You Don't Need an 'India Strategy' — You Need a Strategy for Each State in India." *Harvard Business Review*, 15 December 2017. https://hbr.org/2017/12/you-dont-need-an-india-strategy-you-need-a-strategy-for-each-state-in-india.

"Single households new market for businesses." *Taipei Times*, 4 April 2017. https://www.taipeitimes.com/News/taiwan/archives/2017/04/04/2003668047.

Song, Ligang. "State-owned enterprise Peform in China: past, present and prospects." In *China's 40 Years of Reform and Development: 1978–2018*, edited by Ligang Song, Ross Garnaut, and Cai Fang, 345–374. China Update Series. ANU Press, 2018. http://www.jstor.org/stable/j.ctv5cgbnk.27.

Spierdijk, Laura, Jacob A. Bikker, and Pieter van den Hoek. "Mean Reversion in International Stock Markets: An Empirical Analysis of the 20th Century." De Nederlandsche Bank Working Paper No. 247 (1 April 2010). http://dx.doi.org/10.2139/ssrn.1947305.

Sravanth, K. Reddy Sai, N. Sundaram, and Desti Kannaiah. "PEST Analysis of Present Indian Telecom Sector." *International Journal of Innovative Technology and Exploring Engineering* 9, 2 (December 2019): 4938–4942. https://doi.org/10.35940/ijitee.B6384.129219.

Srivinas, Val, and Urval Goradia. "The future of wealth in the United States: Mapping trends in generational wealth." Deloitte Center for Financial Services research report. Deloitte University Press, 2015. https://www2.deloitte.com/content/dam/insights/us/articles/us-generational-wealth-trends/DUP_1371_Future-wealth-in-America_MASTER.pdf.

Stanley, Leonardo E. "India." In *Emerging Market Economies and Financial Globalization: Argentina, Brazil, China, India and South Korea*, 163–184. London-New York: Anthem Press, 2018. https://doi.org/10.2307/j.ctt216683k.13.

Studwell, Joe. *How Asia Works*. Grove Press, 2014. http://www.vlebooks.com/vleweb/product/openreader?id=none&isbn=9780802193476.

Sugawara, Sandra. "Gangsters Aggravating Japanese Banking Crisis." *The Washington Post*, 15 December 1995. https://www.washingtonpost.com/archive/politics/1995/12/15/gangsters-aggravating-japanese-banking-crisis/7fb1c379-1391-4ecb-8dd9-ff620c91206b/.

Svenson, Ola. "Are we all less risky and more skillful than our fellow drivers?" *Acta Psychologica* 47, 2 (February 1981): 143–148. https://doi.org/10.1016/0001-6918(81)90005-6.

Taleb, Nassim N., and Constantine Sandis. "The Skin In The Game Heuristic for Protection Against Tail Events." *Review of Behavioral Economics* 1, no. 1–2 (2014): 115–135. https://doi.org/10.1561/105.00000006.

Taylor, Bryan. "A Century of Chinese Stocks and Bonds." Global Financial Data, 4 January 2019. http://www.globalfinancialdata.com/a-century-of-chinese-stocks-and-bonds/.

Tetlock, Philip E., and Dan Gardner. *Superforecasting: The Art and Science of Prediction*. First edition. New York: Crown Publishers, 2015.

Thaler, Richard H. *Misbehaving: The Making of Behavioural Economics*. London-New York: W. W. Norton & Co, 2016.

"The Battle of the Business World – Human vs Data." Summit & Friends, 5 December 2019. https://summitandfriends.com/blog/the-battle-of-the-business-world/.

"The History of Bombay Stock Exchange" Video. BSE India, 11 September 2014. https://www.youtube.com/watch?v=oDkiJcRWvRQ.

"The journey of Rakesh Jhunjhunwala." Interview with *The Economic Times*, 23 October 2009. https://economictimes.indiatimes.com/opinion/interviews/the-journey-of-rakesh-jhunjhunwala/articleshow/5145756.cms?utm_source=contentofinterest&utm_medium=text&utm_campaign=cppst.

The Stock Exchange of Thailand official website. "History of the Stock Exchange of Thailand." Accessed 13 November 2020. https://www.set.or.th/en/about/overview/history_p1.html.

Thuy, Ngoc. "Samsung committed to long-term business in Vietnam." *Hanoi Times*, 21 December 2018. http://hanoitimes.vn/samsung-committed-to-long-term-business-in-vietnam-385.html.

Titan Company corporate website. "Titan Company Limited: Earnings Presentation – Q2 FY '21 and H1 FY '21." 28 October 2020. https://www.titancompany.in/sites/default/files/Earnings%20Presentation%20-%20%2028th%20Oct%20-%20Final.pdf.

Toshikuni, Murai, and Muraoka Keiichi. "Order in the Court: Explaining Japan's 99.9% Conviction Rate." Nippon.com, Society, 18 January 2019. https://www.nippon.com/en/japan-topics/c05401/order-in-the-court-explaining-japan's-99-9-conviction-rate.html.

Tsuchida, Akihiko. "Symbolic 'Juliana's Tokyo' disco reborn in Osaka." *The Mainichi*, 27 October 2018. https://mainichi.jp/english/articles/20181027/p2a/00m/0na/020000c.

Tuk, Mirjam A., Debra Trampe, and Luk Warlop. "Inhibitory Spillover: Increased Urination Urgency Facilitates Impulse Control in Unrelated Domains." 2010. http://dx.doi.org/10.2139/ssrn.1720956.

Tyagi, Rachna. "Tata Group History Is Also the History of Indian Industry." *The Week*, 14 October 2018.

United Nations, Department of Economic and Social Affairs, Population Division. *World Urbanization Prospects 2018: Highlights* (ST/ESA/SER.A/421). 2019.

United Nations and Economic and Social Commission for Asia and the Pacific. *The Future of Asian & Pacific Cities Transformative Pathways towards Sustainable Urban Development*. 2019.

"US foolishly fed the rise of China: Famed international relations expert John Mearsheimer." *India Today*, 20 June 2020. https://www.indiatoday.in/india/story/us-foolishly-fed-rise-of-china-international-relations-expert-john-mearsheimer-1691051-2020-06-20.

Uzsoki, David. "Drivers of Sustainable Investing." International Institute for Sustainable Development. 2020. https://doi.org/10.2307/resrep22000.5.

Vaitilingam, Romesh. *The Financial Times Guide to Using the Financial Pages*. Fourth edition. London: Financial Times/Prentice Hall, 2001.

van der Linde, Herald. *Jakarta: History of a misunderstood city*. Singapore: Marshall Cavendish Editions, 2020.

Vasal, V. K. "Corporate Social Responsibility & Shareholder Returns – Evidence from the Indian Capital Market." *Indian Journal of Industrial Relations* 44, no. 3 (2009): 376–85.

Vaswani, Karishma. "Indonesia's love affair with social media." BBC News, 16 February 2012. https://www.bbc.com/news/world-asia-17054056.

Veer, Gerrit de. *A True Description of Three Voyages by the North-East towards Cathay and China: Undertaken by the Dutch in the Years 1594, 1595 and 1596.* Translated by William Phillip. Edited by Charles T Beke.Cambridge: Cambridge University Press, 2010. https://doi.org/10.1017/CBO9780511696022.

Vega, Josseph de la. *Confusion de Confusiones* (1688). Translated by Herman Kellenbenz. Boston: Harvard Graduate School of Business Administration, 1957.

———. *Confusion de Confusiones* (1688). Edited by M. F. J. Smith. Den Haag: Martinus Nijhoff, 1939. https://www.dbnl.org/tekst/vega002conf01_01/

Vijayaraghavan, Nandini, and Umesh Desai. *The Singapore Blue Chips: The Rewards & Risks of Investing in Singapore's Largest Corporates.* New Jersey: World Scientific, 2017.

Wahyudi, Reza. "Indonesia, Pengguna Facebook Terbanyak ke-4 di Dunia." Kompas.com, 2 March 2018. https://tekno.kompas.com/read/2018/03/02/08181617/indonesia-pengguna-facebook-terbanyak-ke-4-di-dunia.

Wang, Levin. "The homecoming of China concept stocks." – DotDotNews, Business, 18 August 2020. Accessed 17 November 2020. https://english.dotdotnews.com/a/202008/18/AP5f3b7733e4b0d6297fa5a897.html.

Wang, Wallis. "Bank's luck will change, say feng shui masters." *The Standard*, 23 October 2020.

Wei, Lingling. "China Blocked Jack Ma's Ant IPO After Investigation Revealed Likely Beneficiaries." *The Wall Street Journal*, 16 February 2021. https://www.wsj.com/articles/china-blocked-jack-mas-ant-ipo-after-an-investigation-revealed-who-stood-to-gain-11613491292.

Weintraub, Andrew N. *Dangdut Stories: A Social and Musical History of Indonesia's Most Popular Music.* New York: Oxford University Press, 2010.

Wielenga, Friso. *Geschiedenis van Nederland: Van de Opstand Tot Heden.* Amsterdam: Boom, 2012.

William III, 1696–1697. An Act to restraine the Number and ill Practice of Brokers and Stock-Jobbers. [Chapter XXXII. Rot. Parl. 8 & 9 Gul. III. p.11.nu.1.]. Statutes of the Realm: Volume 7, 1695–1701. Edited by John Raithby. http://www.british-history.ac.uk/statutes-realm/vol7/pp285-287.

Woetzel, Jonathan, Oliver Tonby, Fraser Thomson, Penny Burtt, and Gillian Lee. "Southeast Asia at the crossroads: Three paths to prosperity." McKinsey Global Institute, November 2014. https://www.mckinsey.com/~/media/McKinsey/Featured%20Insights/Asia%20Pacific/Three%20paths%20to%20sustained%20economic%20growth%20in%20Southeast%20Asia/MGI%20SE%20Asia_Executive%20summary_November%202014.pdf.

Wolff, Edward N. "Household Wealth Trends in the United States, 1962 to 2016: Has Middle Class Weath Recovered?" National Bureau of Economic Research, Working Paper 24085. November 2017. https://doi.org/10.3386/w24085.

———. "Who Owns Stock in American Corporations?" *Proceedings of the American Philosophical Society* 158, no. 4 (2014): 372–91.

World Bank, Development Research Center of the State Council, the People's Republic of China. "China 2030: Building a Modern, Harmonious, and Creative Society." Washington DC: World Bank. © *World Bank* 2013. https://openknowledge.worldbank.org/handle/10986/12925.

"World's most polluted cities 2019." IQAir.com, 2019. https://www.iqair.com/us/world-most-polluted-cities.

Wynand Fockink corporate website. "Our History." Accessed 6 September 2020. https://wynand-fockink.nl/history.

Yeung, Henry Wai-chung. *Strategic Coupling: East Asian Industrial Transformation in the New Global Economy*. Cornell Studies in Political Economy. Ithaca-London: Cornell University Press, 2016.

Yi, Fuxian. "Worse than Japan: how China's looming demographic crisis will doom its economic dream" *South China Morning Post*, 4 January 2019. https://www.scmp.com/comment/insight-opinion/asia/article/2180421/worse-japan-how-chinas-looming-demographic-crisis-will.

Yoon, Gene, and Ki-soo Eun. "Understanding Aging in Korea." *Korea Journal of Population and Development* 24, no. 2 (1995): 301–17.

Zee, Saskia C. van der, Paul H. Fischer, and Gerard Hoek. "Air Pollution in Perspective: Health Risks of Air Pollution Expressed in Equivalent Numbers of Passively Smoked Cigarettes." *Environmental Research* 148 (1 July 2016): 475–83. https://doi.org/10.1016/j.envres.2016.04.001.

Acknowledgements

"Writing is the art of applying the arse to the seat". Those were the words of my friend and colleague, Jon Marsh, after we finished our coffee with a few colleagues early one morning in HSBC's headquarters in Hong Kong. He had borrowed the quote from Dorothy Parker, a witty US writer from the 1930s, but his message was clear – if I wanted to write a book about Asian stock markets, it was best to sit down and just start writing. That is just what I did the next Saturday morning, in the early weeks of 2020. Along the way, Jon provided suggestions, ideas and criticisms, and gave the whole manuscript a thorough edit. I am very grateful for all his help. And as Jon spent part of his weekends going over the manuscript, I would like to thank his wife, Annie, too.

My uncle Dinand, in Amsterdam, proofread early drafts of the manuscript (while undergoing a series of major dental surgical procedures). I thank him for all his suggestions and ideas. For all his efforts, I owe him a trip to Wynand Fockink's gin shop in Amsterdam the next time I am back in The Netherlands.

Many of the ideas in this book originated from discussions with my team of stock market strategists: Devendra Joshi, Barak Hurvitz, Prerna Garg, Nishu Singla and Raymond Liu. I count myself lucky to have them as colleagues and friends.

Many others have, directly or indirectly, contributed ideas to this book, for which I am grateful. Dilip Shahani is never shy of expressing his opinions on markets (he looks at credit markets in Asia, I look at the region's stock markets) and I have other "sparring" partners in Eliot Camplisson, Frederic Neuman, Paul Mackel, Parash Jain, Evan Li, Karen Choi, Ricky See, Anurag Dayal, Amit Sachdeva, Anurag Dayal, Helen Huang, Joey Chew, Ju Wang, Madan Reddy, Jake Lee, Derek Hamilton, Michelle Kwok, Steven Sun, John Lomax, Andre de Silva, Neale Anderson, Helen Fang, Peisan Chow, Karl Redmond and the rest of the Asia research team.

Garry Evans is an old hand in Japanese stocks – it's a market he has been looking at since the 1980s – and I thank him for taking time to read the chapter on Japan. The same gratitude goes to Soeren Addicks, who used to manage Japan-focused investment funds at Fidelity for a long time (and with whom I share a passion for wine). Soeren gave me some feedback on the Japan chapter and for that I will open a bottle of wine with him the next time we meet.

I would also like to thank Nick Thompson and Lareina Wang for reading some of the very early scribbles and drafts, when I was just getting started on the manuscript. It is always good to get feedback early in the writing process. Later, Vinay Chopra and Khoon Li Ong at HSBC looked at the manuscript from a compliance angle and at the end of writing, Piers Butler in London, who is passionate about financial literacy, came up enthusiastically with all sorts of ideas on how best to bring the book to the market. Thanks to all of you.

And then there are former colleagues and friends who helped me crystallise ideas on Asia and its stock markets over the years. Rick Loo and James Brewis in Jakarta hired and brought me into the industry, and Rick showed me the ropes. I would also like to thank James Brewis for a detailed proof reading of the whole book. Roland Haas, who is never tired of discussing Indonesian stocks markets. Stuart Gietel-Basten gets a special mention for his incredible insights into all sorts of demographic issues across the region. Thanks also to friend, former colleague, client, anonymous book writer and financial literacy advocate, Michael Gilmore. Michael is a very good friend, I have known him for three decades now, and it's through all sorts of conversations with him that I've learned a lot about Asian stock markets.

Then there is the group of "dismal illuminati" who regularly meet over a few glasses of wine to talk about Asia – Simon Ogus, Philip Wyatt, Mark MacFarland, Sitao Xu, Ryan Manuel, Michael Kurtz and the honourable Geoff. Michael Kurtz was also helpful (sort of) in sourcing some of the data I used in a few charts. I was also able to talk through some of the ideas with hiking buddy and experienced investor Mike Goldstone, for which I am grateful. And a special mention goes to Leo, Mitch, Mike and Paul for their "off the wall" insights on all matters Asia and what, I suppose, is moral support.

Michelle Ng at Factset got me approval to use their vast database, cartographer Brendan Whyte helped with designing the map (with lightning speed) and the talented Mike McKeever provided the tug of war illustration. Thank you.

A few unlikely characters need to be thanked, too. First up is the Chinese man near Guilin airport, who gave me a bowl of steaming noodles after the minor plane crash I experienced. He probably did not realise then that his kindness made me decide to continue with my journey through China after the rather disastrous start on my first day in the country.

And then there are Mas Yadi, his wife Ati and their children, Miman and Fatma, in south Jakarta. They showed incredible hospitality when they took me into their home on my first trip to Indonesia in 1990. I stayed with them for months and they taught me all things Indonesian, from eating spicy *rendang* to speaking Bahasa Indonesia. It was Fatma who, as a seven-year-old child, took me by the hand and guided me through the narrow alleys in Pasar Minggu. A few years later, I would stay with them again while writing my Master's thesis on Indonesia's central bank.

Anita Teo, Melvin Neo and the team at Marshall Cavendish International (Asia) have been very helpful and efficient with all sorts of technical challenges and issues in getting the book published. Actually, it was Anita who planted the seed of the idea for writing a book about stock markets after we had worked together on my first book, *Jakarta – History of a Misunderstood City*. She also suggested to avoid writing the book as a report for professional investors but to write it "as if you are talking to friends in a bar over a beer". I have kept that in mind and tried to do just that. Thanks a lot.

And then, as always, there is my wife, Teni. She patiently allowed me to spend weekends and evenings on my laptop, but she also knew when it was time to tap me on the shoulder and say, "Enough now," and let me take her out for dinner. I am always grateful to her.

Last but not least, lots of gratitude to my parents who allowed me to set sail for Asia on my first backpacking trip in 1990. They supported me, even when they knew I was leaving my hometown behind. But I must say "*Twente, doar is niks mis met*".

This book is dedicated to them.

Herald van der Linde

About the Author

Herald van der Linde is HSBC's Head of Equity Strategy, Asia Pacific. He joined the bank in 2005 and came to HSBC with 20 years of experience in various roles, including stock analyst, equity strategist and country head of research in Indonesia, South Africa and Taiwan. He is a Chartered Financial Analyst (CFA), speaks seven languages and has an MSc in Economics, for which he wrote a thesis on Indonesia's central bank in Jakarta in 1993. Herald is also an Associate of the Institute of Wine and Spirits and is a certified lecturer for the Wine & Spirit Education Trust (WSET). He sits on the advisory committee for the China Studies programme at Hong Kong's Baptist University and is the author of *Jakarta: History of a Misunderstood City*, published in 2020.